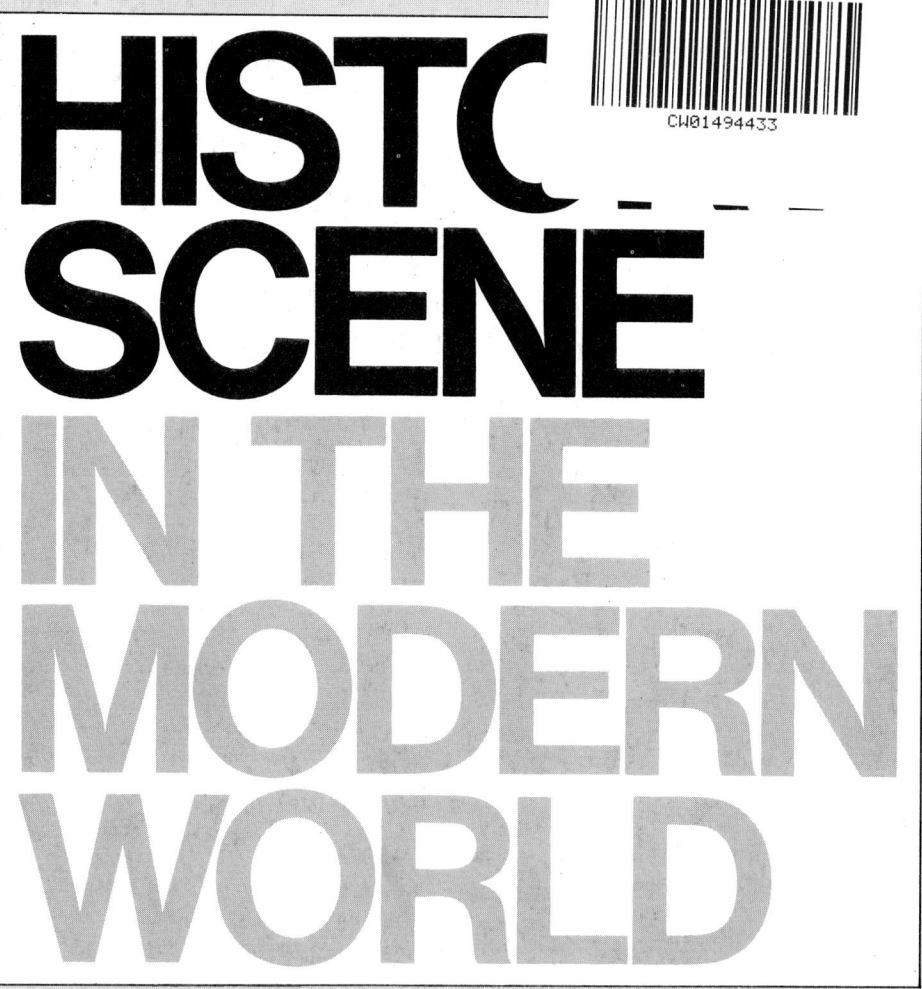

HISTORY SCENE IN THE MODERN WORLD

by PETER MOSS

Illustrated and designed
by Ray Fishwick

COLLINS EDUCATIONAL

Front cover photos, from left to right:
Winston Churchill; Adolf Hitler; Joseph Stalin;
Franklin Roosevelt; Mao Tse-tung; Ghandi.
Back cover photos, from left to right:
Lenin; Martin Luther King; Marie Curie; Mussolini.

The publishers would like to thank the following for permission to reproduce
illustrations:

Age Concern, p128; Associated Press, p49 bottom right, p52 top right, p53 centre, p91
bottom, p99; Barnaby's, p84 bottom, p127 left, p142 top right and bottom right, p143 top
left and bottom right, p151 bottom; BBC Hulton Picture Library, p12, p13, p15 top, p16,
p24 bottom right, p25 top left and bottom left, p29 bottom, p31 top, p32 top and bottom
left, p35 top left, p38 bottom left, p54, p58, p67, p80 top right and top left, p92 bottom,
p97 bottom left, p103 top, p111 top, p114, p115, p122, p123 bottom, p124, p126 left,
p130 bottom, p131, p132 bottom, p134 bottom right, p138 top and bottom right, p142
top left and bottom left, p144 top left; Anne Bolt, p56, p80 bottom left and bottom right,
BP International p66 left; Bournville Village Trust, p141 top right; British Museum, p82,
right; Camera Press Ltd, p77 bottom; CEGB, p66 right, p109; J. Allan Cash, p82 left, p89
top left, p110 right, p143 bottom left, p151 top; Design Council, p126 right; Earthscan,
p89 top left and bottom left, p108; EEC Commission, p59 top; Engineering Design
Council, p126 right; Mary Evans Picture Library, p26 left, p100 centre and bottom, p121,
p134 bottom left, p138 bottom left; Melanie Friend, p61; Chris Gilbert, p125; Imperial
War Museum, p14, p15 bottom, p19 bottom right, p35 top left, p36, p37 top left, p48
centre and bottom, p49 top right, top left, centre left, bottom left, p50 top, p51 top left,
centre, bottom left and bottom right, p52 top left, bottom left and centre right, p53, top
and bottom, p62, p77 top, p104 right, p128 bottom, p144 bottom; Japan Information
Centre, p74; John Hillelson Agency Ltd, p70 bottom; Mansell Collection, p68 right, p75
top and bottom, p101, p102 top, p130 top; Ministry of Defence, p105 right; NASA, p107;
National Library of Ireland, p102 centre; Novosti, p19 bottom left, p24 top left and top
right; p25 bottom right, p29 top left, p35 bottom right, p50 bottom, p59 bottom; Terry
Onslow, p151 centre; Oxfam, p89 bottom right, p111; Photo Source, p33 top, p47, p48
top, p51 top right, p69 bottom left, p93 bottom; Popperfoto, p19 top, p31 bottom, p26
right, p28 top right, p29 top left, p34, p37 top right and bottom, p38 bottom right, p39,
p41, p52 bottom right, p65 left, p67, p70 top, p71 top right, p76, p77 centre, p79, p81,
p84 top, p90, p91 top, p92 top, p96, p97 top right, p104 left, and top, p110 left, p123 top,
p155 top left, bottom left, and bottom right; Press Association p147; Punch, p102
bottom; Robert Harding Picture Library, p141 top left; County of Shropshire, p143 top
right; Syndication International p65 right, p97 top left and centre left, p103 centre and
bottom; Topham, p30 top, p32 bottom right, p35 bottom, p68 left, p69 top, p71 top left,
p72, p73, p97 bottom right, p135, p145, p155 top right and bottom left; Trinity College
Library, Dublin, p100 top; Ullstein Bilderdienst, p50 centre; United Nations, p55; Xinhua
News Agency, p69 bottom left.

©1987 Peter Moss

First published 1987

ISBN-0- 00 327305-9
Printed and bound in Great Britain
by R J Acford, Chichester
Published by Collins Educational, 8 Grafton Street, London W1X 3LA, United Kingdom.
10 9 8 7 6 5 4 3 2 1

Contents

THE WORLD IN THE TWENTIETH CENTURY

The world in 1900

Outside Europe, parts of North America and Japan, the world was almost completely undeveloped, with little or no industry and few good roads or railways. In most places people lived much as their ancestors had done for hundreds of years, grubbing a poor living from tiny farms or plots. Four-fifths of the world was in the hands of European colonial powers, for this was the great Age of Imperialism.

Europe
Europe felt itself to be the centre of the world. 90% of world trade was European. Britain and Germany were the first and second industrial powers in the world. The old European enmities grew as countries struggled for colonies, power and trade. New alliances were formed, and the continent was dividing into unfriendly camps. There was an arms race, and many people felt that a major war was certain in the near future. There had not been a major European war since the defeat of Napoleon in 1815.

North America
The USA consisted of 45 states in the union. Alaska, Arizona, New Mexico, Hawaii and Oklahoma had not yet been admitted. After the Civil War the US had begun a huge programme of development. Roads, railways and canals were built. The population had soared from four million in 1800 to 75 million in 1900, largely because of the flood of immigrants. People had pushed further and further westwards and almost all of the land had now been taken over. The wars with the Indians were over and most of the remaining Indians were living in reservations.

But industrialisation and urbanisation were the most dramatic changes. Great cities sprang up, and industrial output soared. By the early twentieth century US heavy industry and mining were about to pass their world rivals, Britain and Germany. In 1898 the US had fought Spain and had seized Puerto Rico, Hawaii, the Philippines and other Pacific islands, and was in control of Cuba. It also controlled the central American countries because it took almost all of their produce. The US was isolationist. It would not allow any outside state to interfere in the affairs of the whole American continent, and although it had seized the Spanish territories, it would not take part in European wars.

Canada was part of the British Empire and had been a self-governing dominion since 1867.

Africa
Liberia, a small state set up in 1847 for freed slaves from the Americas, and Ethiopia were the only really independent states in Africa. The rest were controlled by colonial powers. In particular, Britain controlled Egypt, where the Suez Canal was the main link with India. In the last quarter of the nineteenth century the Europeans scrambled for Africa. The boundaries of the different colonies had been drawn more or less at random, cutting across black African regions and splitting tribes.

South Africa had very valuable gold and diamond mines. In 1900 there was a war going on between Britain and the white South Africans known as the Boers. Elsewhere the continent was undeveloped, though a few agricultural products were exported, especially from the east.

Central and Latin America
Unstable states, many of them in constant rebellion as one powerful family overthrew another to take control. They were almost all very under-developed and poor, depending often on a single crop such as rubber, coffee or sugar. The ordinary people, many of them descendants of slaves and Indians, were often little more than serfs. A few countries, such as Chile, Argentina and Uruguay, had been partly developed with money from elsewhere — mainly from Germany, Britain and America. The mines and ranches were often owned by foreigners, and provided cheap food and raw materials for the factories of Europe and the USA.

Russia

In spite of its vast size, Russia was not as strong as the main European countries. It had improved production of cloth, coal, iron, steel and oil, and had built important railways. But there were still many very small workshops and transport was poor in many areas. There was no parliament and the country was ruled by an emperor called the tsar. There was a secret police and criminals might be sent to Siberia. Russia had big ideas. It wanted to control eastern countries and also southern countries near the Mediterranean. It had been defeated in the south in the Crimean War of 1854-56, but was still trying to influence the states in that area, known as the Balkans. Although the rule of the tsar was harsh, there were powerful underground movements. There were frequent strikes; politicians were sometimes killed. The unrest was to come to a head in the revolution of 1905.

Japan

Japan had been like a closed medieval state until 1853, when the USA began to force it to open to trade with the western countries. The Japanese then began to modernise. In 50 years they covered the ground that had taken the Europeans four hundred. They built railways, roads, factories, telephones and a powerful new army and navy equipped with the latest weapons. Thousands of technical experts, engineers, doctors, officers and others were recruited from Europe and America to train Japanese workers and military forces. A more European form of government was introduced, and a national educational system was set up. Japan was ambitious and wanted an empire of its own.

China

China was almost entirely undeveloped, with little modern industry. In the last years of the nineteenth century the vast country had been divided up into 'spheres of influence' by the western powers, where they claimed, without any reference to the Chinese, that they had sole rights of trading. Many Chinese did not like the Europeans and there had been several risings. These had been easily put down by the western powers, which had better weapons, and were used as an excuse to squeeze more from the Chinese government. Chinese people wanted to throw out the Europeans and to rebel against the Manchu emperors who ruled China.

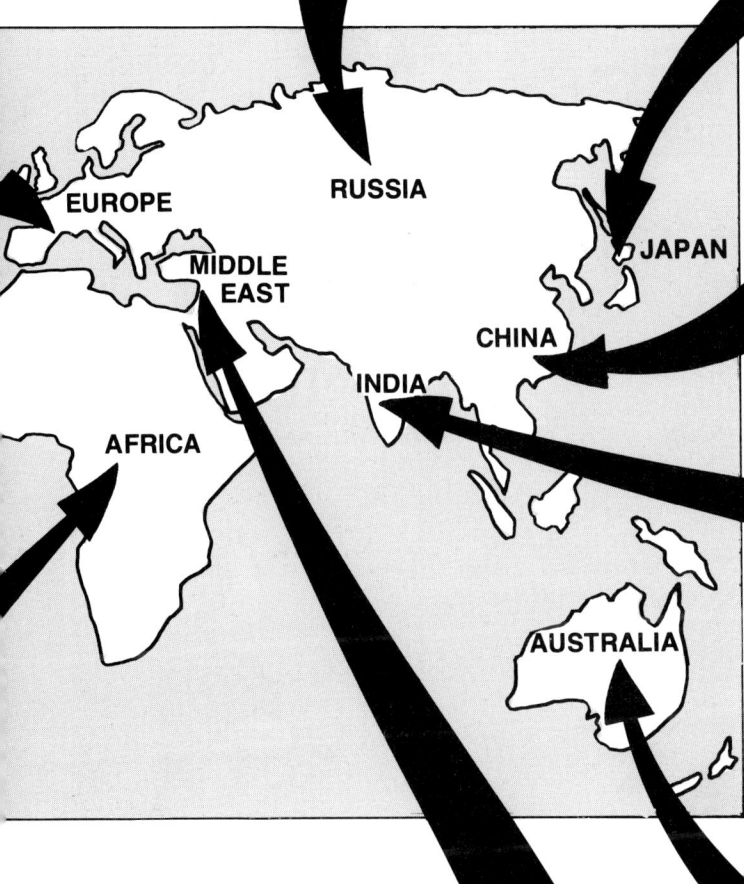

India and South-east Asia

All of these countries except Thailand were colonies of the British, Dutch, French and Portuguese. They were regarded as a source of cheap raw materials for the European factories, and as markets for European manufactured goods. None of the countries was developed. In India there was a growing movement for rule by Indians, but this was largely among educated men, and there were no mass protests yet.

Middle East

Apart from a few places in the river valleys where there was small-scale farming, the Middle East was largely a desert. It was supposed to be under the control of Turkey, 'the sick old man of Europe'. The vast oil reserves had not been tapped. The area was very important, lying at the crossroads from west to east and north to south. The Suez Canal was particularly important: millions of tonnes of shipping passed through it each year with raw materials from the east and goods to trade from the west.

Australia and New Zealand

These were, like Canada, part of the British Empire and governed themselves. There was some mining in Australia, but they were generally agricultural countries, producing wool, meat and dairy produce for Britain. When refrigerated ships were invented in the last quarter of the nineteenth century, food cargoes could be brought to Britain very cheaply. They had low populations. Apart from aborigines (Australia) and Maoris (New Zealand), almost all the people had come from Britain, or were descended from British people.

Britain and Europe in 1900

Britain

The richest and most powerful nation on earth. The British Empire covered about a quarter of the world's land surface and contained about a quarter of the world's population. Britain was the most industrialised nation. British skills and money were found everywhere on earth, not only in the empire. British companies owned and ran railways in South America, and industry in Russia. The British navy was the most powerful fleet in the world, ready in every ocean to protect the trade routes. The army, though small, was very efficient.

Germany

Was second in strength and industrialisation, and growing richer. It had been late in the race for colonies, and had been able to get only a few parts of Africa and some Pacific islands. Under the leadership of Prussia Germany was the most aggressive state in Europe. Germany felt that it should have a greater part as a world leader.

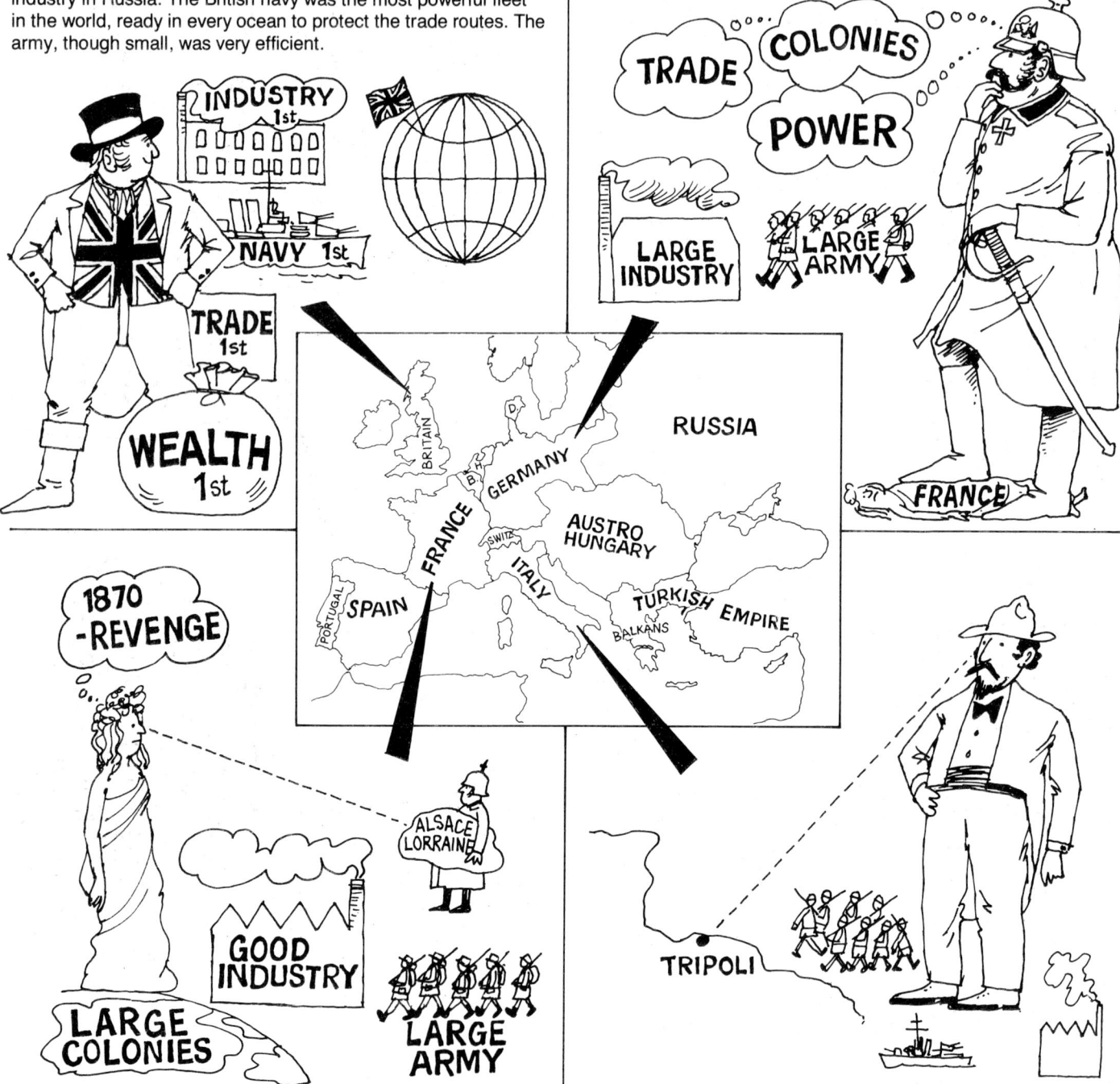

France

Was industrialised, but not as much as Britain or Germany. It had large colonies in Africa and some in the Far East, but in 1900 it was more interested in north Africa where it hoped to add Morocco to its colonies of Algeria and Tunisia. After 1870 it had become a republic again but was very unstable and in the following 25 years had 34 prime ministers.

Italy

Like Germany a 'new' nation, having been made into a single state only in 1866. Unlike Germany it was very under-developed and industrialisation was only just beginning, and then only in the north. It had almost no overseas territory (but had its eye on Tripoli) and little trade. Its army was large and not very efficient, but its small navy was more effective.

Russia

Russia stretches across both Europe and Asia. The Turkish empire was very weak and Russia wanted to control the European states in the Balkans which had been controlled by Turkey. Austria-Hungary was also very interested in the Balkans, and was trying to keep and increase its influence there.

Turkey

Turkey had been the most powerful nation in the eastern Mediterranean, with an empire which stretched from Italy to the Persian Gulf and along the north of Africa. By the nineteenth century it had become weak and one by one the outer parts of the empire had more or less gained independence or were fighting for it.

Austro-Hungarian empire

A great, scattered empire made up of modern Austria, Hungary, Czechoslovakia and parts of northern Italy, Yugoslavia, Poland and Russia. There were Muslims, Jews, orthodox and catholic Christians, and the different races and creeds did not mix well together. There was almost no industrialisation. The army was large but inefficient, and the 70-year-old emperor, Franz Joseph, tried to do too much on his own. The whole empire was ready to fall apart.

Balkans

These were a group of small, unstable countries of many different peoples and religions. There were Serbs, Croats, Albanians, Macedonians, Greeks, Bulgarians, Romanians. They had once all been part of the Turkish empire. Greece became independent in 1829, and Romania, Bulgaria and Serbia later on. Most of the rest were still part of the Turkish empire. The tiny states were constantly quarrelling.

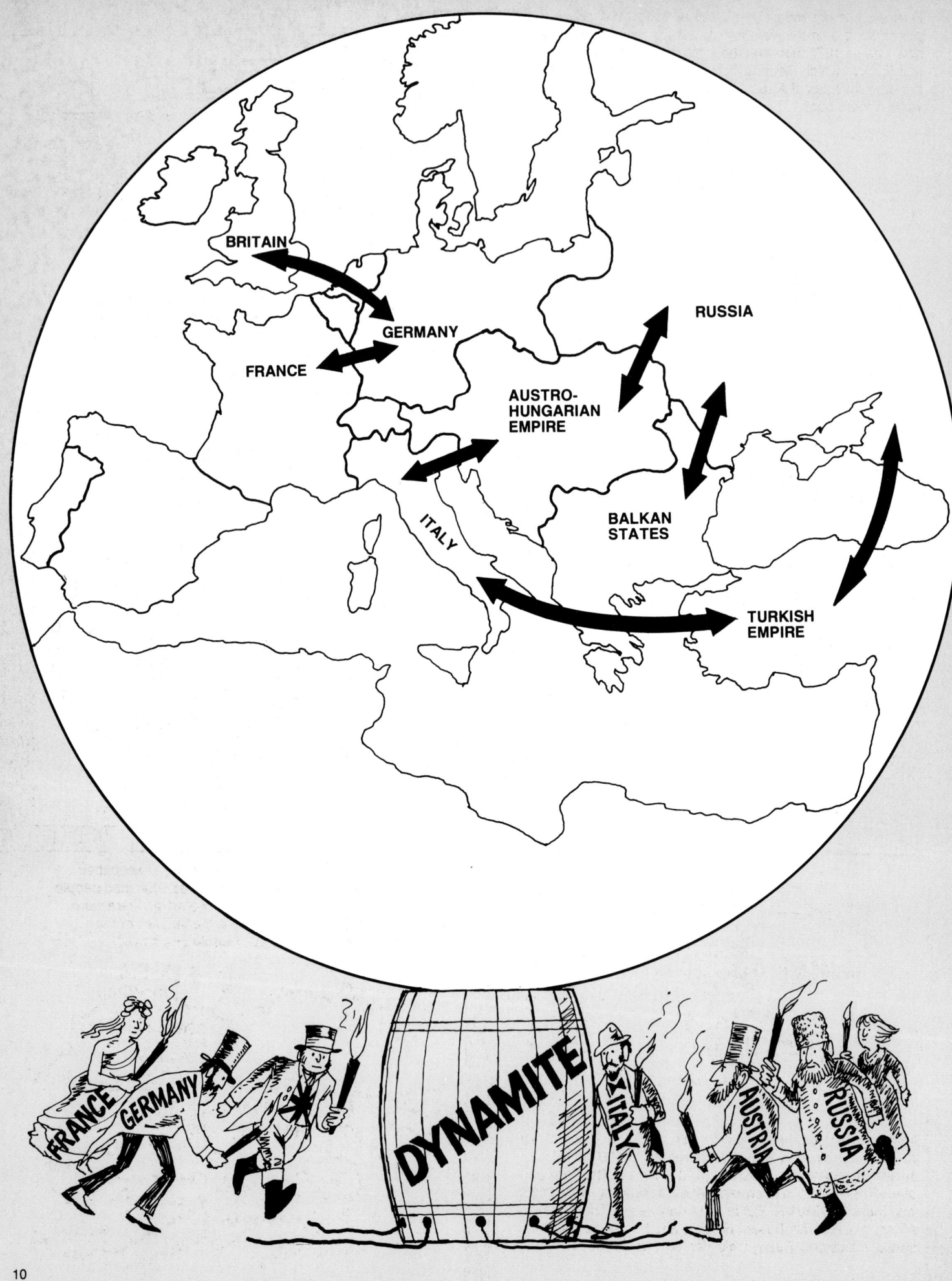

France could not accept that it was no longer the most powerful state on the mainland of Europe, and that Germany now was. In 1870 there had been a war between Germany and France, which Germany had won. The French had lost the two provinces of Alsace and Lorraine to Germany and wanted them back.

Rivalries before the First World War

Russia had always needed an outlet to the warm Mediterranean Sea as all its northern ports were frozen in winter. The Black Sea harbours were useless in wartime because ships using them had to go through the narrow Bosphorus, which was controlled by Turkey. Turkish guns on both sides could stop any ships going in or out.

Millions of people in the Austro-Hungarian empire and in the Balkans were Slavs, like many of the Russians themselves. Russia encouraged these people to plan for independence, so that it could have a strong influence over them.

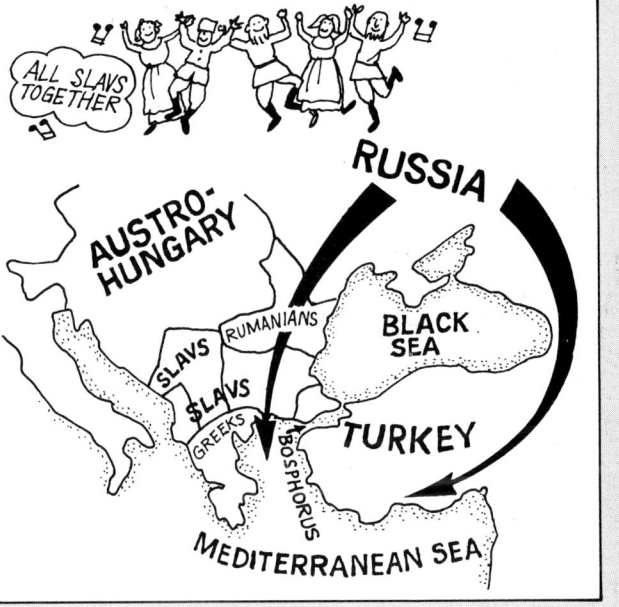

Britain and Germany were trade rivals. Germany was very envious of Britain's empire and all the trade advantages it gave. Germany had been late in the scramble for colonies as it had become a united nation only in 1870, when most of the 'spare' land had been taken. Britain was very suspicious of Germany, which was building a huge navy although it did not have any major shipping routes to protect.

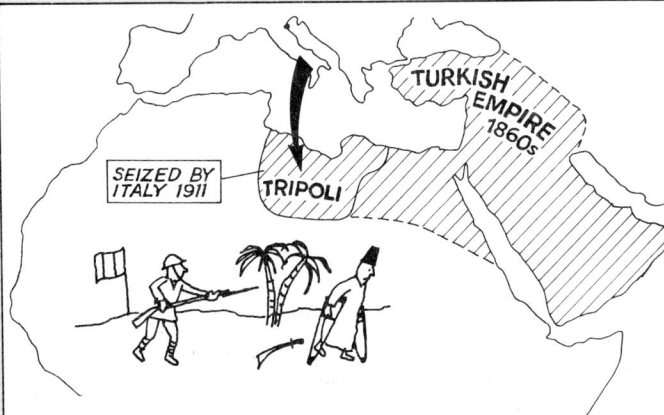

Italy, like Germany, was a young nation. It wanted colonies in Africa, and had been badly beaten when in 1896 it tried to invade the country of Abyssinia (now Ethiopia). Italy was part of the Triple Alliance (Germany, Austria-Hungary, Italy) which was friendly to Turkey. But in 1911 Italy seized Tripoli in North Africa, a part of the Turkish Empire, and there was a war between Italy and Turkey which lasted a year.

Both Austria-Hungary and Turkey were trying to keep their ramshackle empires together. Both empires contained people of different races and countries. In both empires there were movements for Nationalism — that is the peoples of the different races and countries each wanted their own government.

GERMANS 11.5m
MAGYARS 11m
CZECHS 6m
POLES 5m
UKRAINIANS 3.5m
RUMANIANS 3m
SLOVAKS 2m
SERBS 1m
OTHERS 2.5m

11

The rival countries of Europe tried to keep the balance of power by forming groups, or alliances. Germany, Austria and Italy formed the Triple Alliance. Russia, France and Britain joined in the Triple Entente. They hoped that both sides would be equally powerful and neither side would dare to start a war.

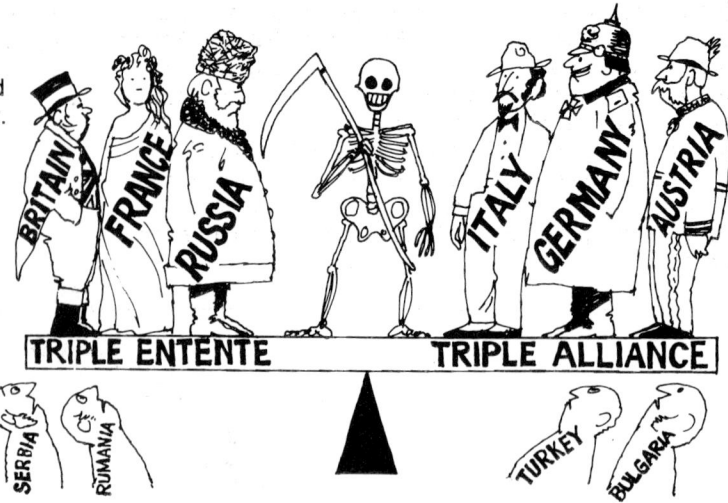

EUROPE SLIDES INTO WAR

1905   **1908**

War could have broken out in 1905, when Germany threatened France, which was trying to increase its influence in Morocco. The quarrel was patched up. In 1911 Germany again threatened France in Morocco, and sent a warship, The Panther, to the main port of Morocco. This quarrel was settled by France giving Germany a strip of jungle in Africa. In 1911, too, Italy nearly caused a general war by seizing the Turkish province of Tripoli. As both the Alliance and the Entente wanted Italy's help, nothing was done by either side.

In 1908 Austria had seized the two little states of Bosnia and Herzegovina. Many of the people there were Serbians and Serbia thought that it ought to rule them. Secret groups were working against Austria in Bosnia and Herzegovina, some of them organised by the Serbian government. One important group was known as The Black Hand.

In 1912 the Greeks, Bulgarians and Serbians attacked and drove most of the remaining Turks from the Balkans. For the next two years the tiny states fought among themselves. Some of them were friendly towards the Triple Entente, and Bulgaria was friendly towards the Triple Alliance. The bigger states, such as Britain, France, Austria and Russia, did not really want a major war, but the smaller Balkan states did not have so much to lose. There was a great danger that the fighting among the smaller states would draw in the larger ones.

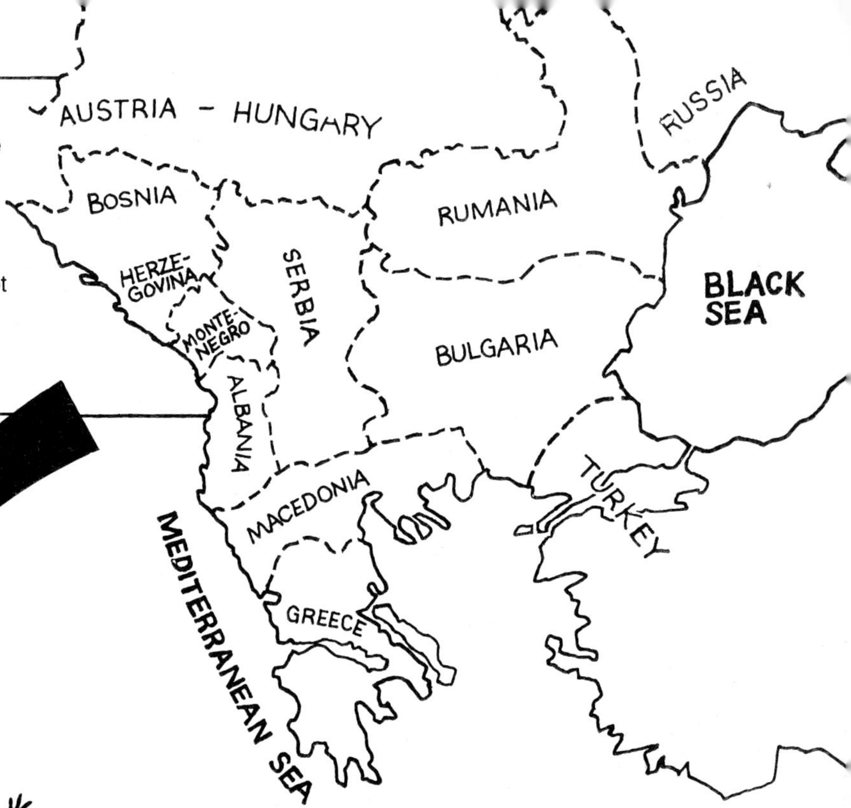

1912

1914

Archduke Ferdinand and Duchess Sophie on the day of their assassination.

In June 1914 the heir to the Austrian empire, Archduke Ferdinand, was on a visit to Sarajevo in Bosnia. There he was murdered by a 19-year-old Bosnian student called Gavrilo Princep. Austria believed that the Serbian government knew about the plot and invaded Serbia. Germany sided with her ally, Austria, and Russia got ready to help hers, Serbia. The other nations were quickly drawn into the quarrel, and by August 1914 the two sides had lined up.

WESTERN ALLIES	CENTRAL POWERS
France	Germany
Belgium	Austria-Hungary
Britain	Turkey
Russia	Bulgaria (after 1915)

Italy joined the Western Allies in 1915, Portugal and Romania in 1916, and most important of all, the USA in 1917.

So began World War I. No one in August 1914 realised that the war would drag on for four years or that it would kill between 10 and 20 million people. No one knew that it would bring to an end a whole way of life in Europe. No one thought that this war, which was called 'the war to end all wars', would be followed by an even worse one twenty years later.

Gavrilo Princep, who fired the shot that killed so many millions of people, was too young to be executed, and died of TB in prison in 1918.

13

World War 1

Although the war of 1914-1918 is called World War 1, most of the fighting was done in Europe. There were a few minor skirmishes in Africa, where German colonies were seized, and much more serious fighting in the Middle East against the Turks. There were some naval battles in the Pacific, but most of the war at sea was in the Atlantic and the North Sea.

The Western Front

German armies invaded Belgium and northern France, but could not get any further. Both sides dug deep trenches and spent most of the next four years trying to kill the men in the opposite trench and capture it. Conditions were dreadful, and the front lines moved backwards and forwards only a few miles in the whole war. By 1917 both sides had fought themselves to a standstill, but then the United States entered the war on the side of the Allies. They did not take a great part in the actual fighting, but they seemed to have limitless supplies of equipment and men. Although Germany made a tremendous effort in 1918, the Central Powers were defeated.

The last major European war had been a hundred years earlier, when there had been great charges on horseback on land, and battles between wooden sailing ships at sea. Between 1815 and 1914 there had been the vast technical changes and inventions of the industrial revolution, so that World War 1 was completely different from anything that had happened before. Some of these changes in the way of fighting and the organisation of the armed forces are shown here.

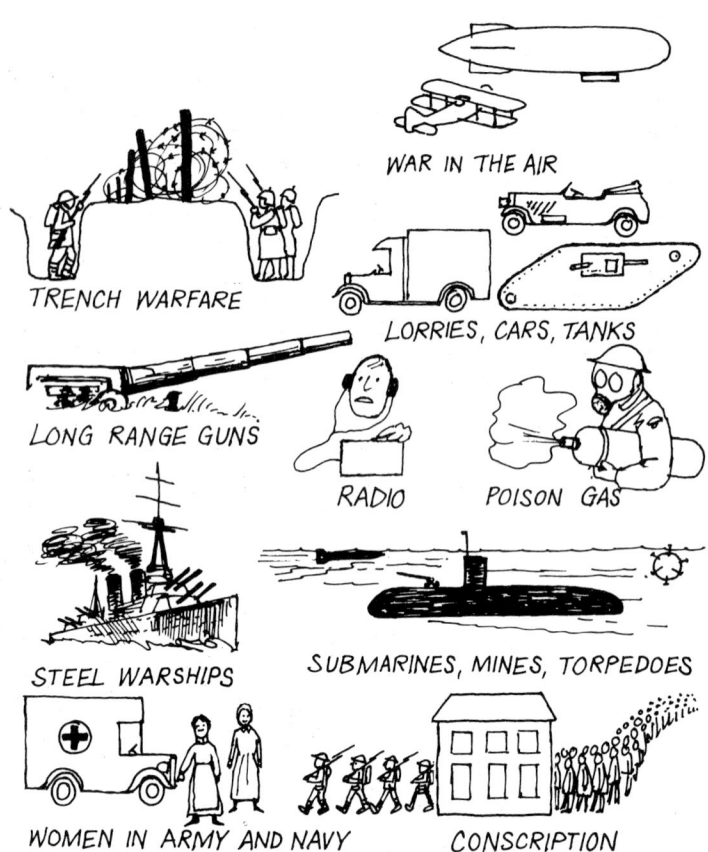

A corner of the trenches in good weather. More often the trench would have had several inches of water and mud in the bottom.

Carrying wounded back from the front line in northern France 1916. Note the tape which shows where the path was safe from mines and other dangers.

The Eastern Front

The Russian army was huge, but it was very badly equipped. Often there was only one rifle between five or six soldiers. Many of the junior officers were badly trained, while the senior officers stayed safely in St Petersburg, far from the fighting. Medical care often did not exist; food and clothing were desperately short. At first sheer weight of numbers carried the Russian army into parts of Germany and Austria, but by the end of 1914 it was being driven back everywhere with terrible casualties. At two battles alone the Russians are thought to have lost a million men. By 1916 the German and Austrian armies were deep into Russia. Hundreds of thousands of starving Russian soldiers shot their officers and deserted. The Russian army was no longer a real fighting force. In October 1917 the communist revolution (see pages 24-25) took place and Russia made peace with Germany in 1918.

Artillery on the Russian front. The soldiers are not wearing steel helmets — probably because there were none.

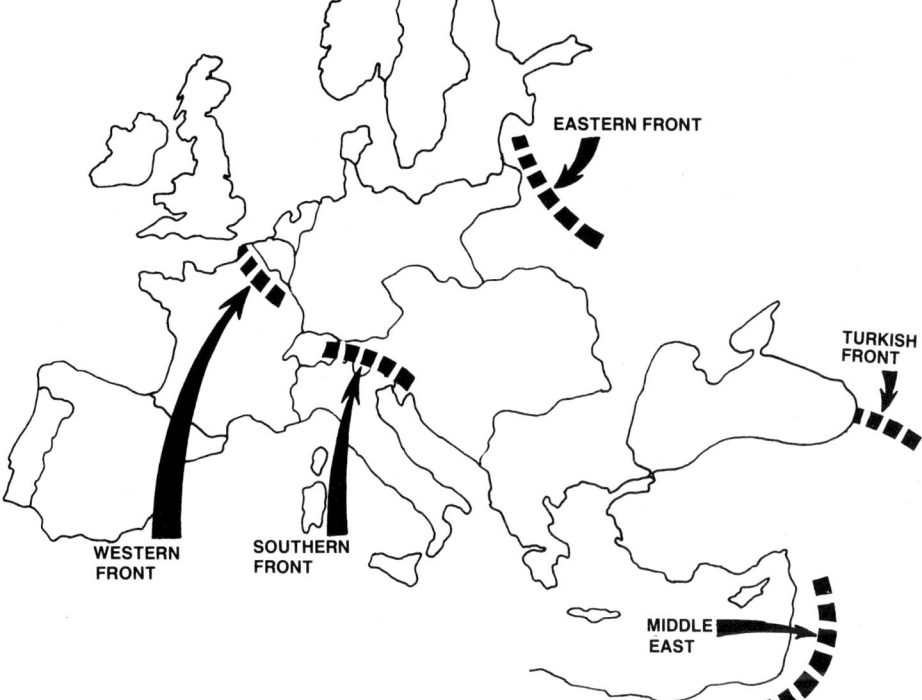

The war at sea

The British navy was so much stronger than the German navy that there was only one major naval battle between Britain and Germany, at Jutland in 1916. The British lost more ships in this battle, but the German fleet fled to its harbour and for the rest of the war never went to sea again. Germany then used submarines and laid minefields round the coasts. Warships and troopships were attacked, but — more important — Germany tried to starve Britain into surrender by using submarines to sink merchant ships bringing food and other supplies from overseas. This method was almost successful, until in 1917 the convoy system was introduced.

Battleships of the Royal Navy: Royal Sovereign (nearest camera); Resolution, Revenge (in front). Note the 15 inch guns on Royal Sovereign ready to fire a broadside.

The Middle East

In 1914 the Turkish empire covered today's Turkey, Syria, Lebanon, Israel, Jordan, Iraq, Cyprus, Yemen and large parts of Saudi Arabia. Turkey was the weakest of the Central Powers.

It was attacked by Russia in the north, and by Britain and France from the Mediterranean. T. E. Lawrence (Lawrence of Arabia) led many Arab tribesmen, who hated their Turkish masters, in a guerilla war against the Turkish army in the desert. In 1915, to make sure of the support of the Arabs, the British government said they would help them gain their independence from the Turks. Two years later Britain also told the Jewish people that it thought that they should have their own country in Palestine when the war was over. So both Arabs and Jews believed they had Britain's support to live in Palestine. These British statements are still causing a great deal of trouble in the Middle East. By 1918 the Turkish armies were beginning to collapse. The British captured Jerusalem, and the Turkish government asked for peace.

The Treaty of Versailles

The war ended in November 1918, and in 1919 a conference met at Versailles near Paris to try to sort out the terrible mess that the war had caused. Although the conference wanted a lasting peace, the members made serious mistakes and laid the foundations for an even worse war 20 years later.

The Paris peace conference, 1919. The British prime minister, Lloyd George, is seated fourth from the left.

The beaten countries were not allowed to take part and put their points of view. Russia was in the middle of a bitter civil war, and did not attend. The main conference was far too big, so that all the important decisions were made by the Big Four — Clemenceau for France, President Wilson for the USA, Orlando for Italy and Lloyd George for Britain. Even they could not agree. France, which had suffered most, wanted to punish the Germans; the USA had had no damage and few men killed, and President Wilson wanted to be generous to the Germans. Britain and Italy had to try to find a middle way. The main points of the Treaty of Versailles were:

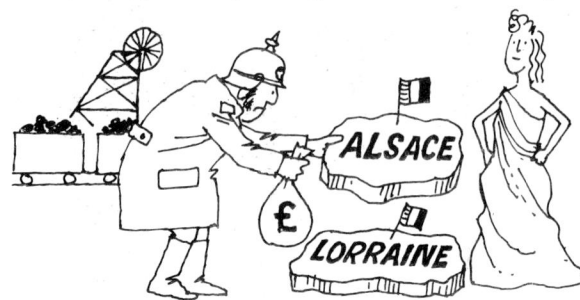

Germany was to blame for the war and must pay for the damage to the Allies, especially France. Germany must also give Alsace and Lorraine back to France.

Germany must be made weak so that it could not start another war. It was not allowed to have an air force at all, and only a tiny army and navy.

To try to stop any more wars and to help the world in general the League of Nations was set up. This was based on plans put forward by President Wilson.

The Central Powers were to lose their colonies and overseas possessions. These were given to the winning countries as mandates from the League of Nations. This meant that they did not own the ex-colonies, but had to agree to make them independent in the future.

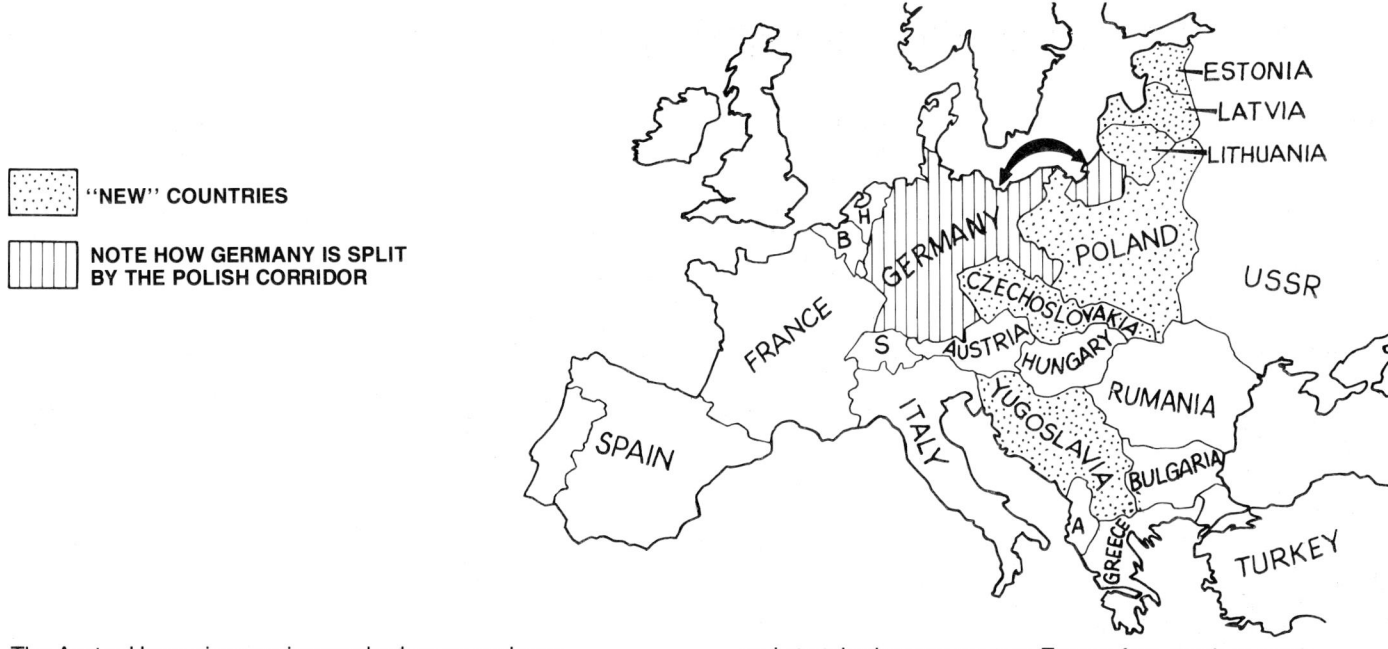

"NEW" COUNTRIES

NOTE HOW GERMANY IS SPLIT
BY THE POLISH CORRIDOR

The Austro-Hungarian empire was broken up and new countries made from territory taken from Austria-Hungary, Germany and Russia. Each new state was supposed to have a large majority of people of one nationality but this proved to be impossible. The new states had their own governments, and stretched across eastern Europe from north to south. They formed a barrier between the west and Russia because the people of western Europe were afraid that communism (see pages 22-23) would spread.

Germany was bitter because all the blame for the war was put on it and because it was forced to pay immense sums for damages.

Germany was angry at not being allowed to put its case. Later on, when it defied the treaty, it said that it had not helped to make it so it was not bound by it.

The peoples of the new countries of eastern Europe could not be properly sorted out into separate nations. There were large minorities of one people in countries ruled by another, especially Germans in Czechoslovakia, and Hungarians in Rumania.

Britain ruled Israel and Jordan as mandates from the League of Nations, and controlled Egypt. France took Syria. The Arabs, who felt that they had been promised these lands, were angry, especially when more and more Jewish people were allowed to settle in Israel.

The League of Nations

The League of Nations was the first attempt to set up a world body to deal with world problems. Each member country, whatever its size, sent one representative to the General Assembly each year. The main work was done by a small Council, which was made up largely of Europeans. The chief aim of the League was to stop wars, but it also did much other good work.

The committee appointed by the Peace Conference to draw up plans for the League of Nations. President Wilson of the USA, whose idea it was, is number 9. Other important members are 1 — Japan; 2 — France; 3 — Britain; 4 — Italy; 11 — China.

It tried to settle quarrels peacefully by discussion.

If wars started it tried to stop them by getting members to cut off supplies to the fighting nations.

The International Labour Organisation tried to improve working conditions all over the world.

The Court of International Justice tried to settle disputes between countries over such things as boundaries, fishing rights, etc.

The League had Agencies to stop slavery and drug traffic, to help refugees and minorities, to look after mandates, to

help poor nations with money, and to tackle world health problems.

BUT . . .

Fewer than half the countries of the world belonged to the League, and those that did could leave whenever they wanted to. The USA, which had put forward the idea in the first place, never joined; Russia and Germany belonged only for a few years. In any case the League had no real power. If a country defied it, there was very little that could be done. Even so, the League did some good work, especially through the Agencies. Many of these were taken over by the United Nations when it was set up in 1945 after World War 2.

The effects of World War 1

World War 1 caused terrible suffering, damage and death in Europe, and its effects were world-wide. Some were good and some bad.

The League of Nations

In the end the League was largely a failure, but it was the first time that anyone had tried to make an organisation for the whole world instead of for one country or a group of countries. After World War 2, when the United Nations was set up, people tried to avoid the mistakes made by the League.

The end of the old way of life

The war destroyed much of the old way of life. Peasants and workers had fought and died alongside people from the middle and upper classes and now ordinary people wanted a larger share in running their lives and their countries. Many of the old customs and ideas had gone for ever.

Nationalism

In Europe some nations had thrown off their foreign rulers and were governing themselves. Now people in other parts of the world, especially Egypt and other Arab countries, India and China, began to fight for their freedom and the right to have their own governments.

Rise of the USA and Japan

For four years European industry had been making weapons and equipment for war. But the world still wanted other goods, and the USA and Japan built up their factories to supply them when Europe could not. Their factories were new and more efficient, so that when the war ended they could make and sell things more effectively than Europe.

The smaller world

Air transport, radio, motor cars and all forms of communication developed rapidly during the war because the armies needed them. Now these could be adapted to peaceful purposes, and it was easier and quicker to travel and send messages.

A British airliner in 1938 at London's chief airport at Croydon.

New political ideas

The old forms of government and politics seemed to have failed because they had resulted in the terrible war. People began to look for new ways of running their countries, usually without royalty. These were sometimes extreme forms of politics such as communism and fascism (see pages 22-23, 30-33).

Joseph Stalin.

Adolf Hitler making a speech at the famous Nuremberg Rally.

Some good results for Britain from World War 1

Women had few freedoms. Very few were employed and most of those were domestic servants.

◀ *A young housemaid.*

There were gaps in understanding between the upper, middle and working classes. Often they had little to do with each other.

THE WAR

Women showed that they could work in industry, agriculture, business and in the forces, and could take great responsibility.

◀ *Working in the shell casing department of a munitions factory.*

War material was needed quickly and in large amounts so that new methods such as mass production on conveyor lines had to be used.

AFTER 1918

Women were given more freedom, partly as a reward and partly because they took it. More joined the professions and those of 30 and over were allowed to have the vote in 1919, and some even stood for Parliament.

Women Labour candidates, 1924.

Classes began to mix a little more freely. There was a growth of union power and the first Labour government was elected in 1924.

No one can say how much the war actually cost Britain in materials and damage. Nor can we put a value on the 750 000 men from Britain and Ireland who were killed and the 1 700 000 who were wounded. But in the long term there were some benefits.

Most goods were made by machines, but many of these were inefficient. A lot of time and manpower were wasted.

Medicine was improving very steadily, but the expectation of life at birth in 1900 was only 44 years for men and 48 for women.

Visiting the wounded ▶ at St Mary's hospital, London, after explosions on the underground railway, 1883.

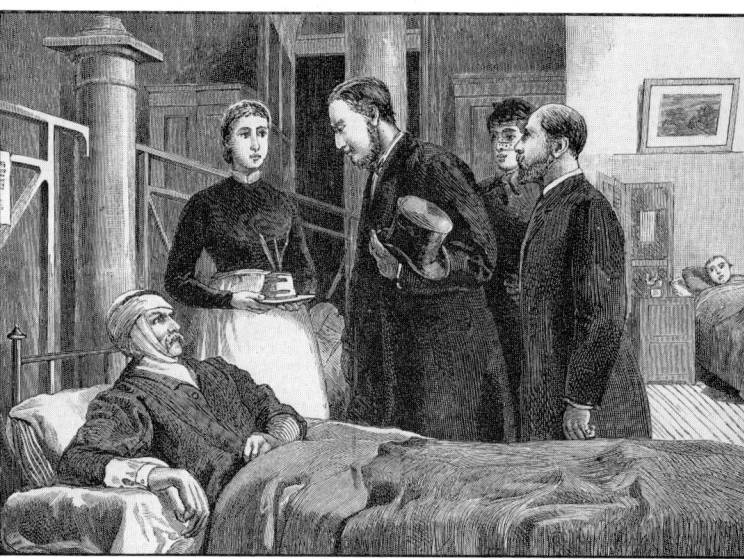

Men of all classes fought side by side in terrible conditions, and shared danger. They began to understand other people's points of view.

Doctors had to cope with large numbers of wounded and surgery and drugs improved. New methods of treatment were worked out.

An operating theatre ▶ in a Casualty Clearing Station on the Italian front.

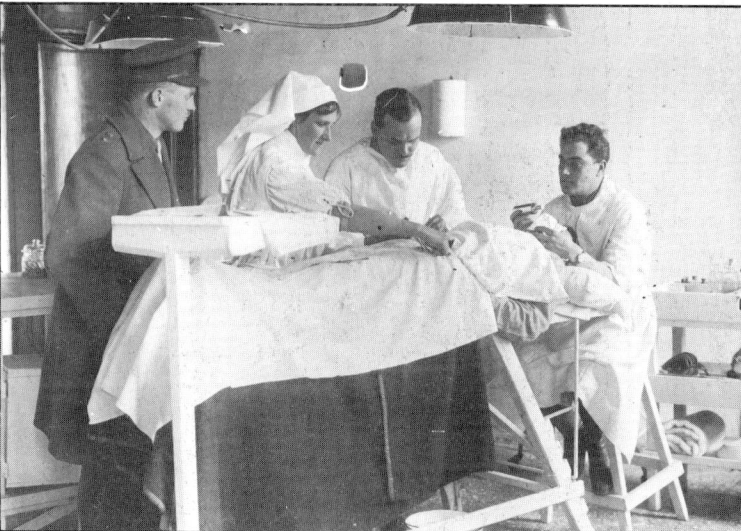

A car production line, 1928.

Mass production methods were used to make household goods, cars and clothes. This made them cheaper so that more people could afford more of them.

There were advances in all branches of medicine. By 1930 the expectation of life at birth had risen to 59 years for men and 63 for women.

Communism and capitalism

The two main political and economic systems in the world today are communism and capitalism. In many ways they are completely opposite methods of running a state and each have advantages and disadvantages, strengths and weaknesses.

Many states today have mixed economies. Some communist countries have small free-enterprise markets, and many capitalist countries have state controlled (nationalised) industries and services.

Communist

Communist governments believe that the state should own everything — land, industry, mines, transport, shops, communications.

Communism has a planned economy. The government works out how much the state needs — food, fuel, manufactured goods, transport, etc. — and orders that amount to be produced, so that there is no over-production or under-production. Prices of all goods are controlled, and profits go back to the state, not to private individuals.

Communism, with its planned economy and everyone working for the state, means that there is a much more equal society. Not everyone is paid the same but the differences are less than in capitalist societies. No one can be allowed to become very rich while others are poor.

A communist government is strong and can get things done because it is a one-party state without any opposition parties. People who disagree with the basic ideas of communism seem like traitors who are trying to ruin a fair system which gives everyone freedom from poverty.

Capitalist

Except in its most extreme form (national socialism) capitalism means a parliamentary system with two or more parties putting forward different ideas about running the country. People can change their government at general elections if they do not like the present government's policies.

Capitalism encourages competition and allows people to use their initiative. This can lead to more money and a better standard of living. It can benefit everyone because new ideas are encouraged. People work hard if they think they are likely to reach a better standard of living by doing so.

Parliamentary systems can change more quickly than centrally-controlled ones. The commercial world especially can change quickly to make use of new ideas.

Most production is controlled by private people or companies. Manufacturers compete with each other to make profits. Competition keeps prices down and quality has to be good enough to persuade people to buy at a price they can afford.

balance

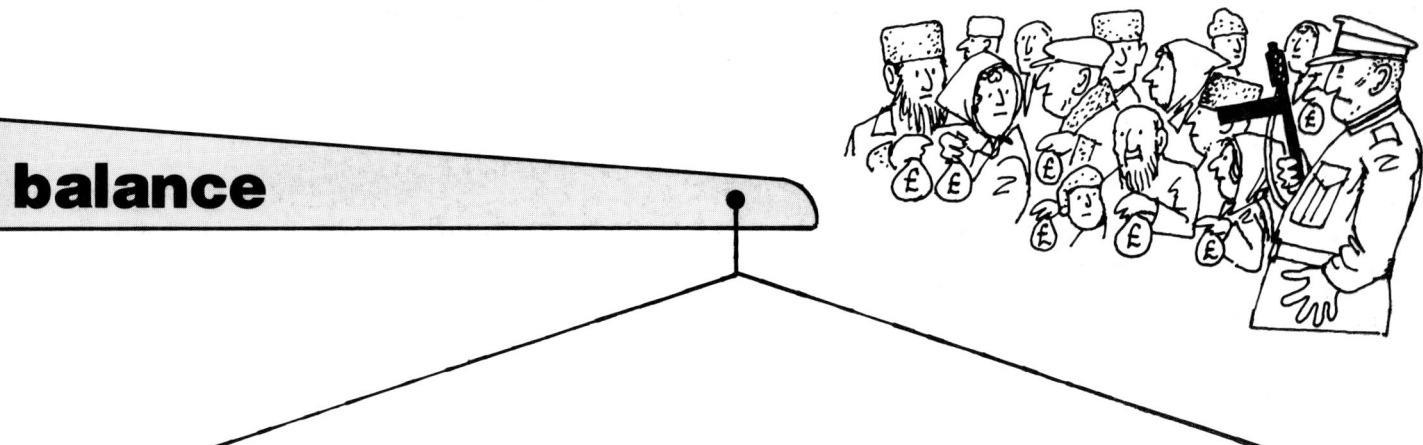

Because the communist system depends on central control it can become very rigid. Large plans have to be approved by the communist party, so that there is usually much less opportunity for initiative than in the capitalist system.

Because the party has to keep itself in power it cannot allow serious opposition. This means secret police and political trials. People cannot say in public what they really believe if they disagree with the system, or publish books which oppose it.

Although people living under communist governments may have freedom from poverty, they are not free to change their government peacefully. They often have little choice of goods in shops because the government decides what may be produced. Because communist governments maintain strict control over foreign currency, ordinary people cannot buy foreign money easily, and this makes it difficult for them to visit non-communist countries except on official business.

balance

Parliamentary systems can result in weak governments, especially when two or more parties have to join in a coalition. Governments often avoid strong measures in case they are defeated in parliament or voted out at the next election.

A new government may reverse laws made by the previous one. This can be costly and wasteful.

Capitalism can lead to an unequal and unjust society. A few people can become very rich, while others, through no fault of their own, are very poor with little chance of improving their lives.

Rich and powerful people can sometimes influence the government to do what they want. Unless there is a fair government or strong trade unions they can exploit the majority of working people by giving low wages and bad conditions.

Russia's road to revolution

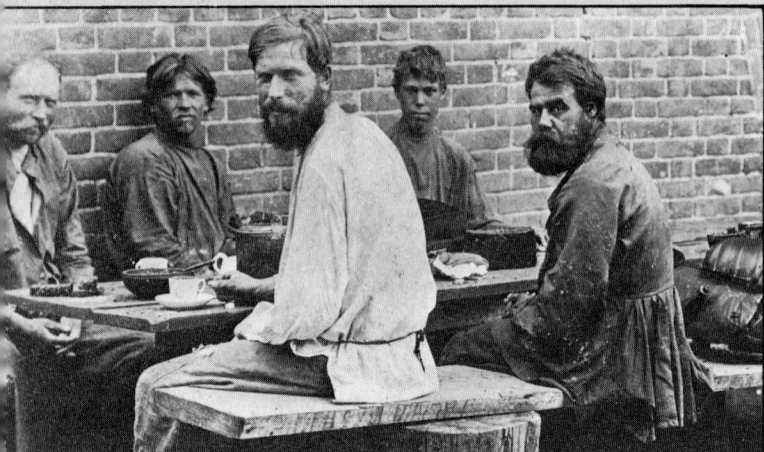

Russian serfs at the end of the nineteenth century.

In the middle of the nineteenth century Russia was very backward. Industrialisation had scarcely started and there were few large towns. The country was ruled by the tsar and the upper classes, who kept order by secret police and savage punishments including exile to Siberia. Civil servants and judges could often be bribed — if you had any money. Most people did not. Three quarters of all Russians were serfs, that is, almost slaves, working for the government or the nobility on their vast estates. These peasants lived harsh lives. They could not move from their own village and had to do what their master told them.

Lenin speaking at a Military Training Festival in Moscow, 1919.

Many left-wing political parties were formed among the workers, even though there was no parliament. Some of them wanted to work slowly towards better conditions through elections and a parliament. Some wanted to use violence and began a campaign of bombing and murder. But the most important group was the Social Democratic Party, formed in 1898. It later split into two wings. Lenin became the leader of what was called the Bolshevik wing. He believed in the communist ideas of Karl Marx and tried to unite all the left-wing parties to overthrow the tsar and set up a workers' government. In 1900 Lenin was forced to leave Russia as he was known to the secret police as a man with dangerous ideas who had already been in prison.

1850s   1860s   1890s   1905

In 1856 the Russians were defeated in the Crimean war. The tsar, Alexander II, realised that his country was behind much of Europe, and began to make reforms. He abolished serfdom and improved education. Peasants now had to buy their land from the landowners. There were loan schemes to help them do so. But as a result many became even poorer than before. Tsar Alexander tried to expand industry. Towns began to grow. Workers in the industrial cities were very different from peasants. They met and discussed the bad conditions of the working class, whereas peasants on the great estates rarely saw outsiders.

In 1905 the Russians were badly defeated by the Japanese in a war and there was a general uprising led by the left-wing parties. Police, politicians and aristocrats were murdered and land seized by peasants. The army was on the point of mutiny and the tsar, Nicholas, gave in. In the October Manifesto, he allowed the people to have elections for a parliament called the Duma. But now all the left-wing groups quarrelled. A Duma was elected but was quickly dismissed because it would not agree with the tsar. A second Duma was chosen — and dismissed. A third was elected and this one lasted for five years.

The tsar and family, 1905.

In 1904 the tsar's wife, the tsaritsa, had had a son, the heir to the throne. He had haemophilia, a condition which prevents blood from clotting. He might bleed to death from a scratch. There was no medical cure, but the tsaritsa believed that a monk, Rasputin, could control the bleeding. The royal family allowed Rasputin to influence politics, though many people hated him.

1850 – 1917

Gregory Rasputin, who greatly influenced the tsaritsa.

When World War 1 broke out in 1914, the Russians were very excited but within a few months the people realised just how badly things were going. Transport and production collapsed. Everyone was short of food and everything else. In 1915 the tsar made himself commander-in-chief of the forces, though he knew little about war. The tsaritsa tried to persuade the tsar to take Rasputin's advice. Every day tens of thousands of men died in battle, of disease or of starvation. Everything was in confusion as the Germans and Austrians forced the Russian armies further and further backwards.

The Germans saw a way of getting Russia out of the war. In the summer of 1917 they helped Lenin leave Switzerland, where he had been in exile, and smuggled him across Europe in a secret train to Russia. At once he gathered his Bolsheviks together and tried to take over from Kerensky's government. The confusion was worse than ever: peasants seized the land and killed aristocrats; workers seized their factories and tried to run them; soldiers poured back from the front when they heard what was happening at home. The whole of Russia was in complete collapse. Kerensky realised too late that the Bolsheviks were about to take over.

1914   **February 1917**   **Summer 1917**   **October 1917**

In February 1917 the starving people of St Petersburg (now Leningrad) rioted. The troops in the city mutinied and joined the people. The revolution had begun. A new government took over from the tsar's ministers, and at the same time a committee (in Russian, a soviet) of workers and soldiers was set up in St Petersburg to run the city. The most important man in the new government was Kerensky, but by this time the army was electing its own officers and he could not control it. The tsar abdicated in March, and with his family was murdered a year later. And the war dragged on. Food grew shorter.

Dead and wounded Leninist soldiers after the siege of the Duma, 1917.

At dawn on 25th October 1917 the Bolshevik Red Guards seized railway stations, the bridges, the telephone exchanges and other important places in St Petersburg. They stormed the Winter Palace, where Kerensky's government was meeting. The surprise was so complete that the building was defended only by a few soldiers with young officers. In a few hours Lenin had taken control of St Petersburg, and soon controlled much of central Russia. The first phase of the communist revolution was complete.

Lenin's followers storming the Winter Palace, 1917.

Russia 1921-1940

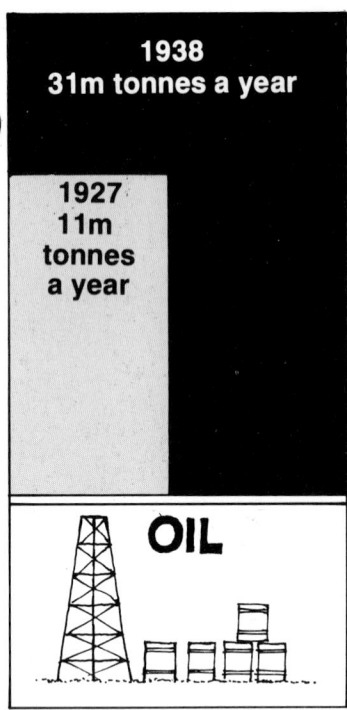

OIL
1938 31m tonnes a year
1927 11m tonnes a year

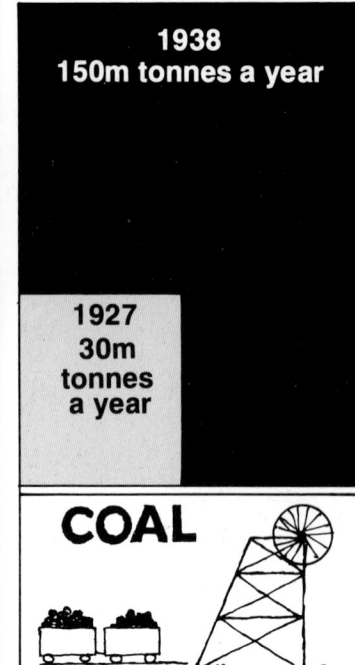

COAL
1938 150m tonnes a year
1927 30m tonnes a year

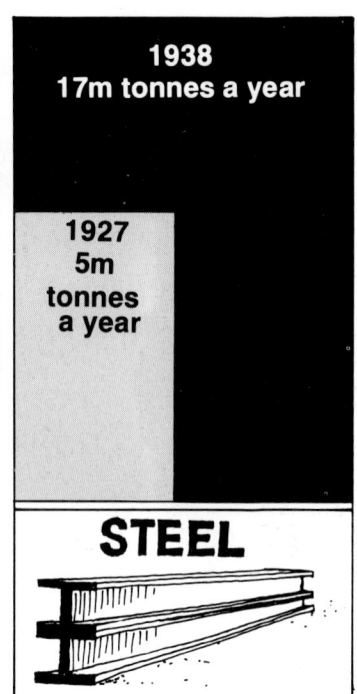

STEEL
1938 17m tonnes a year
1927 5m tonnes a year

Lenin was only in control of a small but very important part of Russia. Early in 1918 he signed a peace treaty with Germany (the treaty of Brest-Litovsk), and was forced to give up large parts of the country with most of the industry and the best farm lands. Starvation became worse, and then a civil war broke out between those who wanted to bring back the old form of government (the Whites) and the new communist government (the Reds). Trotsky, a brilliant communist leader, managed to organise the Red Army so well that the Whites were defeated. The communists now controlled a shattered, starving country where industrial output was only a fraction of what it had been in 1913. The task facing the communist government seemed impossible.

Slowly Lenin and the communist party pulled Russia from the edge of total collapse, but life was desperately hard. People worked very long hours in farming, or in heavy industry (coal, iron, steel and machinery) for low wages and without holidays. In 1924 Lenin died. Stalin and Trotsky were both possible leaders and Lenin had seen faults in both, but Stalin managed to take power. Trotsky, who wanted to keep the revolution going until the whole world was communist, was sent into exile and finally killed on Stalin's orders in 1940. So began Stalin's long rule, which, though it was very harsh and cruel, made the Soviet Union one of the most powerful countries on earth in less than 20 years. (Russia is now often called the USSR, the Union of Soviet Socialist Republics, or the Soviet Union.)

Stalin (left) in 1919, and Trotsky (right) in 1918.

Stalin said that if Russia was strong and prosperous other countries would copy her and become communist without fighting. But he knew that first Russia must build its industry and so in 1928 he began the First Five-Year Plan. This was a crash programme to build factories, power stations, mines, oil wells and heavy transport. To try to make farming more efficient, he joined tiny peasant holdings and made them into huge farms of many thousands of hectares. The peasants worked for the government on these 'collective' farms, growing what the government ordered. Although the collectives could have machinery that peasants could not afford on their own, output was low, because people wanted to work for themselves. Many even killed their farm animals rather than hand them over to the state.

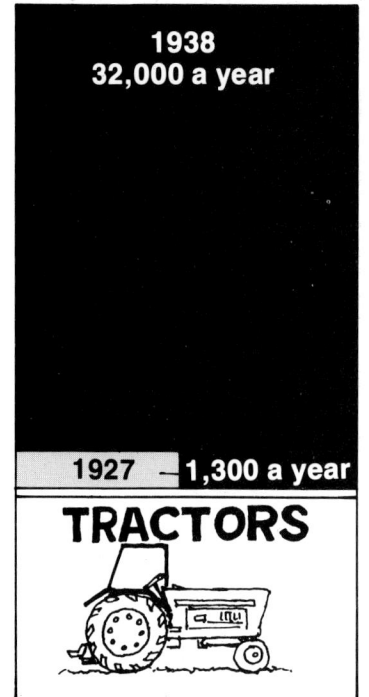

TRACTORS

1938
32,000 a year

1927 — 1,300 a year

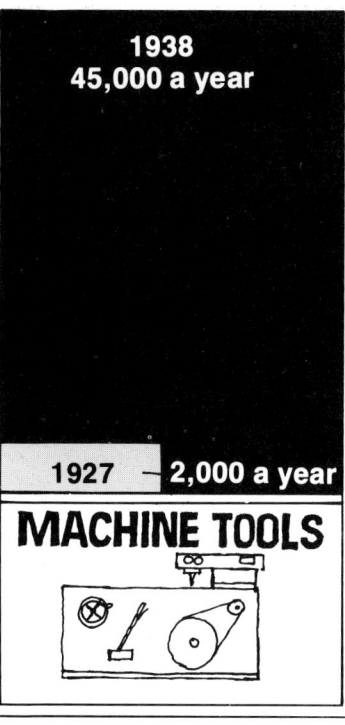

MACHINE TOOLS

1938
45,000 a year

1927 — 2,000 a year

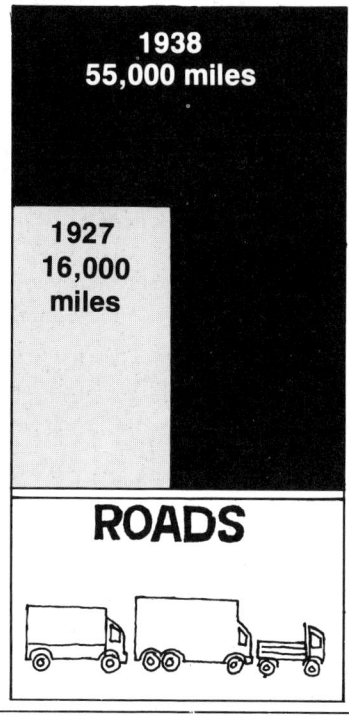

ROADS

1938
55,000 miles

1927
16,000
miles

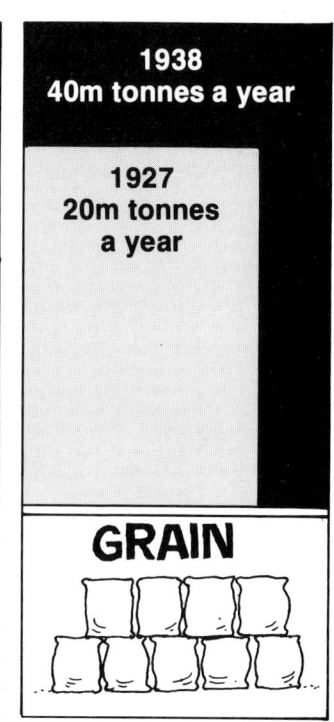

GRAIN

1938
40m tonnes a year

1927
20m tonnes
a year

The better-off peasants, called kulaks, rebelled against the collectives, but Stalin forced them into the state farms. In three or four years about four million kulaks were killed or had died in labour camps. More than half of the country's animals were dead and much land was not being farmed.

Stalin now turned to attack other groups he thought were threatening him. Many of his old friends in the party who had fought through the revolution were executed on fake charges because Stalin thought they might try to take over power from him. Thousands of Red Army officers were shot, tens of thousands of ordinary people were killed, sometimes for no real reason, sometimes because they had criticised Stalin's government. He now had total control.

The First Five-Year Plan had some success, but the second (1933-1937) continued to drive the people hard. The secret police were everywhere, spying on workers who after years of very hard work were asking when they were going to get something for all their sacrifices. By the end of the Second Five-Year Plan, however, Russia was the third largest industrial power in the world, after the USA and Germany. The Third Five-Year Plan (1938-1942) began to allow factories to make a few more goods to make life more comfortable — bicycles, furniture, clothes and household goods. But by 1939 it was clear that war was coming and the factories had to make weapons.

Communist Russia and Nazi Germany were bitter enemies. Britain and France hoped that fear of Russia would stop Germany attacking Poland and so prevent a European war. Then in August 1939 a horrified world heard that Stalin and Hitler had signed a treaty not to fight each other, and also to share Poland between them. In September Poland was invaded by Germany from the west and by Russia from the east. Russia seized Lithuania, Estonia and Latvia and also invaded Finland.

Russia 1945-1970

When World War 2 ended in 1945 Russia was shattered. Millions of citizens were dead; hundreds of towns and cities and much of industry and agriculture had been destroyed. It seemed that 25 years of desperate struggle had been in vain, and Russia had to start from nothing.

Stalingrad after the battle showing the terrible devastation facing the USSR when the war ended.

The Berlin airlift, 1948-9. Unloading food supplies from a British flying boat on a lake in Berlin.

We call the years from 1945 to 1953 the time of the Cold War (pages 56-57). Poland, Czechoslovakia, Hungary, Romania, Bulgaria, Yugoslavia, Albania and Eastern Germany had communist governments and became 'satellites' of the USSR, forming a barrier between Russia and the west. Each side made threats, blocked radio broadcasts, closed roads and railways and did many other things to upset the other. There was always a terrible danger that one side or the other would do something to turn the cold war into a hot war with nuclear weapons, as Russia soon had its own.

WARTIME ALLIES — IRON CURTAIN — COLD WAR — COMMUNIST CHINA

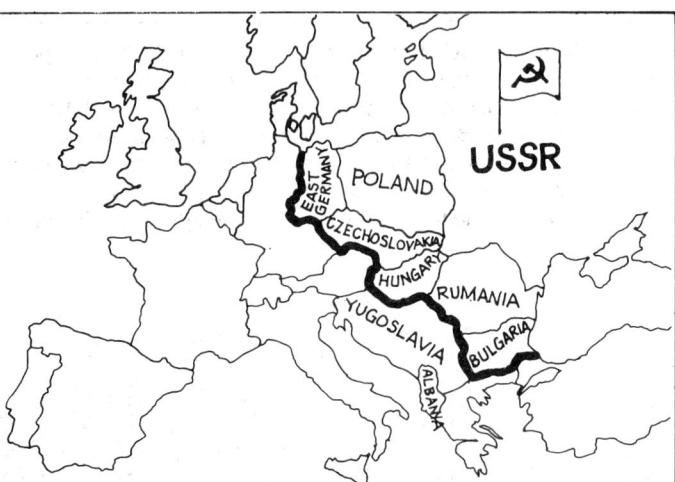

To make matters worse the wartime alliance broke up: the USA, Britain and France on one side and the USSR on the other. The USA alone had the atom bomb, and most of her forces intact. Russia suspected that the United States, which hated communism, would attack it. Europe became divided into two parts by what Churchill called the Iron Curtain — a communist east and a parliamentary west. The two formed military alliances: Nato in the west and the Warsaw Pact in the east. The world seemed on the brink of another war.

The western nations felt that the danger was even greater when in 1949 the communists under Mao-tse-tung won the civil war in China (page 70) and set up the Marxist People's Republic. Now almost 40% of the people in the world were under communist governments, and if they united they would be almost unstoppable.

The Soviet premier, Kruschev, pounding the table at the General Assembly of the UN in 1971.

Matters were getting worse when Stalin died in 1953. He was succeeded first by Malenkov and then in 1955 by Krushchev. Krushchev especially travelled all over the world, talking of 'peaceful co-existence' — the idea that although communism and western governments were so different, they did not have to fight and should be able to live peacefully side by side. The threat of nuclear war seemed to fade.

In 1960 a quarrel broke out between the two great communist powers, Russia and China (page 70). Western countries now felt that they were unlikely to work together. But Russia saw itself as surrounded by enemies. The Soviet Union gave way to the west on some important matters, such as the Cuban missile crisis in 1961 (page 41) and signed a nuclear test ban treaty in 1963. Once again the world relaxed a little.

PEACEFUL COEXISTENCE

HUNGARIAN RISING

MISSILE CRISIS

CHINA — SOVIET QUARREL
MISSILE CRISIS RESOLVED
NUCLEAR TEST BAN TREATY

CZECHOSLOVAKIA INVADED

But in 1956 the communist Hungarian government began to make reforms such as freeing political prisoners and asked the United Nations for independence. The Soviet Union did not wish a satellite state to have that freedom, and the Red Army invaded the country. The Hungarian rising was put down with great loss of life. To the west it seemed that Russia had not really changed at all, and that the threat of war was as great as ever.

Hungarian demonstrators smash a statue of Lenin and fly their national flag in the uprising of 1956.

In 1964 Krushchev fell from power and was followed by Kosygin and Brezhnev. When in 1968 Czechoslovakia, like Hungary twelve years earlier, tried to make some reforms, the Red Army again marched in. But this time there was no serious bloodshed. The Czech leader was removed but allowed to go free, and some of the Warsaw Pact nations even refused to take part in the invasion. Russia had made considerable changes since the worst days of Stalin.

Prague during the Czech rising in 1968. Russian soldiers are collecting propaganda leaflets while Czech people look on.

Germany 1919 - 1939

After World War 1 Germany was in a state of chaos with many political parties fighting for power. At last a parliamentary government was set up at Weimar (1919) to try to get Germany on its feet again. One problem was that Germany had to pay France vast sums of money for damages. As Germany could not do this, France seized the rich industrial Ruhr area (1923). Inflation was terrible. In 1923 you had to pay 21 billion German marks to buy one pound sterling! In 1915 the mark had been worth 15 to the pound.

Inflation gone mad. Bank notes, like newspapers, were worth only what they would fetch as pulp.

After 1924 things began to improve. The money problem was settled and huge loans from the United States allowed Germany to get industry going again with the latest machinery. As things got better people left extreme political parties and concentrated on making a living. But the extreme parties of both right and left — Nazis (fascists) and communists — were still there, waiting for the right moment.

WORLD WAR 1 — 1919 — 1923 — 1924-28 — 1929-32

As the government struggled with the problems, many people turned to extreme political parties which said they could offer quick and easy answers. On one side were the communists and on the other right-wing parties such as the National Socialist Workers' Party — Nazis for short. One of the early members of this party was Adolf Hitler. In 1923 he attempted a revolution in Munich, but his small 'army' was quickly defeated and he was sent to prison. While he was there he wrote Mein Kampf (My Struggle), which explained how he would run the country.

In 1929 the Depression (page 34) hit Germany very badly. It could not sell its products so there was much unemployment. America stopped lending it money and asked for repayment of loans. By early 1932 one man in three was out of work, and people began again to turn to anyone who promised to solve the problems. In the elections of 1933 Hitler and his Nazi party took 45% of the seats but this was not enough to allow him to take over.

Adolf Hitler after his appointment as Chancellor in 1933. General Goering stands next to him.

The Reichstag on fire, February 1933.

In February 1933 the German parliament building (the Reichstag) was burned down. Hitler claimed that it had been done by the communists, and all the communist members of parliament were arrested. Without them Hitler had a large enough majority to pass a law making himself dictator — the Führer or Leader. The Weimar government had gone and the evil Third Reich of the Nazis had begun.

Hitler began to re-arm Germany in defiance of the Treaty of Versailles, which many other governments now realised had been very unfair. He began to build an air force, submarines, warships and many new weapons. Children and young people were given compulsory military training. Many of the unemployed were put to work building the first motorways in Europe (the autobahns) which would be important for moving troops and supplies when war came.

1933   **1934-39**   WORLD WAR 2

All opposition was forbidden. Everyone who was suspected of being against Hitler was seized by the secret police (the Gestapo) and sent to concentration camps or executed. Trade unions were abolished; there was no freedom of the press; artists were not allowed to express themselves freely. Schools taught children to believe in Hitler and his ideas. Hitler blamed the Jews and the Treaty of Versailles for Germany's problems. The Nazis said that Jews were an inferior race. They were not allowed to be doctors or civil servants. Their shops were attacked. Later the Gestapo rounded up Jews and they were killed in concentration camps. (See also page 90.)

An anti-Jewish poster in Vienna. It says 'All Jews are criminals'.

With Germany itself in his power, Hitler began to threaten neighbouring countries. The Germans, he said, were the Master Race, and must have more land. All Germans must be united under the Nazis and Nazi parties were formed in countries such as Austria, Czechoslovakia and Poland, where there were a good many German people. Hitler demanded that land taken from Germany by the Treaty of Versailles should be returned. It was only a matter of time before war broke out.

Italy staggers between the wars

Mussolini (immediately under the white flag on the right) with some of his senior staff in 1923 celebrate the march on Rome in 1922.

After World War 1 Italy, like Germany, was in a desperate state. It too had many different political parties, each with different ideas. Among them was an extreme right-wing party, the Fascists, led by Benito Mussolini. He promised to destroy communism and to make Italy the centre of a great empire as it had been 2000 years earlier.

Once in power Mussolini outlawed all other parties and the trade unions, and after a few years abolished all elections. He became dictator and called himself Il Duce (The Leader).

 **1919**  **1921**  **1923**  **1924**

In 1921 the Fascist party won a few seats in the Italian parliament, but the political situation became so bad that in 1922 Mussolini's men (called Blackshirts because of the black uniform they wore) went to Rome to demand that their leader be made prime minister. The weak king, who thought anything was worth trying, agreed.

Mussolini addressing a crowd. He liked to be photographed from low down because he was short and this made him seem taller.

For a time Fascism seemed the answer to Italy's problems. The strong man got things done, which had not happened before. Roads and railways were built; pensions and social security started; schools were built and education made compulsory; marshes were drained to make new farms. As a sign of the new times the Forum of the Caesars of ancient Rome was restored after centuries of neglect.

Fascism did some good for Italy. Here, Mussolini lays the foundation stone of a new film centre, modelled on Hollywood.

Crack Abyssinian troops armed with rifles and wooden spears on their way to fight Italian tanks, heavy guns, bomber aeroplanes and poison gas.

But there was a bad side too. Opponents of Fascism often disappeared mysteriously; everything was censored; there was no freedom of speech; children were compulsorily drafted into military training and legal rights were taken away. Many Italian people accepted this as the price they had to pay for better conditions.

In 1935, to divert people's minds from the difficulties at home, Mussolini sent his troops to Africa 'to capture an empire'. They attacked the backward state of Ethiopia which had defeated an Italian army 30 years earlier. The Ethiopian tribesmen fought with spears and bows against the Italian bombers, poison gas and machine guns. Naturally the Italians won and Ethiopia was added to Mussolini's 'empire'.

1930-32  **1934**  **1936**

The Depression hit Italy very badly. Its industry was already weak, and the new difficulties resulted in terrible unemployment. To try to disguise this, Mussolini drafted tens of thousands of men into the army.

The League of Nations made only the feeblest effort to stop Mussolini's attack on Ethiopia, with the result that smaller nations saw that it was useless and left. It was really the end of the League. Most countries were disgusted with Mussolini, but Hitler completely approved of his aggression. When other nations refused to have much to do with Italy, Germany signed a treaty of friendship with it — the Rome-Berlin Axis (1936). Another important step towards World War 2 had been taken.

The Great Depression 1929 - 1932

Trade does not normally go on at a steady level. It has booms, when most people have plenty of work and money, many goods are sold and business prospers. Then there are recessions, when there is little trade, much unemployment and poverty. Booms and recessions tend to follow each other fairly regularly, and one of the biggest problems of governments in the modern world is to try to keep trade steady.

Factories and shops busy. Plenty of jobs and money. Many goods bought. High living standards.

Still more goods sold = more jobs = more money = yet more jobs.

Slight drop in demand = less wages = further drop in demand.

BOOM

A few more goods sold = a few more jobs = more wages = more demand.

Still fewer goods sold = less wages = less money.

RECESSION

Mass unemployment = factories and shops closed = low income = few goods bought.

RECESSION AGAIN

Depression in the USA. A free soup kitchen in Chicago run by the gangster, Al Capone.

After World War 1 there were great shortages to be made up. People had been without many goods for years and now wanted them. There were repairs to be done; new things such as motor cars and household goods were being made by mass production methods so that they were cheaper and more people could buy them. For a few years there was great prosperity, especially in America. There was plenty of work for everyone, with good wages.

Then in 1929 it came to a sudden end. Businesses had been growing too fast. Too many goods were being made and many could not be sold. Profits started falling. The prices of shares on the New York stock exchange fell and many people lost money. Thousands of businesses went bankrupt. As the USA was the biggest industrial country in the world, the depression spread everywhere. In Europe thousands of factories closed, and millions were unemployed.

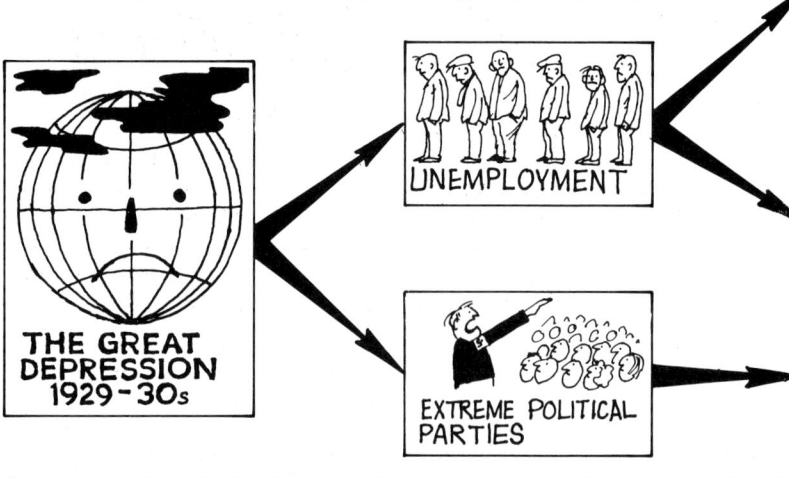

Governments thought that the recession would soon end, but it just got worse. Some countries, like Germany, voted extreme political parties into power because they thought strong dictators would put things right. Some countries, like the USA, tried to reduce unemployment by getting men to work on government schemes for building such things as roads, dams and railways. Some countries enrolled unemployed men in their armies, or (like Italy) turned attention from the troubles at home by starting wars abroad.

About 1932-35 things began to improve — but largely because many countries were beginning to prepare for war, and industry was making weapons and equipment. The effects of the Great Depression, as it is called, were felt all round the world, but especially among the industrial nations.

The rise of the dictatorships

When countries are in serious trouble it often seems that parliaments are too slow and too weak to get anything done. The different political parties discuss and argue, and often come to an arrangement which suits no one. A very strong government, with one man in complete power and no opposition party at all seems a better way to get decision and action.

After World War 1 most countries in Europe had very serious problems — shortages, inflation, unemployment, quarrelling political parties — and many of them became one-party states ruled by dictators. In 1914 almost all of Europe was ruled by parliamentary governments or monarchs. By the mid-1930s all except 11 were ruled by dictators.

Germany: Hitler 1933

USSR: Lenin 1917

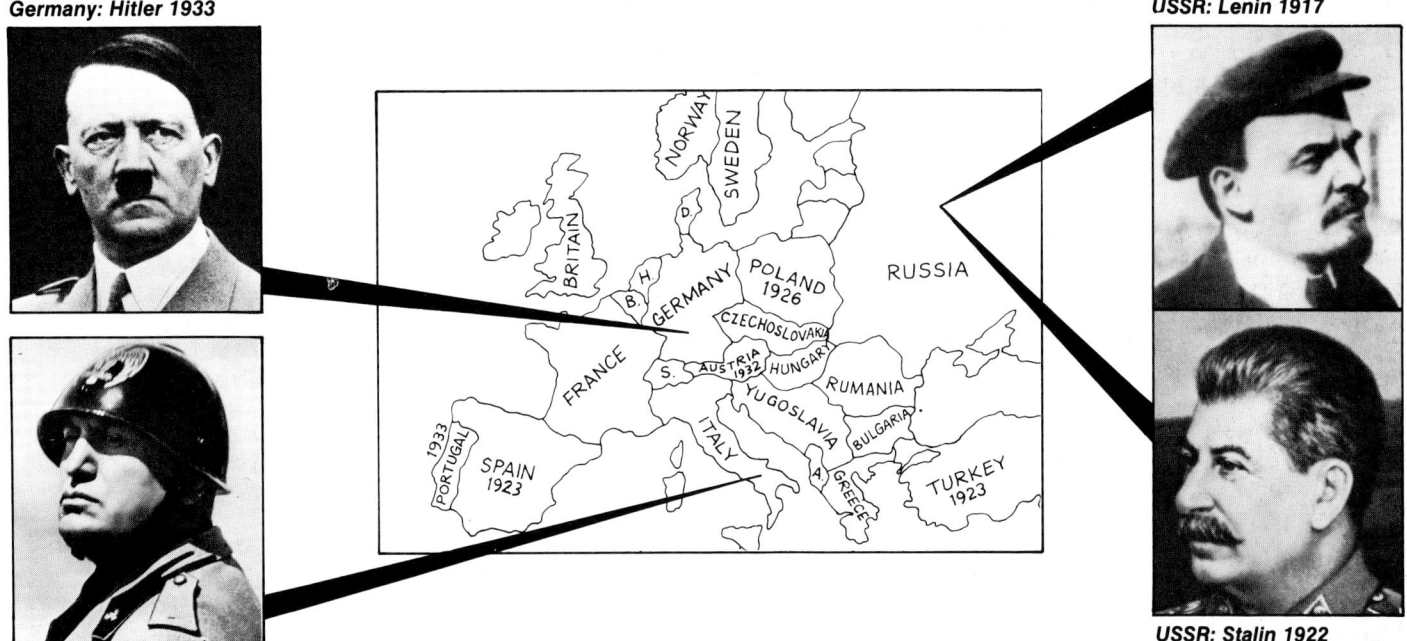

Italy: Mussolini 1922

USSR: Stalin 1922

Dictatorships are strong because

All opposition is silenced — either in prison or executed. Secret police use torture to find people who have different ideas from the leader.

One party controls education completely so that pupils are taught only those things the leader wants them to know.

One party controls newspapers, radio, TV and books so that nothing appears which opposes it.

There is military training of children and young people, who are taught to believe that the leader can do no wrong.

Hitler Youth on a six-week march to a training camp in 1935.

35

The USA: 1823 - 1939

The development of the United States after the War of Independence was fairly slow. In 1823 President Monroe warned European countries against trying to interfere in any part of the American continent. This Monroe Doctrine was the beginning of isolationism — the policy of staying out of world affairs. By 1850 the limits of the present USA were more or less settled, but most of the land west of the Mississippi was empty and unexplored.

After 1865 there was a great expansion of industry and transport, and many people moved westwards. Railways and canals were built. New cities and factories sprang up. Millions of immigrants poured into the US from Europe, especially from Britain, Ireland, Germany, Italy and Russia. Hunters, trappers and pioneers travelled into the empty lands, driving out the Indians. After them came merchants and traders. Settlements grew into villages, then into towns and cities, until the whole country from coast to coast was settled.

ISOLATIONIST WALL

1823

1861-5

1865-

1898

From 1861-1865 the US was torn by the bitter Civil War. The industrial northern states, where slavery was illegal, wanted it abolished in the southern cotton-growing ones. President Lincoln declared all slaves free in 1863, but the southern states did not surrender for another two years. It was the worst war in US history. More Americans were killed than in World Wars 1 and 2 put together.

One of the earliest wartime photographs (1863). It shows railway engines used in the Civil War for transporting troops and materials.

From 1865 to 1890 the US was completely occupied with its own affairs, and its industries grew to challenge those of Britain and Germany. But it had problems with overseas markets. In the 1890s it began a little European-style aggression to help its trade. In 1898 in a war with Spain it seized Puerto Rico, Hawaii, the Philippines and other Pacific islands as well as control of Cuba. In the next few years it gained control of Panama, Nicaragua, San Domingo and Haiti.

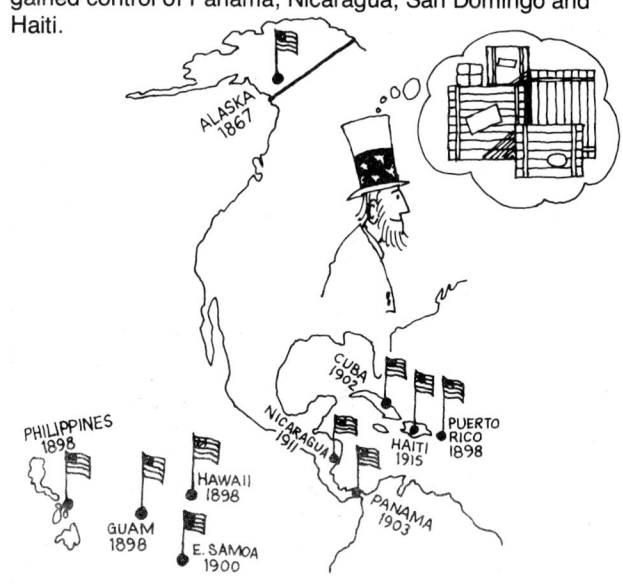

US troops landing in Le Havre, France, July 1917.

When World War 1 broke out in Europe the US was determined to stay out of the fighting. Its industry and agriculture enjoyed a great boom supplying Europe with food and war materials. But President Wilson began to feel that it would be better for the US to give up isolationism and join the war on the side of the Allies. When German submarines sank several ships with American passengers the US entered the war in 1917. Although its troops did not do much actual fighting their numbers and equipment worried the German leaders and so the USA played an important part in ending the war.

An armour-plated police car in Chicago, 1933. The sheriff is in the centre. The holes in the windscreen are for guns.

The 1920s were the greatest boom period ever in US history. This was the Jazz Age: mass-produced cars, famous Hollywood films and stars and a high standard of living for most people. But the prosperity was not based on a firm foundation, and in 1929 came the great Wall Street Crash (page 34). By 1930 in the Great Depression over 20% of workers were unemployed and many others worked for starvation wages. People wandered the streets begging or offering to work just for food and shelter. Thousands of businesses became bankrupt.

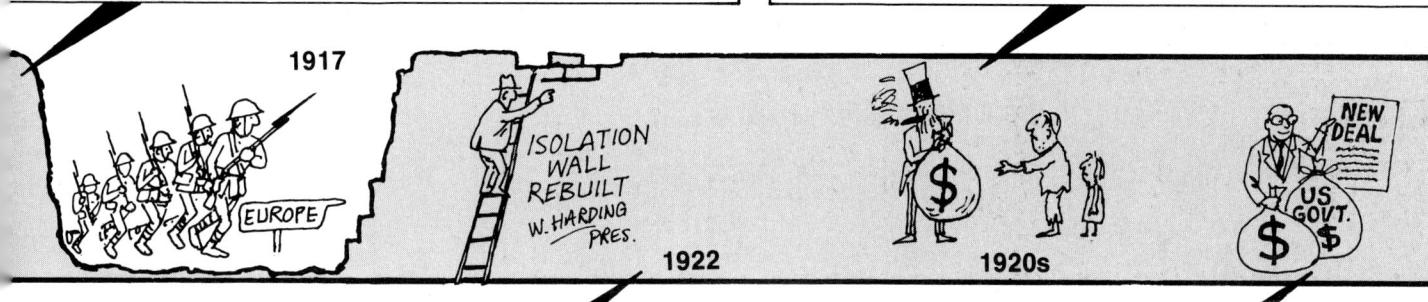

President Wilson was one of the most important people at the peace conference at Versailles. His Fourteen Points tried to give something to everyone, but in the end pleased no one. The US government refused to sign the treaty, and in the 1922 elections Wilson was voted out. Americans were disgusted with what they saw as greed in the European states. They wanted only to get back to isolationism. The US would not join the League of Nations and this made the League much weaker than it might have been.

The government seemed helpless, but in 1932 Franklin D Roosevelt became president. At once he began his New Deal programme. Billions of dollars were spent to start public works such as building new roads and schools and planting new forests. The biggest scheme was the Tennessee Valley Authority, which covered seven states with great hydro-electric schemes to provide electricity for farms and industry, and made it possible to farm new areas by irrigation. By 1936 the country was moving out of the depression, and settled back into isolationism, watching the growing threat of war in Europe — determined not to be involved this time.

One of the smaller dams (Pickwick Landing, Tennessee) in the TVA scheme.

The United States after 1945

After World War 2 both the main political parties in the United States agreed on the main aim of foreign policy: to stop communism spreading. But on home problems they had different views, though they were closer than they had been in the past. The Republicans supported big business and the power of state governments over the Federal government. They did not like the idea of large welfare schemes (such as free health care), and they did not want to increase civil liberties very much. The Democrats felt that the Federal government should have more power and that welfare schemes and civil liberties should be increased.

In the 40 years between 1945 and 1985 there were four Democrat presidents and four Republicans. With each there was a movement one way or the other on the major issues. But the most important home problem in the post-war years was civil liberties — especially for the blacks.

CIVIL LIBERTIES

A segregated drinking fountain in one of the southern states in the 1950s

Olympic Games, 1968. Two black US athletes give the 'Black power' salute on the rostrum after winning gold and bronze medals in the 200 metre race.

After the war black people formed 10% of the population, but they had few civil liberties, especially those living in the southern states. Many were not allowed to vote. They had the worst schools, the worst housing and the worst jobs. In many places they were not allowed on the same buses and trains as white people. They were forbidden to go to the same restaurants and places of entertainment. Black children were forced to go to black-only schools.

Black soldiers had fought and died beside the whites in the war, and felt that they deserved something better in peace. There were militant groups like Black Power which wanted violence to get justice, as well as those which wanted more peaceful methods such as strikes and sit-ins. The rest of the world, especially communist countries, criticised the US, which wanted freedom for people abroad, but would not give it to their own black citizens.

38

The federal government of the USA is called the Congress. It consists of a president (elected for four years), 100 senators (six years) and 435 representatives (two years). The people vote for all of these, but at different times, and the public may change its mind between elections. Having elected a republican president one year, they may elect a democratic House of Representatives and Senate two years later. This can make government difficult, for each can stop any law the others try to bring in. In addition the USA has the Supreme Court, which consists of a number of senior judges who can decide whether any law, even if passed by the other three parts of the government, is legal or not. The 1983 congress had a republican president, a democratic majority in the House of Representatives and a republican majority in the Senate.

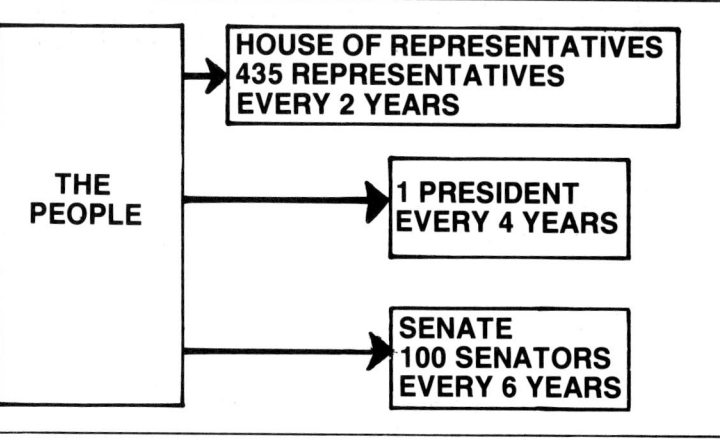

THE PEOPLE

→ HOUSE OF REPRESENTATIVES
435 REPRESENTATIVES
EVERY 2 YEARS

→ 1 PRESIDENT
EVERY 4 YEARS

→ SENATE
100 SENATORS
EVERY 6 YEARS

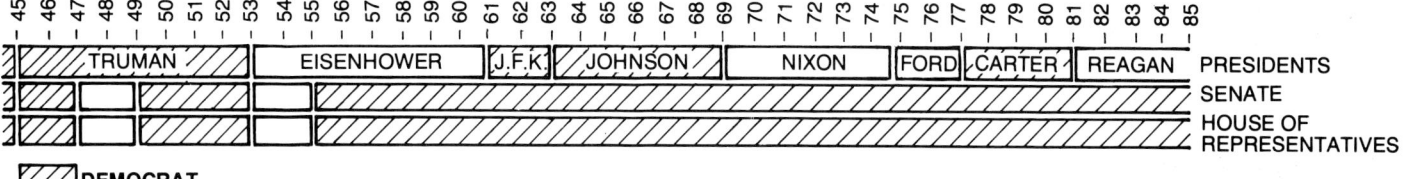

	45	46	47	48	49	50	51	52	53	54	55	56	57	58	59	60	61	62	63	64	65	66	67	68	69	70	71	72	73	74	75	76	77	78	79	80	81	82	83	84	85	
	TRUMAN									EISENHOWER							J.F.K.			JOHNSON					NIXON						FORD		CARTER				REAGAN					PRESIDENTS

SENATE

HOUSE OF REPRESENTATIVES

▨ DEMOCRAT
☐ REPUBLICAN

For 22 out of the 40 years, 1945-1985, the president and the majority in Congress have been of opposite political parties.

The first sign of change came when, in 1947, President Truman de-segregated the armed forces. This meant that in theory everyone, black and white, stood equal chance of promotion in the army, navy and airforce.

After much violence and protest the Supreme Court ruled in 1954 that segregated schools were illegal. That is, that schools to which only blacks or only whites could go could not be allowed. When some schools in the south refused to let black pupils in troops were sent to force them to do so.

In 1955, after peaceful protests by blacks led by the civil rights leader the Reverend Martin Luther King (who was later murdered), the Supreme Court ruled that segregated transport was illegal, and that blacks and whites must travel together on the same buses and trains. But fighting each issue one at a time was too slow; what was needed was a bill which outlawed all segregation and discrimination.

This bill came in 1963 when President Kennedy introduced his Civil Rights Bill, which made any kind of segregation illegal in a public place, and gave equal rights of work, education and opportunity to everyone. The bill was defeated by the Congress. In that same year, 1963, President Kennedy was assassinated. The whole world was horrified, and in 1964 President Johnson managed to get the

Civil Rights Bill passed almost as a memorial to the dead president. The bill is the basis of civil rights in the USA today, but though many non-whites do reach very important positions, there is still a great deal to do.

Rev. Martin Luther King (centre) leads a civil rights protest march in Montgomery, Alabama in 1965.

The United States after 1945: foreign policy

The USA has given thousands of billions of dollars to poorer nations. The Marshall Plan of 1947 gave large sums of money to western European countries to help them after World War 2. Nations in eastern Europe refused to take American money. Since then vast sums have been given to countries in Asia, Africa and especially in Latin America. The USA hopes that the money will help the countries to become richer so that they will not turn to communism. Sometimes the US asks for bases for its forces in return for the money.

Although the US did not want to join in another war, she was drawn into World War 2 (pages 44-53). At the end of it, in 1945, the USA was the most powerful nation on earth. It alone had the atom bomb in a usable form. The country had not been touched by a single bomb, and its industry was stronger than it had ever been. But the USA did not go back into isolationism, mainly because of its great dislike of communism.

Although the Soviet Union had been so terribly battered in the war, communist ideas were spreading rapidly in eastern Europe, Asia, Africa and even in South America. The US believed that it must stop communism from spreading any further. The history of America in foreign affairs since 1945 has been largely concerned with this problem and with the prevention of another world war. The US has tried to work by making alliances and treaties with other countries, giving aid to poorer nations, and sometimes by using force. (See also pages 56-58, 96-97.)

 AID

CONFRONTATION

 TREATIES

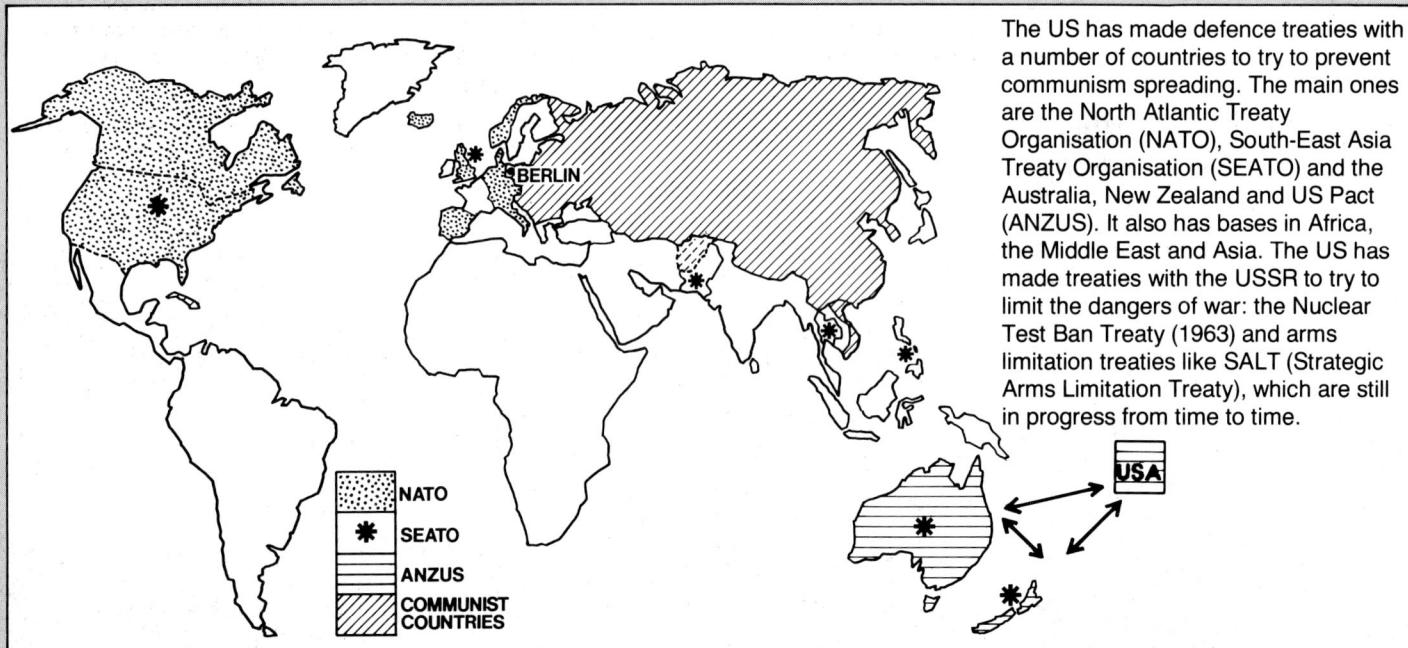

The US has made defence treaties with a number of countries to try to prevent communism spreading. The main ones are the North Atlantic Treaty Organisation (NATO), South-East Asia Treaty Organisation (SEATO) and the Australia, New Zealand and US Pact (ANZUS). It also has bases in Africa, the Middle East and Asia. The US has made treaties with the USSR to try to limit the dangers of war: the Nuclear Test Ban Treaty (1963) and arms limitation treaties like SALT (Strategic Arms Limitation Treaty), which are still in progress from time to time.

BERLIN

NATO
SEATO
ANZUS
COMMUNIST COUNTRIES

USA

Berlin airlift 1948

After World War 2, Poland, Czechoslovakia, Hungary, Bulgaria, Romania, Albania, Yugoslavia and East Germany became communist. It seemed that the rest of the western European countries would fall one by one under Soviet influence. The test came in Berlin. France, Britain, the USSR and the USA had agreed that although the city was deep inside East (communist) Germany it should be shared equally between east and west. In 1948 the Russians decided to starve the western powers out. They closed road, rail and canal links to West Germany and cut off many food supplies. The western powers decided not to be driven out, but to supply the city of two million people with food, coal, oil and everything else by air. For almost twelve months planes landed every 90 seconds, keeping the western zone alive. Then the Russians gave up, and reopened the surface links with western Germany.

US troops covering an advance in the Korean War, 1950.

Korean War 1950-1953

After World War 2 the northern half of Korea was occupied by Russia which set up a communist government, and the southern half by the USA which set up its own kind of government. When the two major powers withdrew North Korean forces invaded the south. China, which had now become communist, helped North Korea, while the USA stood by to help the south. The forces in the south eventually became a United Nations army, but they were mainly American. Savage fighting raged up and down the country for three years, before an armistice was signed, and Korea was divided where it had been before the war.

Cuban missile crisis 1961

In 1959 the communist Fidel Castro overthrew the corrupt right-wing dictator of Cuba and became ruler himself. The US was not pleased at having a communist state so close — the US mainland was only 150 km away. When in 1961 the US found that the USSR was building missile bases in Cuba, from which it could attack almost any part of the US, there was panic. When Russian ships were seen with missiles on board, President Kennedy told the Soviet Union that US warships would stop them. The world seemed on the brink of nuclear war. But at the last moment the USSR backed down, and the ships returned home.

An official US spy-plane photograph of the missile sites being built in Cuba in 1961.

Vietnam 1957-1973

Vietnam belonged to France before World War 2, but after the war the French were driven out (1954) mainly by Vietnamese communists under Ho Chi Minh. An international conference at Geneva decided that the country should be split, like Korea, into a communist north and a non-communist south. Again, as in Korea, the north Vietnamese began to move into the south, and again the US forces moved in. Although the US had many tanks, aeroplanes and chemical weapons, they could not defeat the lightly-armed North Vietnamese. After terrible losses they were forced to withdraw (1973) and later (1975) the communists occupied the whole country.

Vietnam War, 1968. Vietnamese villagers fleeing as they are caught in crossfire between US troops in the foreground, and Vietcong (Vietnam communists) in the jungle behind.

Europe between the wars

After World War 1 Europe was in a state of shock and poverty. Billions of pounds were owed, particularly to the USA. Twelve or more million men, among them many who would have been leaders, had been killed. The old way of life had been destroyed for ever. Most countries struggled from crisis to crisis, and from government to government. France, for example, had nine prime ministers and cabinets between 1920 and 1929. Old allies fell out, and tried to grab what they could from the mess. Quarrels over the Treaty of Versailles kept breaking out. In 1920 Poland, which had been given large areas formerly German by the treaty, attacked Russia. By the Treaty of Riga (1921) it received an area of Ukrainian territory (part of Russia), and so was hated by both Germany and the Soviet Union.

The rise of the dictatorships (pages 30-33, 35), especially in Germany and Italy, seemed to give some kind of improvement in the countries which had them, but by the mid-1930s many people believed that this, and the improving prosperity were merely the run-up to the next world war. The Spanish Civil War (1936-1939) seemed to be the beginning.

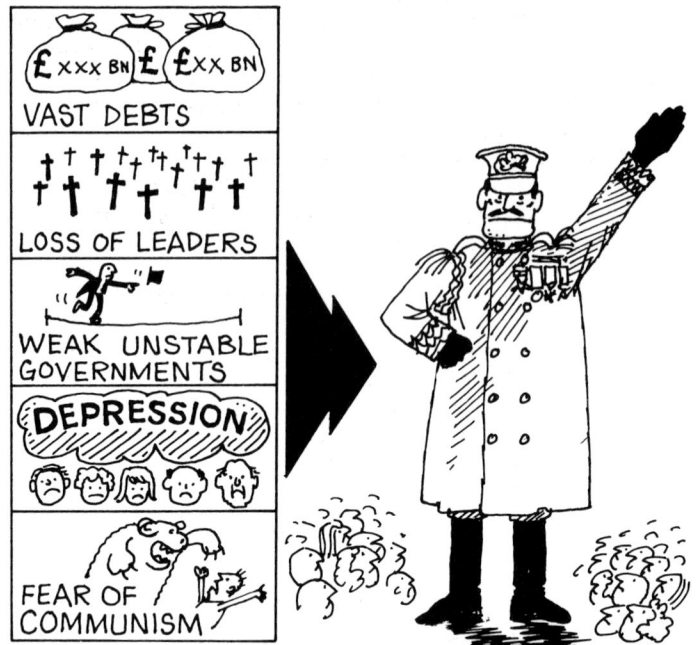

42

From 1923-1936 the Spaniards had democratic governments, though they forced the king to leave in 1931. In 1936 the republican socialist and communist parties came to power in the election, and at once were faced with a military uprising under General Franco, who was supported by the Catholics, the fascist party (extreme right-wing) and those who wanted the return of the king. His forces were helped by Germany, Italy and Portugal. The socialist-communist government was helped by the USSR and by about 60,000 people from all over Europe who formed International Brigades to fight on the government side. These were mostly from left-wing movements.

Three years of bitter fighting ended in 1939 with total victory for Franco and the fascists, who remained neutral in World War 2, though they had signed treaties with Hitler. The Spanish Civil War did help Hitler, however, because he used it to test new weapons — guns, tanks, aircraft, as well as dive bombing and parachute landings. Germany's rapid victory in Europe in 1940-41 was partly due to the fact that methods of fighting had been tried out in Spain.

Victims of an air raid on Barcelona in the Spanish Civil War.

Below: Picasso's famous painting 'Guernica' Guernica was a market town in northern Spain. It was destroyed by German bombers in the world's first all-out air raid in 1937, in an effort to terrorise the Basque people into surrender. Picasso conveys the horror of this terrible new form of warfare.

Below: Spanish government soldiers try desperately to hold up General Franco's troops advancing on Madrid. The soldier in the centre seems to be firing at an attacking aeroplane — probably German.

Events leading to World War 2

After 1930 there were a number of reasons why another major war seemed likely, and once the fuse had been lit it burned steadily towards World War 2.

Worldwide depression. Countries increased armies and weapons

Hatred between communism and fascism

German anger about the Treaty of Versailles

Growing strength of Japan in military power and trade

League of nations weak and unable to stop wars. US isolationism

1931 The Japanese army invaded northern China and brought a large part of it under its control. The League of Nations and the world did nothing except condemn the attack, so that it seemed that aggression was quite safe and paid the aggressor well.

1934-35 Italy invaded Ethiopia (page 33). Again, the League and most of the world took little action. A few countries did try to stop trade with Italy but others, especially Germany and the USA, increased trade with Italy. Again, aggression seemed quite safe, and well worth while.

1934 Germany began to re-arm, defying the Treaty of Versailles. It built warships, submarines, aeroplanes, tanks and trained a large army. As children did military training as part of their education, there were large reserves of soldiers.

1936 The Spanish Civil War between the right-wing General Franco and the left-wing government began. Germany helped Franco, and tried out new weapons and new ways of fighting, such as divebombing and tank attacks. The battle-experience was very valuable when World War 2 came.

1936 Germany, Italy and Japan signed the Anti-Comintern Pact, agreeing to fight against communism everywhere.

1938 Germany claimed part of Czechoslovakia (Sudetenland) where many Germans were living. There was a conference at Munich in Germany between the British prime minister, Neville Chamberlain, Hitler and the French prime minister. Without consulting the Czech government, the French and British told Hitler he could have Sudetenland as long as he did not take any more territory. This was called 'appeasement'.

1939 (August) People hoped that Germany might not attack Poland because that would bring it face to face with its biggest enemy, Russia. This hope vanished when Germany and the USSR signed a friendship treaty. They promised not to attack each other, but to invade Poland and share it between them.

WORLD WAR 2

1938 Germany invaded and took over Austria, which it said was part of Germany. Once more the world did nothing about it, and aggression seemed more profitable than ever.

1939 In spite of his promise, Hitler occupied the rest of Czechoslovakia. Poland (see page 27) seemed next on the list even though Britain and France said that if Poland was attacked they would help it. Mussolini, copying Hitler, invaded Albania. War now seemed unavoidable, and Europe frantically began to prepare.

1939 (September) Germany invaded Poland. Britain and France kept their promise and said that if Germany did not withdraw, they would declare war. Germany did not withdraw. World War 2 had begun.

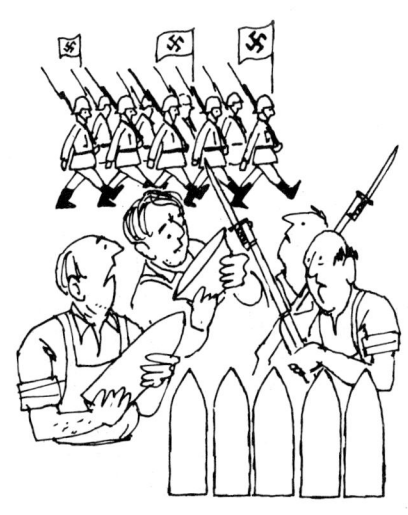

World War 2

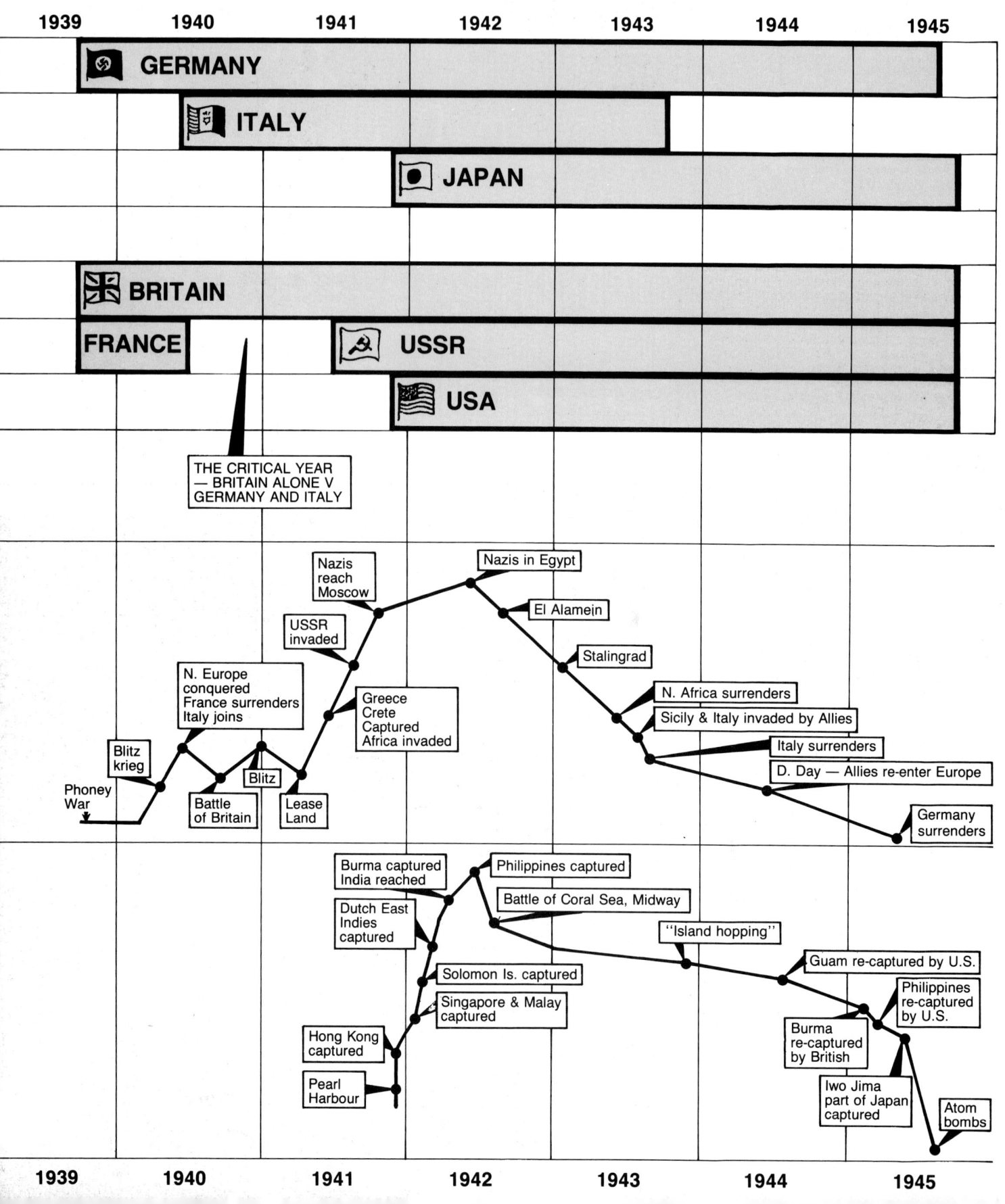

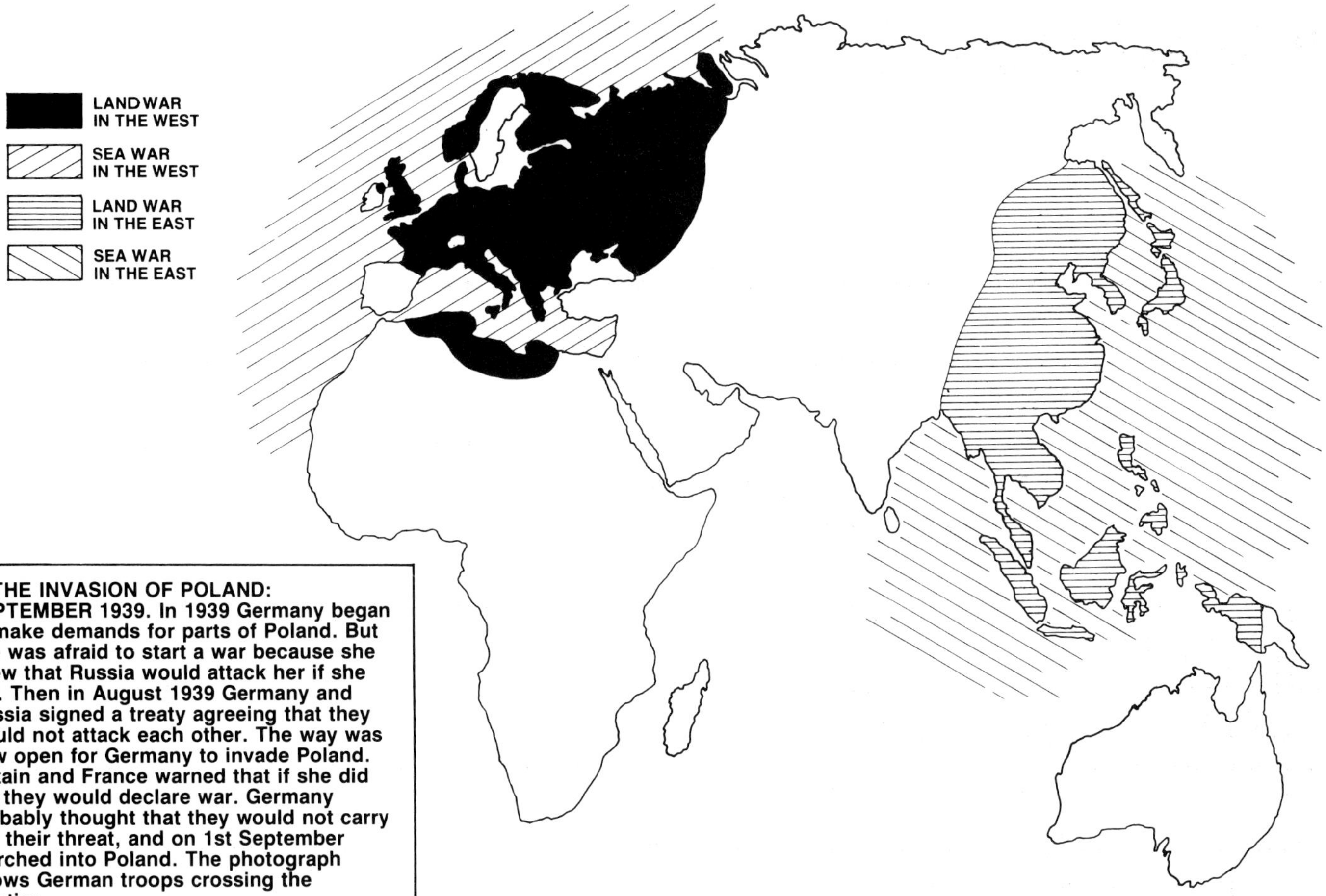

Key:
- **LAND WAR IN THE WEST**
- **SEA WAR IN THE WEST**
- **LAND WAR IN THE EAST**
- **SEA WAR IN THE EAST**

1. THE INVASION OF POLAND: SEPTEMBER 1939. In 1939 Germany began to make demands for parts of Poland. But she was afraid to start a war because she knew that Russia would attack her if she did. Then in August 1939 Germany and Russia signed a treaty agreeing that they would not attack each other. The way was now open for Germany to invade Poland. Britain and France warned that if she did so, they would declare war. Germany probably thought that they would not carry out their threat, and on 1st September marched into Poland. The photograph shows German troops crossing the frontier.

2. THE WAR IN EUROPE: 1939 - 1940. Germany quickly conquered half of Poland, and Russia invaded the other half. But in the west nothing happened for six months. Then suddenly in three months (April -June 1940) Germany conquered Denmark, Norway, Belgium, Holland and France, using 'blitzkrieg' methods. The German armies used high-speed tanks and by-passed fortifications. The British and French armies suffered a humiliating defeat as France surrendered. The photograph shows a Belgian street corner on fire after a Nazi bombing raid.

3. DUNKIRK: 1940. About 300 000 British and French troops reached Britain after a desperate rescue from the beaches of Dunkirk in northern France. Every craft available, from warships to paddle steamers and rowing boats, was used to bring back the shattered armies which had lost almost all their equipment and weapons. Britain began frantically to prepare for the German invasion which she thought would come very soon.

4, 5. THE BATTLE OF BRITAIN: AUGUST-SEPTEMBER 1940. Before Germany could invade she had to get control of the air, and began an attack on the aerodromes along the Channel. Britain had only a few hundred fighter planes and about 1500 fighter pilots. Germany had many more planes but the British had a much better radio system, and — even more important — radar. They were also successfully breaking the German secret codes. So the British airforce knew in advance of German bombers coming and were waiting for them. German losses in the fighting in the skies above southern Britain were too great, and the invasion was called off. Hitler was planning to invade Russia and needed all the planes he had.

6, 7. THE BLITZ: 1940 - 1941. Germany now turned to the bombing of cities, especially at night, hoping to destroy enough industry, railways, roads, and docks to force Britain to surrender. About 150 000 civilians were killed and injured and the air raids caused a vast amount of damage. The photograph shows two German bombers over the dock area of London. You can see fires started in Victoria Docks, and in the centre of the photograph West Ham football ground.

8. THE WAR AT SEA. At the same time Germany began an all-out attack on merchant shipping, hoping to starve Britain into surrender. Losses were enormous. In 1940 4½ million tonnes of allied ships were sunk, and in 1941 about the same. Losses almost doubled in 1942 to 8½ million tonnes. In 1943 by a lucky chance Britain managed to crack the code used by the German U-boats. New anti-submarine devices helped them to sink about 300 U-boats. Merchant ships travelled in convoy protected by warships and barrage balloons.

9. LEND-LEASE HELP: 1941. For twelve months Britain was alone against Germany. She was desperate for food, oil and weapons, but the United States Neutrality Acts did not allow American weapons to be sold to countries at war, or anything else except on a cash-down basis. In 1941 the US president, F.D. Roosevelt, persuaded Congress to sell arms and other goods to Britain, but to delay payment until after the war. A number of old warships were also 'given' to Britain to protect the shipping lanes. This enabled Britain to survive this critical period.

The United Nations

Before World War 1 countries tried to keep the peace by the balance of power. Nations believed that if they and their enemies were about equal in strength neither side would start a war. So states made alliances to keep their strengths about equal. World War 1 showed that the balance of power system did not work.

The League of Nations tried to stop wars by 'collective security'. That is, if all nations joined together they could bring pressure to bear on any country which started a war. This too failed because countries thought only of themselves, and some of the most powerful nations did not belong to the League.

World War 2 left at least 40 million people dead and ended with the first atom bombs being dropped on Japan. Weapons were now so terrible that the whole idea of war was different. Another war might easily destroy civilisation or even the earth itself. People just had to find a way of preventing another major war from breaking out.

The Atlantic Charter

In 1941 the British prime minister, Winston Churchill (below, right), met Franklin D Roosevelt (below, left), the president of the USA, in the middle of the Atlantic to discuss the future of the two countries. Britain was alone against Germany, and seemed on the verge of defeat, and the USA was still neutral. The two men agreed that if there was a future after the war all nations must be allowed to have their own governments and no changes must be made without the agreement of the people. There must be some way of keeping peace and reducing the numbers of weapons. Working conditions and social security must be improved for everyone. Five months later the US was at war.

On January 1st, 1942, 26 nations, including the USSR, signed the Declaration of the United Nations, in which they all agreed to the ideas of the Atlantic Charter. The leaders of the USA, USSR and Britain met again several times to discuss the plans, and a committee of all the 26 nations drew up details of the new organisation. In June 1945 53 countries signed the Charter of the United Nations, with provision for other countries to join. Today the membership is 157 countries, and every country of any size belongs to it. Switzerland is an exception as it has had a policy of complete neutrality for a very long time.

The United Nations Organisation took over some of the better parts of the League of Nations, such as the ILO and the International Court, and tried to avoid some of the mistakes the League had made. The UN, for example, recognised that some states were more powerful than others and though in the General Assembly every member state has one vote, in the Security Council, which is more important, the major countries have a right of veto. But by using the veto a single powerful country could block the work of the UN. In 1950 it was decided that if the Security Council could not agree, the General Assembly would take over and decide what to do.

GENERAL ASSEMBLY
Meets once a year unless there is an emergency. All member nations attend and have one vote each. Important matters are decided by a two-thirds majority.

SECRETARIAT
The permanent civil service of the UN, which carries out the decisions of the Assembly and Security Council.

SECURITY COUNCIL
The 'cabinet' of the UN. Five permanent members (USSR, USA, China, France and Britain) who have the right of veto, and ten other members chosen in turn for 2-year periods.

COURT OF INTERNATIONAL JUSTICE
15 international judges sit to settle disputes such as those about fishing limits and frontiers between states.

SOCIAL AND ECONOMIC COUNCIL
The most important body after the Security Council. Has many different 'agencies' as shown below.

TRUSTEESHIP COUNCIL
Looks after the interests of smaller countries and territories which do not yet have self-government.

Financial organisations such as the International Monetary Fund (IMF), International Bank, General Agreement on Tariffs and Trade. These try to regulate world trade and economic problems and lend money to poorer nations for development.

Marine Consultative Organisation co-ordinates world shipping and tries to solve problems of pollution at sea, etc.

International Labour Office (ILO) tries to settle problems of working conditions, wages, etc.

United Nations Scientific and Cultural Organisation (UNESCO) deals with education and helps in the exchange of ideas. It sends orchestras, theatre and dance companies and artists to different countries.

World Meterological Organisation (WMO) pools information about weather so that all nations can use it.

Universal Postal Union and International Telecommunications Union help states to use each others' post and telephone services.

World Health Organisation (WHO) offers information on health, sanitation, etc. It sends teams to help in major epidemics and to control such things as malaria.

Food and Agriculture Organisation (FAO) looks after farming, fishing and forestry worldwide. Helps developing countries to improve agriculture and control pests.

International Civil Airlines Organisation (ICAO) tries to get air communications, traffic control and safety regulations standardised throughout the world.

The Cold War

When the fighting ended in 1945 the armies of the western nations were left facing the Russians. The western powers were afraid that communism might spread right through Europe. The Russians, who had suffered terrible losses, were afraid that the western nations would attack them — and indeed some leaders wanted to. So began the Cold War. It was really between the USA and the USSR, the two 'super-powers'. Both sides threatened and boasted, tried to outdo the other, broadcast propaganda and hoped to get the other to make a mistake or back down. They never actually fought each other. The 'hot' wars involved other countries backed by one or other of the super-powers.

Fidel Castro

The desperately poor countries of Latin America were an obvious target for communist power. There were a number of revolutions. Fidel Castro seized power in Cuba in 1958 and made the island a communist state. This frightened the Americans as now the Russians could have a base only 150 km from the US mainland. In 1970 the communist party was voted into power in democratic elections in Chile, but three years later was overthrown in a right-wing revolution.

At first the main 'battlefield' was Europe. In 1947 the USA offered large sums of money (Marshall Aid) to try to get Europe's shattered industry working again. The western nations accepted, but those in the east were compelled by Russia to refuse. Instead, Russia (1955) offered them aid through an agreement called Comecon. Between 1945 and 1953 Yugoslavia, Albania, Bulgaria, Romania, Poland, East Germany and Hungary all had communist governments and became Soviet 'satellites'. In Greece between 1945 and 1947

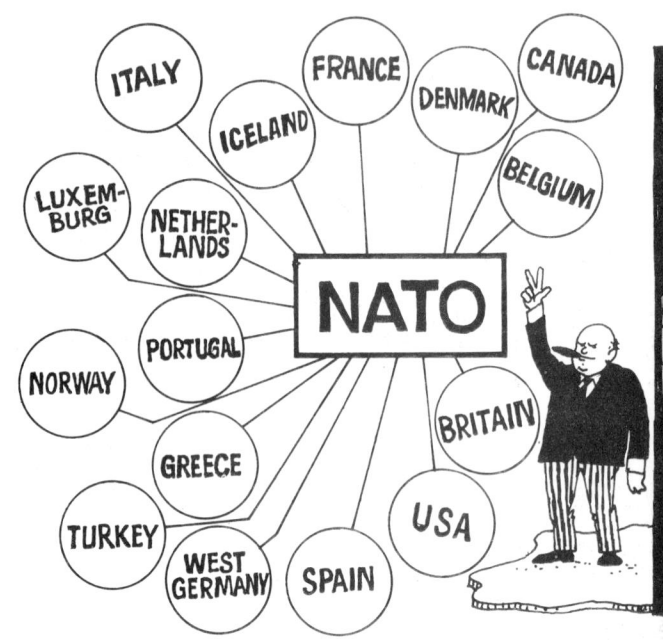

When the colonial powers gave independence to the African states (pages 82-83) the communist parties tried to gain control, but were only successful in the former Portuguese colony of Angola, where communist Cuba sent many troops.

The Cold War also appears in the Middle East, where the Israelis are supported by the USA and some Arab states, such as Syria, by the USSR. There is always a great danger that the smaller wars between the Israelis and the Arabs could drag in the super-powers.

there was a civil war in which the communists were defeated. In 1949 the military alliance called NATO (North Atlantic Treaty Organisation) was formed by the western powers, and in 1955 the Warsaw Pact was formed by Russia, East Germany, Poland, Czechoslovakia, Hungary, Romania, Bulgaria and Albania (pages 60-61). Europe seemed to be divided into two groups of enemies as it had been in 1914. Winston Churchill said that there was an Iron Curtain between them.

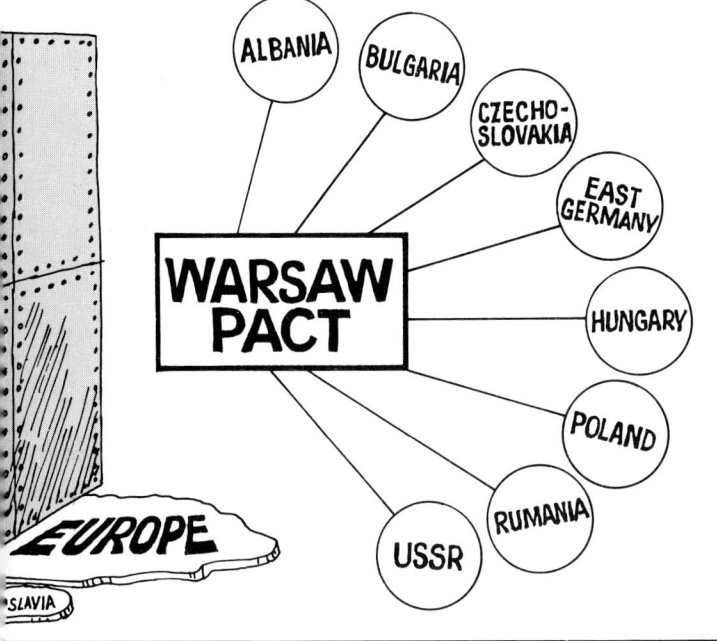

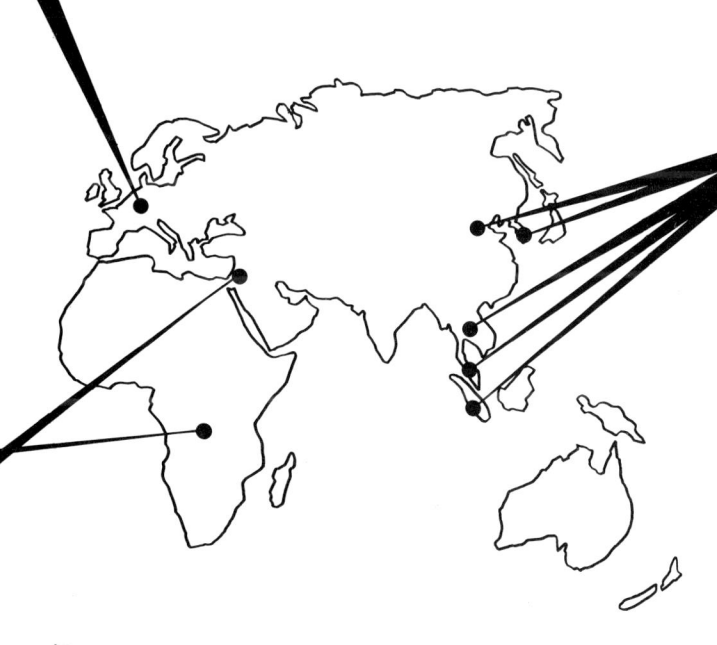

Chairman Mao in 1947.

In 1949 the Chinese communists under Mao-tse-tung won the civil war and signed a treaty of friendship with Russia (page 70). The Cold War had now begun to freeze parts of Asia. The old colonial powers (France, Britain and Holland) had been driven out and there was a struggle for power between communists and non-communists. The Americans were afraid that countries would fall to the communists one after another. In the Korean and Vietnam wars (pages 96-97) half of Korea and all of Vietnam, Laos and Cambodia became communist. There was also a civil war in Malaysia in which the communists were eventually defeated. Communist parties fought for power in Indonesia and to a lesser extent in India.

Since Stalin died in 1953 the Cold War has alternately thawed and frozen. Sometimes the two great groups of nations seem a little more friendly, sometimes on the edge of real war again. The victory of the Chinese communists (1949), the invasions by Russia of Hungary (1956) and Czechoslovakia (1968), the Korean war (1953), the Vietnam war (1960s), the Cuban missile crisis (1961) were among the most dangerous moments. Relations were better under Krushchev's 'peaceful coexistence' (1953-56), during the quarrel between Russia and China (1960), and when a number of nuclear and other arms treaties were signed between the USSR and the west.

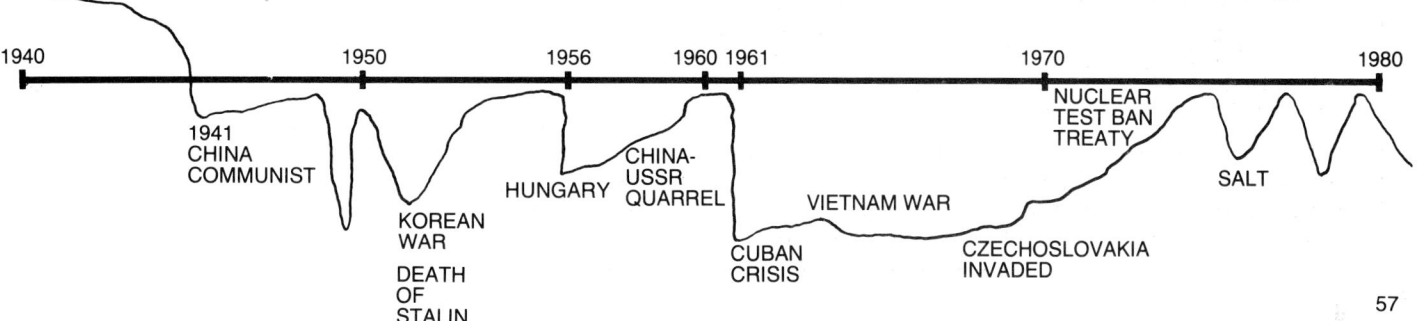

Europe: some important steps

In 1945 Europe was in ruins. Four hundred years of western European domination of the world had ended and power had gone to the USSR and the USA. Thirty years later a new kind of Europe was being born. These are some of the main steps in that process.

Winston Churchill (Britain), President Truman (USA) and Joseph Stalin (USSR) meeting at Potsdam to decide the fate of Europe after World War 2.

1945 Potsdam conference

Britain, USA and USSR met to decide the fate of Europe after the war. Poland lost land in the east, which went to Russia, and received some in the west from Germany. Germany was divided, the western part to be under the influence of the western allies, the eastern part dominated by Russia. In effect this meant that before long the whole of eastern Europe would be communist.

1947 Marshall Aid

It was obvious that Europe could not recover on its own, and under the Marshall Aid programme billions of dollars were poured in from America to get the economy moving again. The Organisation for European Economic Cooperation (OEEC) was set up to organise the programme. The USSR, though just as much in need of money, refused to accept Marshall Aid or to allow any of its satellites to do so.

1947 Truman Doctrine

Britain could no longer afford to help the Greek government fight the communist rebellion which was going on there, and withdrew its aid. The Truman Doctrine pledged US help to Greece and Turkey, and any other non-communist country fighting against communism. This was the final proof that the USA had given up isolationism, and had accepted its role as a leader in world affairs.

1947 The Cold War begins

The division of the world into two opposing camps, communist and non-communist, hardened. The military alliances NATO and the Warsaw Pact were formed and though the actual fighting took place in Korea and Vietnam, the heart of the conflict was in Europe. If the Cold War developed into a Hot War, it would be across the Iron Curtain in Europe, where both sides were now well-equipped with nuclear weapons.

1948 Decolonisation

From about this time the European colonial nations — Britain, France, Belgium and the Netherlands — began to lose their empires. In the far east the Dutch and French fought to keep theirs, but lost. Almost all of the British colonies, and the French empire in Africa became independent peacefully. The end of the colonial system marked the end of an era for Europe.

The European parliament in session at Strasbourg.

1952 European Parliament

Originally a parliament for all of the members of the ECSC (European Coal and Steel Community, pages 62-63) which meets at Strasbourg. Its members were at first nominated by the national parliaments but are now elected by the people. The twelve countries of the EEC (European Economic Community) are represented, and although it does not have great power at the moment, this does seem to be increasing. It is the first serious attempt at one assembly for much of the continent.

1956 Suez crisis

The withdrawal of the British and French forces from Suez after threats from the USA and the USSR marked the end of the old form of European imperialism. Western Europe was no longer the leader of the world. This also helped to push the nations of Europe closer.

1956 Hungarian crisis

The USSR invaded Hungary to put down a liberal rising. This confirmed that the Soviet Union was not prepared to allow any freedom in its satellites, and that Europe was very firmly divided into two hostile groups.

Communist policemen executed in the Hungarian rising of 1956.

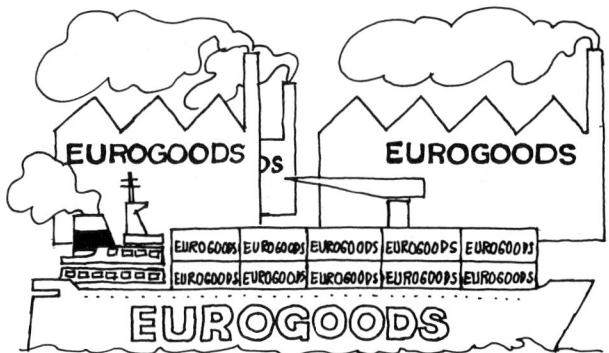

1957 Treaty of Rome

This turned the limited ECSC into the more important EEC or common market. It was the first practical attempt to unite the economies of the major western nations and to make the separate states of Europe into a large block capable of competing with the USA or the USSR.

1968 Czech invasion

The Warsaw Pact invasion to put down a more liberal government in Czechoslovakia was done with much less bloodshed than in Hungary in 1956. Two communist countries, Romania and Yugoslavia, refused to take part and condemned the invasion. The Soviet grip on the satellites, though still firm, seemed to have loosened a little.

1973 Enlarged EEC

With Britain, Eire and Denmark admitted to the EEC and Spain, Greece and Portugal later to be, the common market contained well over 90% of the non-communist population of Europe. Increasing economic cooperation gives hopes of closer political unity.

NATO and the WARSAW pact

When World War 2 ended the two superpowers, the USA and the USSR, faced each other across the world. The USA alone had a workable atom bomb at the time, its homeland had not been touched and its industry was at a peak. The USSR had lost 20 million people, much of its industry and agriculture had been destroyed, and hundreds of its towns and cities were in ruins. The USA was terrified of communism coming to America, and the USSR was even more terrified that the USA might attack it while it was still weak. Both sides wanted allies.

The North Atlantic Treaty Organisation (NATO) treaty was signed in 1949 by Belgium, Canada, Denmark, France, Iceland, Italy, Luxembourg, Netherlands, Norway, Portugal, Britain and the USA. Greece and Turkey joined in 1952, West Germany in 1955 and Spain in 1982.

The Warsaw Pact (1955) nations are Albania, Bulgaria, Czechoslovakia, East Germany, Hungary, Poland, Romania and the USSR.

Both groups aim at having unified commands, joint planning and standardised equipment and weapons so that operations in war would be simpler. Both groups have bases, radar stations and other defences in the member countries but intercontinental missiles have changed the traditional patterns. The map shows just how close the major partners in the alliances, the USSR and the USA are, so that nuclear weapons could be hurled across the north pole from the heart of America to Russia and equally from Russia to America.

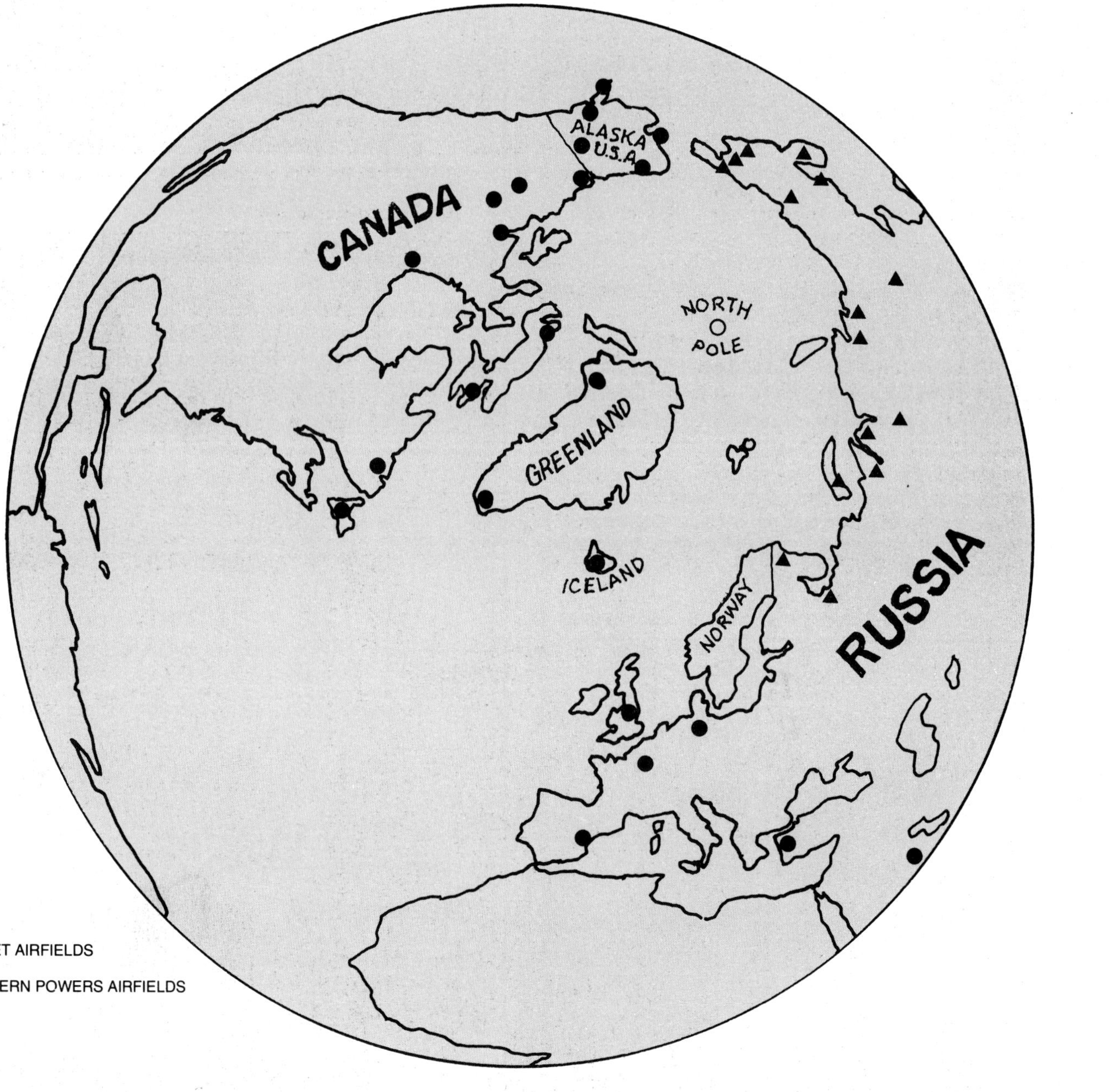

▲ SOVIET AIRFIELDS

● WESTERN POWERS AIRFIELDS

Above: a demonstration in Cologne, West Germany by peace groups and war veterans to mark the 40th anniversary of V.E. (Victory in Europe) day. Their banner says 'No more fascism, no more war'.

Below: a CND rally in Hyde Park, 1985. Demonstrators are showing their strong feeling against nuclear war.

The EEC

For over a thousand years the countries of Europe had fought one another for many different reasons — territory, raw materials, religion, monarchy. At the end of World War 2 in 1945 the whole continent was shattered. Much of the industry and communications had been destroyed, and countries such as Canada, South Africa, Australia, India and the USA, where there had been no fighting, had taken much of the foreign trade. On top of all this Europe itself was divided by the Iron Curtain into the communist east and the western allies. It seemed almost impossible for each of the countries to get back on its feet again on its own, in spite of the aid given by the United States to the west and by Russia to the east.

The Krupps armaments works in Essen, Germany, destroyed by allied bombing in the war. This scene was repeated all over Europe.

A big step towards collaboration came in 1952 when the greatest enemies, France and Germany, which had fought each other three times in 80 years, agreed, together with Belgium, Holland, Luxembourg and Italy, to pool their coal and steel resources.

1952	1957

Five years later the European Coal and Steel Community turned into the European Economic Community (EEC or Common Market) when the six countries signed the Treaty of Rome (1957). This pledged the members to work towards a much closer union than in just coal and steel. They hoped they would eventually become linked in more and more aspects of life, and have a single parliament for the whole community as well as separate ones of their own.

TREATY OF ROME 1957

MARCHÉ COMMUN

AIMS OF THE EEC

To reduce and eventually to abolish customs duties. This would make goods cheaper, especially in countries which put high taxes on such things as spirits, wine and cars.

To allow freer movement of people and goods across frontiers within the EEC. This reduces official delays and speeds up traffic. It allows people to travel to different parts of the EEC to take up jobs. Eventually there will be a common passport.

To have standard weights, measures and specifications. The weights and measures will be in the metric system which is in use in all countries except Britain (though Britain does have some parts of it). Standard specifications will apply to packaging, industrial parts, etc.

To have a common policy for agriculture, transport and tariffs. Much of this is already working, but the farming policy in particular is giving problems because highly efficient agriculture as in Britain and Denmark is badly affected by the inefficient farming of other countries such as Greece and parts of France.

Britain would not join the EEC at first because it conflicted with its close trading ties with the Commonwealth. However, when in the 1960s the Commonwealth began to trade less with Britain and more with Asia and the USA, Britain tried to become a member. France blocked her entry three times, but in 1973 Britain, Eire and Denmark were admitted.

1973

In 1981 Greece became a member of the EEC, and in 1986 Spain and Portugal. Over 90% of the population of non-communist Europe are within the Common Market. This can lead to strains when, for example, the interests of rich Germany and poor Greece, or of highly-industrial Belgium and agricultural Eire are in conflict.

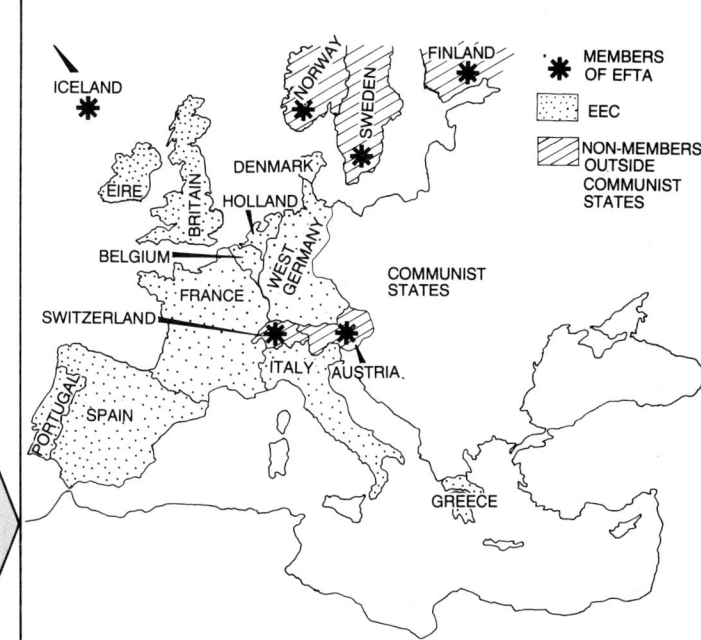

Many countries hope that the European ECONOMIC Community will eventually turn into the European POLITICAL Community — a United States of Europe on the lines of the United States of America or the Union of Soviet Socialist Republics. There would be separate parliaments in each of the countries for business that concerned that country alone, and a federal parliament which decided major issues that concerned the whole community. Such a dream is a long way away. A thousand years of rivalry, bitterness, hatred and war cannot be wiped out in a few years. But if it could, the European community would be a third 'superpower' of 320 million people, perhaps able to balance the Soviet Union's 270 million and the USA's 230 million.

While abolishing tariffs between members, to keep them high against outside countries. This means more trade between members and allows firms to set up shops and factories in other countries — for example Marks and Spencers and Mothercare in France, Carrefour in Britain.

To have common social, health, pension and welfare schemes. Health schemes are already in operation. All of these would make it easier for people to live and work in another country, but make problems because of the different standards in different countries — in wealthy Germany and poor Portugal, for example.

To recognise academic and professional qualifications — doctors, architects, engineers, scientists can all work in other EEC countries without taking extra examinations. Lawyers cannot because the legal systems are so different.

To have a single parliament to co-ordinate major policies for the whole community. This would allow the EEC to speak with one voice in international affairs, but it would mean that the individual members would lose some of their own sovereignty.

The Middle East 1900 - 1965

The Middle East is largely barren land, but people have fought over it for thousands of years. This is because it stands at the crossroads of the world's trade routes — from Europe to Asia, and from Asia to Africa. People who controlled this crossroads could control much of the trade passing through it. It became more important when the Suez Canal opened in 1875, and much more important still in the twentieth century because it contains the world's largest known reserves of oil.

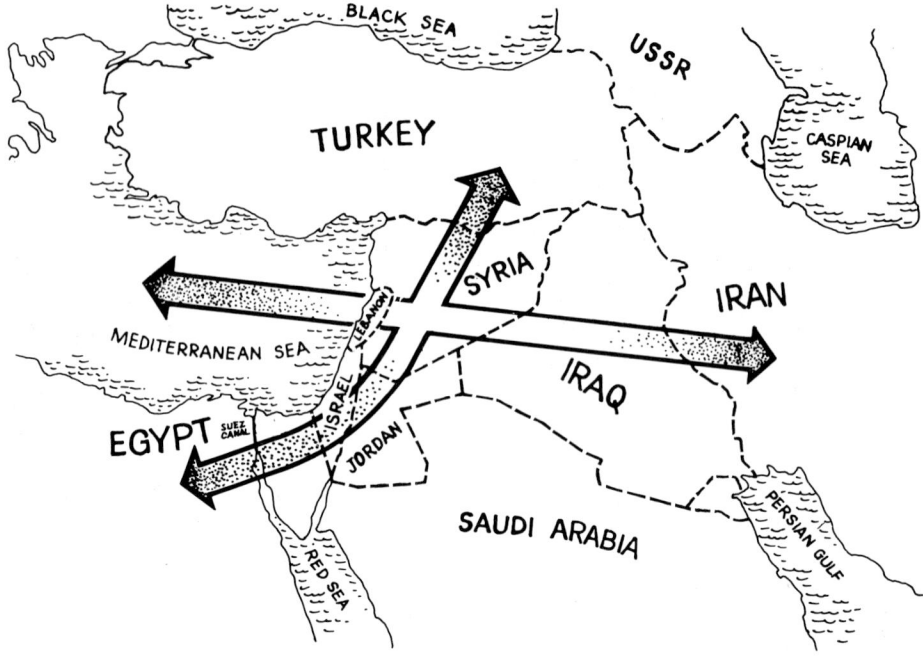

When World War 1 began the area was controlled by the Turks. Many Arabs who lived there wanted to throw out their Turkish masters and rule the land themselves. The Jews had been driven out of Palestine by the Romans centuries before, but many of them hoped that it would one day be their national homeland again. The British were fighting the Turks in the Middle East and wanted help from both Jews and Arabs. So they allowed both to believe that Britain would support their claims to parts of the Middle East after the war.

When the war ended the Turkish empire was split up. Britain took Palestine, Jordan and Iraq as mandates from the League of Nations, and France took Syria and Lebanon. Both Arabs and Jews were furious as they felt they had been cheated. Between World War 1 and World War 2 many Jews came to Palestine to settle, especially after the rise of Hitler. Jews and Arabs fought the British forces and each other. As World War 2 approached, Britain said that it would protect Arab rights and that Jews would never form more than a third of the population.

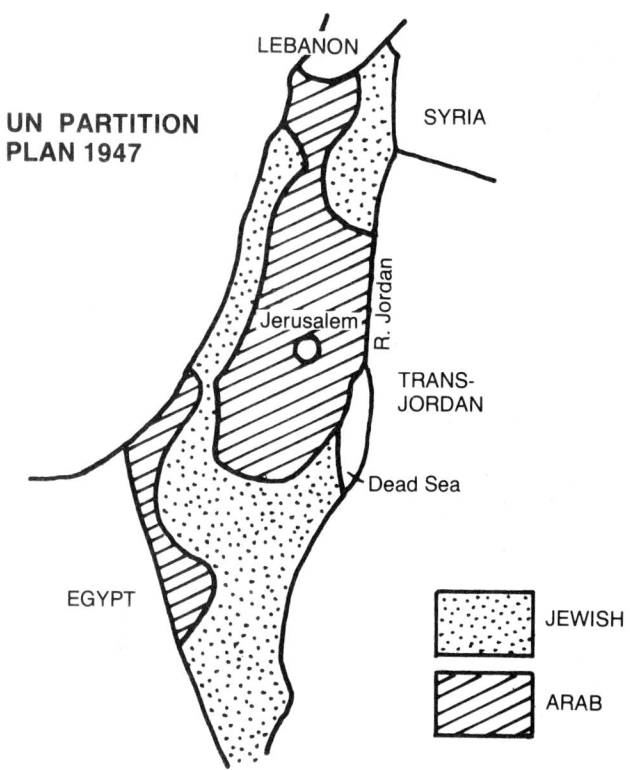

UN PARTITION PLAN 1947

LEBANON
SYRIA
Jerusalem
R. Jordan
TRANS-JORDAN
Dead Sea
EGYPT

▫ JEWISH
▨ ARAB

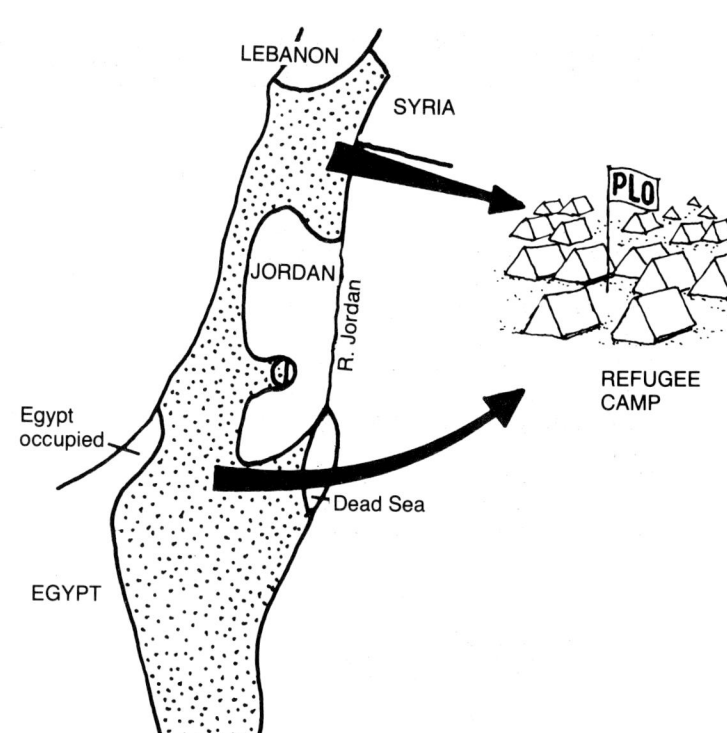

LEBANON
SYRIA
JORDAN
R. Jordan
Egypt occupied
Dead Sea
EGYPT
PLO
REFUGEE CAMP

After the war terrorism increased rapidly until Britain decided that it could no longer be responsible for the mandate, and asked the United Nations to take over. The UN suggested dividing Palestine into three parts — Arab, Jewish and the free city of Jerusalem, which was holy to Jews, Arabs and Christians. The Arabs would not accept this, and fighting broke out again, but in 1948 the Jewish leaders announced that they had created the state of Israel, the Jewish homeland. (See also page 90.) Immediately Egypt, Syria, Jordan and Iraq joined forces with the Palestinian Arabs to attack the new state.

The Arab armies were thrown back almost everywhere. Israel seized half of Jerusalem and land in the north which the UN had wanted to give to the Arabs. Jordan occupied the other half of Jerusalem and the west bank of the river Jordan, which had also been Palestinian Arab territory. Hundreds of thousands of Arabs from Jewish occupied areas left their homes and went to refugee camps in Jordan. Here the Palestinian Liberation Army (PLO) was formed by Arabs who were determined to regain what they felt was their own homeland.

A Palestinian Arab woman takes a few possessions from her home, destroyed by the Israeli army searching for terrorists.

In 1956 Egypt nationalised the Suez Canal which had been controlled by Britain and France. British and French troops, helped by Israelis, attacked Egypt and seized the Canal Zone. Only when the USA threatened to intervene did the British and French withdraw. This last empire-building war marked the end of Britain as colonial power.

A British tank rumbles through Port Said during the Anglo-French invasion. An Arab refugee family rescue what they can from their shattered home.

In 1967 a second war between Israel and Arab countries broke out, but in six days the Arab forces were beaten. Israel now seized all of Jerusalem and the west bank of the Jordan. Hundreds of thousands more Arab refugees were driven into camps in other Arab countries, and the bitter hatred between Arabs and Jews grew stronger.

Egypt, Syria and Iraq attacked Israel again in 1973. At first they made some progress, but were later halted. The UN arranged a ceasefire but Israel refused to move from the west bank of the Jordan or to give up the Golan Heights in Syria which it had occupied. In 1978 Egypt, Israel and President Carter of the USA worked out a peace treaty between Israel and Egypt under which Israel returned to Egypt land it had captured in previous wars.

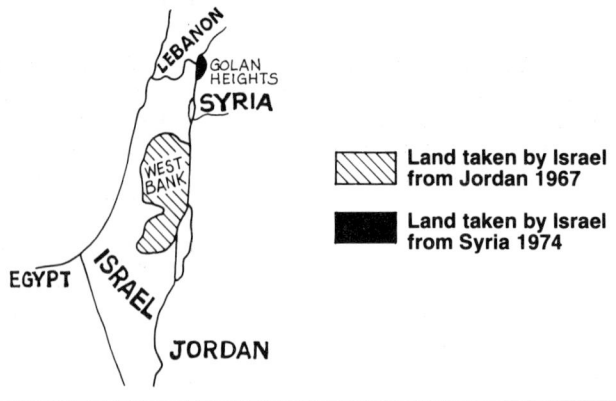

Land taken by Israel from Jordan 1967

Land taken by Israel from Syria 1974

THE OIL WAR

The 1973 Arab-Israel war was a turning point in the history of the twentieth century. To put pressure on the countries which were supplying arms to Israel the oil-producing Arab states cut back their output and raised the price by as much as 4 times. The effect was dramatic, as the west was so dependent on oil from the Middle East. Petrol in many countries was rationed, and in others private motoring was forbidden on Sundays. Speed limits were reduced in most countries to save fuel. Prices of most goods rose rapidly because of the cost of transport and energy. Plastics, which are made from oil, rocketed in price. The use of the oil-weapon was perhaps more effective than the Arab states had expected and they realised that they could hold the world to ransom at almost any time they liked.

But the oil war had some good effects. The world was forced to consider that supplies of oil, coal and timber would not last for ever, and that something must be done to save them. Energy was the main problem and there began a frantic search for sources of supply. New oilfields were explored, and Britain was lucky to find a huge one in the North Sea. Research into nuclear power was increased, as well as experiments in making electricity by using water, wind and the sun. Rapid developments were made into conserving energy by insulating buildings of all kinds and recycling materials which before had been wasted.

An oil rig in the North Sea. The discovery of oil in the North Sea made Britain the fifth largest oil-producing country in the world outside the communist bloc. The present reserves are expected to last at least until the end of the century.

The inside of the nuclear power station at Sizewell in Suffolk. The machine in the centre is for refuelling the nuclear reactor with uranium. About one-fifth of Britain's electricity is generated by nuclear power.

Israel is powerfully backed by the USA, and Syria and Libya by the USSR. There is always a danger that a war between Arabs and Jews might get out of hand. If one side seemed to be winning, or if oil supplies seemed likely to be cut off, the major powers might intervene, and perhaps start World War 3.

Although Egypt has reached a kind of agreement with Israel, much of the Arab world (especially Syria, Libya and Iraq) is still opposed to the existence of the state of Israel. Syria and Israel fought on opposite sides in the terrible civil war in Lebanon (1981 onwards). A very uneasy peace exists (1986) and any incident might result in another all-out conflict.

President Sadat (Egypt), President Carter (USA) and Prime Minister Begin (Israel) in Washington when the Israeli-Egyptian peace treaty was signed.

There is another problem not directly connected with the Arab-Israeli problem. This is the religious conflict between two branches of the Muslim faith, Sunni and Shia. A revolution in Iran in 1979 overthrew the Shah and the country is now (1986) ruled by the very strict Shiite priests. They wish to force religious rule on other Arab states. The Iraq-Iran war is one result of this.

The problems of the west bank of the Jordan and of the refugee Palestinian Arabs have increased, as the Israeli authorities build Jewish settlements, villages and towns all over former Arab land, thus making it less likely that the Palestinian Arabs will ever be allowed to return to places which they think of as their homes.

An Israeli soldier stands guard as Jewish settlers in trailers move into the mainly Arab town of Hebron on the west bank.

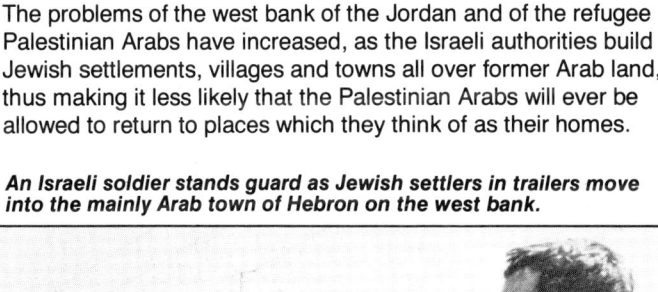

Iranian students in London demonstrate outside the US Embassy against the Shah. The posters are of the leader of the Islamic Revolution, the Shiite leader Ayatollah Khomeini.

China

China reached a high standard of civilisation while most of western Europe was still in the stone and bronze ages. While Europe was still in the middle ages the Chinese had invented paper, gunpowder, printing with type and were making beautiful works of art, especially in porcelain. The Venetian explorer Marco Polo reached China about 1300AD, and a tiny trickle of trade began, but China itself remained an almost closed country. It was ruled by a succession of families (dynasties) whose names are familiar from their pottery — Sung, Tang, Ming, etc. In 1644 the Manchu emperors seized power and remained in control until 1911. For most of this time China seemed to stand still. The local nobles (warlords) ruled their own areas ruthlessly, crushing the peasants with heavy taxes.

Trade with China increased in the eighteenth century as rich Europeans grew to like Chinese furniture, pictures, pottery, tea and silks, but the Chinese thought that Europe had little they wanted in return. In the nineteenth century the western countries began to increase the trade in opium and the Chinese tried to stop it. There was a war with the Europeans, who won, and began to force the Chinese to open the country to trade with them.

For centuries the Chinese leaders had believed that China was better than any other country in the world and did not need to change. So at the time of the industrial revolution in Europe China fell behind the western countries because it did not adopt European methods.

Fishing junks moored along the coast of Hong Kong island, with modern, high-rise office blocks in the background.

Anti-foreigner Chinese officials being executed by the Europeans during the Boxer Rising, 1900.

In the nineteenth century the Europeans forced the Chinese to give them important but very unfair trading rights. The Chinese landlords taxed the peasants even more heavily to get money to buy foreign goods. But although the peasants hated the landlords, they hated even more the Manchu rulers who had allowed the foreigners to get such a grip on the country. In 1900 the peasants rebelled in the Boxer Rising and killed many Europeans. European soldiers put down the rising but the Chinese were forced to pay large sums of money for the damage caused.

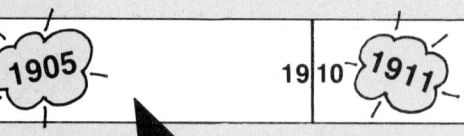

The people blamed the Manchu rulers, and in 1905 Dr Sun Yat Sen formed a revolutionary party — the Nationalists — to drive out the hated Manchus and foreigners. The Nationalists also wanted to have elections for a president and parliament and to share the rich landowners' land among the people. After several terrible harvests a revolution came in 1911 and Dr Sun Yat Sen set up a republic in southern China. General Yuan, head of the emperor's army, was persuaded to join Dr Sun, and they drove out the Manchu rulers. Sun Yat Sen was elected president of the new republic, but after a few weeks was replaced by Yuan. Violent quarrels broke out between Yuan and the revolutionaries and by 1914 Yuan was almost dictator of China.

In 1915 the Japanese began to invade parts of China, and promised Yuan they would make him emperor if he would let them share in running the country. This was too much for the people, who again rose in rebellion, and the whole country was torn apart by years of civil war, as the great warlords struggled for power. After 1917 some Chinese looked towards the new communist state in Russia, where a revolution seemed to have succeeded — unlike their own of 1911. A Chinese communist party was started in 1921 by Mao tse-tung and Chou en-lai.

Japanese front line awaiting Chinese attack.

In 1931 the Japanese invaded the north-east of China and soon captured Manchuria because the Nationalists were too busy attacking the communists and the warlords. In 1934 Chiang surrounded the communist region with half a million troops. A quarter of the communists, including women and children, broke out and began the terrible Long March through the mountains and desert to an even more remote area in the north-west, 13,000 km away. The journey took a year, and though thousands of people died on it, the behaviour of the communists won great respect from the peasants. They did not loot and destroy the countryside as the Nationalists did, and so many thousands of recruits joined them.

915 | 1920 1921 | 1924 | 1930 1931 | 1934 | 1940 1941

At first the tiny communist party and the Nationalists worked together to break the power of the warlords and to bring peace to China. In 1925 Dr Sun died, and Chiang kai-shek, who became leader of the Nationalists, soon quarrelled with his communist allies.

By 1928 the Nationalists controlled a large part of China, though there were still big areas where warlords still ruled. But the communists threatened Chiang's position and he was forced to attack them. They fled to a remote mountainous area in the south-west of the country. Here they set up a communist state, with the land shared among the peasants.

General Chiang kai-shek, leader of the Nationalists of China.

When he was safe in the distant corner of China, Mao appealed to the Nationalists to help him throw out the Japanese invaders. At first Chiang refused to join forces with the communists, but in 1936 his own party threatened to kill him if he did not. But even together communists and Nationalists were no match for the Japanese army, and soon afterwards World War 2 broke out. The fighting in China died down — the Japanese were busy elsewhere, and the Nationalists and communists were preparing for the next stage in the civil war which everyone knew would come.

The young communist leader, Mao tse-tung, talking to peasants in 1939.

Mao with communist party officials inspecting a co-operative farm. Again the peasants are in their best clothes for the occasion.

When Japan surrendered in 1945 (page 51) Mao's Red Army seized the weapons of their Manchurian army. The USA tried to get Mao and Chiang to work together, but the gap was too wide and in 1947 the civil war began again. It did not last long because most Chinese people had seen how corrupt the Nationalists had become. By 1949 the Nationalists were defeated. Chiang and his army fled to the island of Taiwan, where they were protected by the US navy and still called themselves the government of China. Mao became the first president of the People's Republic of China in 1949, and Chou en-lai his prime minister.

The communists immediately began many reforms. Land was taken from the peasants, and the farms made into collectives similar to those in Russia. There were great efforts to get industry going, but there were serious mistakes because so many of the people were not ready for industrial work. Progress was very slow. Millions of peasants with spades dug canals, made roads and railways, built dams. To help her new communist ally the Soviet Union poured in vast sums of money, millions of tonnes of equipment and supplies, and thousands of engineers, technicians, scientists and advisers.

  **19 50**   

China was in a desperate state. Forty years of almost non-stop war had almost destroyed the little industry and communications that had existed; farming was at a terribly low level, and government had nearly disappeared. Millions of peasants with hand tools had to try to rebuild the country. On top of this the world refused to recognise Mao's People's Republic as the real China. Chiang kai-shek's Nationalists in Taiwan still sat in the United Nations and on other world bodies. 600,000,000 people on the mainland had no say in world affairs. The world seemed to pretend that they did not exist.

Volunteer labourers (in their best clothes for this photograph) digging a sewerage ditch in central China.

In 1960 there was a quarrel between China and Russia. The causes were very complicated but an important one was that the Soviet Union would not give China the atom bomb. The Soviet advisers and technicians left China, leaving roads, bridges, factories and other large projects half complete. The west, which had been terrified that Russia and China, the two great communist countries, might be united, breathed a sigh of relief.

In 1963 China exploded its own atom bomb, showing that in some things it could manage alone, but the economy, industry and agriculture were still at a very low level.

Young people during the Cultural Revolution, waving the Little Red Book of Mao's thoughts at a rally.

In 1967 Mao felt that communist leaders were becoming out of touch with ordinary people. Experts were taking over and getting the best jobs for themselves and their children. Young people did not know what their parents and grand-parents had suffered to bring communism to China. Mao called on young people to start a Cultural Revolution. Millions of them became Red Guards and attacked people who they felt were not behaving according to the teachings of Marx, Lenin and Mao. Factories were reorganised to make sure that they were run by the workers; students went to work with peasants on the farms. Thousands of officials, scholars and important people were either killed or disgraced. The Cultural Revolution got completely out of hand. Food production dropped, industries were becoming less efficient. It was almost 10 years before the government really got control of the country again.

70 **1971** **19 80**

In 1971 the People's Republic of China was admitted to its rightful place in the world. It became a member of the United Nations and Taiwan was expelled. Links with other nations were set up, though there is still a great coolness towards Russia. Help to establish industry and other projects came to China from other countries, and Chinese scholars, scientists and technicians went to foreign universities to study the latest advances. In the late 1970s tourism opened in a small way, and an increasing number of people from the west can now see China for themselves.

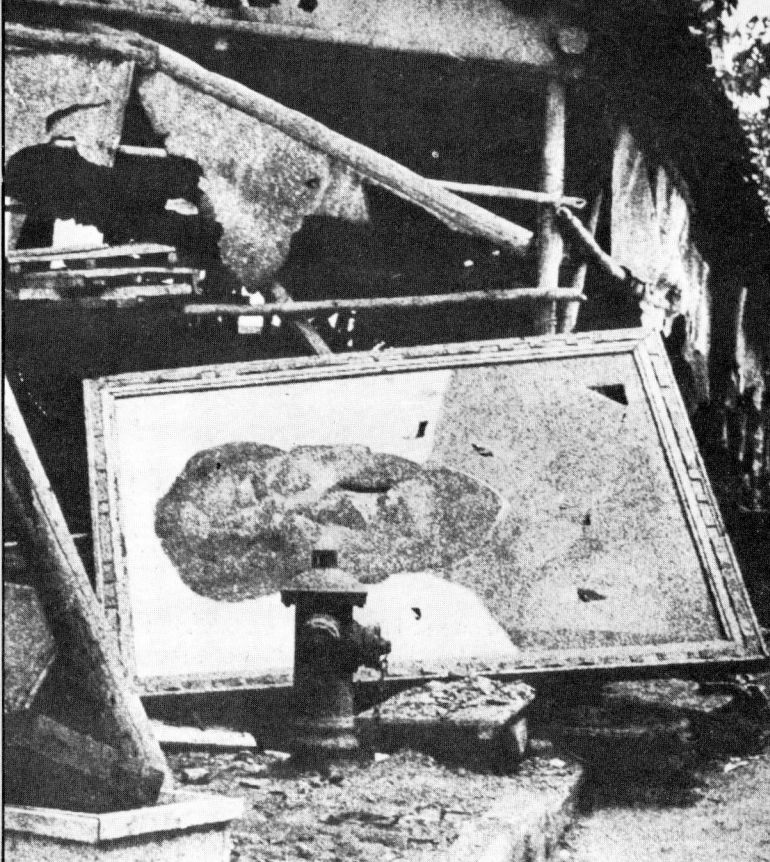

After Mao's death many people's ideas about him began to change. Statues and pictures of him were sometimes pulled down and broken up, like this one in Canton.

China today has about 1 000 000 000 people — a quarter of the total population of the world. She is desperately poor, with little more than 10% of her land really fertile, but 80% of the people work in agriculture. Unlike communist systems elsewhere in the world, which are based on industrial workers, Chinese communism is based on the peasants.

Chinese industry is small and relatively inefficient, and because she has so little to export, she has very little foreign exchange to buy equipment and skills from abroad. Since the death of Mao (1976), however, the communist government has become more flexible. Some business from industrial countries are invited to set up factories, hotels and other operations on a sharing basis. A small amount of private capitalism is being permitted. On the collective farms, for example, peasants no longer work together in great communal fields, but are given individual holdings. They have to provide a certain amount of crops for the commune, but after that they can grow what they like for the local free market. By this method some peasants are becoming more prosperous as they rear poultry or grow 'luxury' crops such as tomatoes. There are some small-scale capitalist industries too. These are generally family concerns, or groups of people who form themselves into a 'collective' to make and sell such things as clothing, furniture or food, or to provide services such as shoe repairing, meals or transport.

Despite this the system is very much a communist one and all of China's efforts are geared to the 'Four Modernisations' — industry, agriculture, defence and science and technology. But there is still a very long way to go.

The ups and downs of Japan

Japan is a string of islands about one and a half times the size of Britain, but because of its many mountains only about one sixth of the land is suitable for growing crops. It was always a secret country, but from the early seventeenth century it shut itself off from the world completely, and was much as Europe had been in the middle ages, with feudal nobles and poor peasants. After the country was opened to outsiders in 1853 (see page 74) the speed of change was amazing. In 90 years it changed from an undeveloped, feudal state, to an empire controlling one twelfth of the world's surface. But two years later it was again a group of off-shore islands. Then within another 30 years it rose to be the third largest industrial power in the world, after the USA and the USSR.

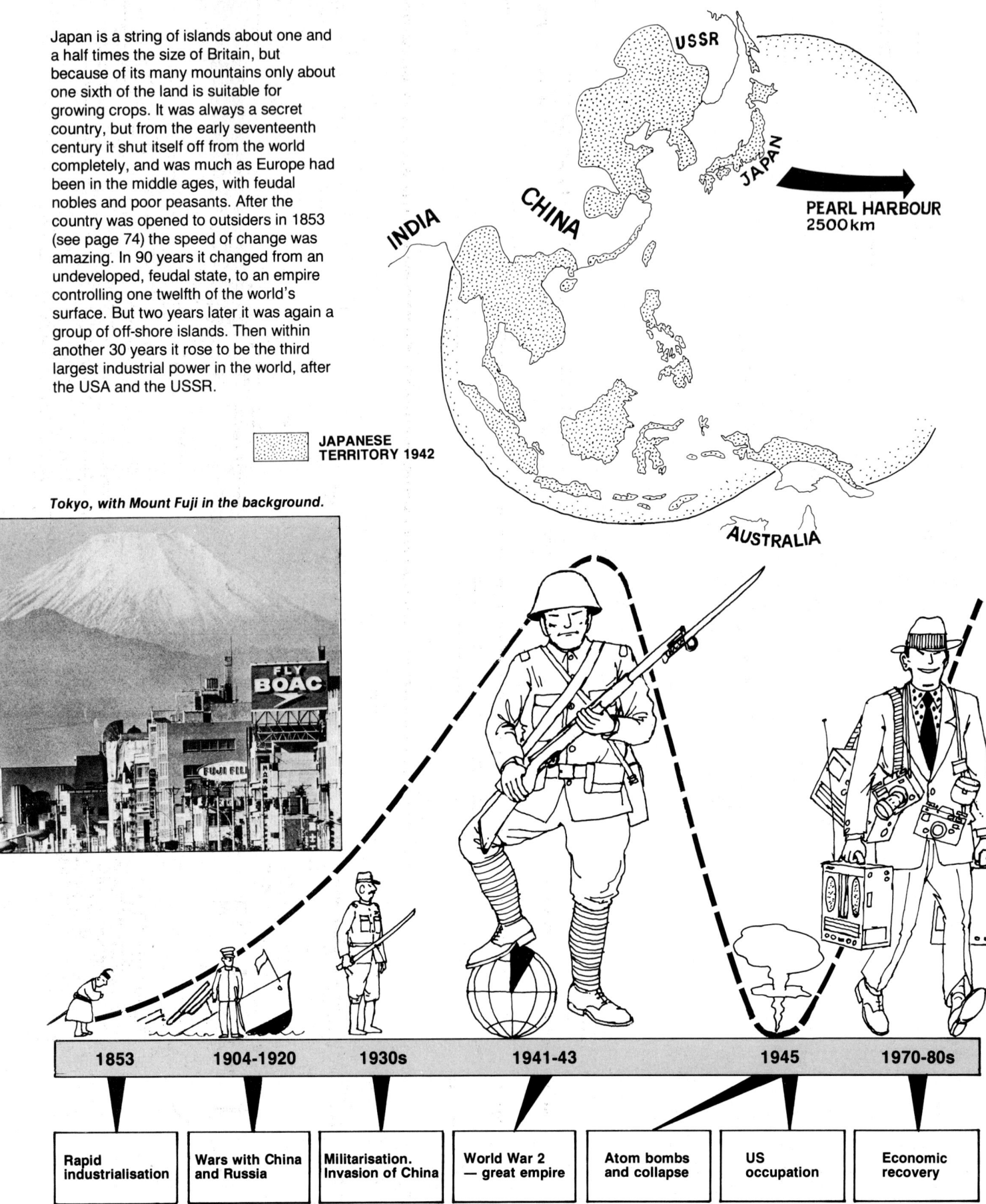

PEARL HARBOUR
2500 km

JAPANESE TERRITORY 1942

Tokyo, with Mount Fuji in the background.

| 1853 | 1904-1920 | 1930s | 1941-43 | 1945 | 1970-80s |

| Rapid industrialisation | Wars with China and Russia | Militarisation. Invasion of China | World War 2 — great empire | Atom bombs and collapse | US occupation | Economic recovery |

A tiny 'shop' in the electronics district of Tokyo is jammed with goods of all kinds at very low prices.

Japanese industrialists use many methods to increase output. The factory loudspeaker at this electronics factory orders the girls to stop work, breathe deeply, yawn and stretch every sixty minutes. It is claimed that the girls work harder for this.

Girls in this textile factory are equipped with roller skates so that they can move quickly from one loom to another. The owners say it is less tiring and increases output.

The Black Ship. The Japanese writing explains that it is a steamship.

In the nineteenth century the chief European industrial nations 'shared out' China among themselves for trading purposes. The USA did not have a share in the China markets and turned towards Japan, which had been closed to the outside world for centuries and which was still much like medieval Europe. In 1854 the US sent warships into Tokyo Bay and demanded that the emperor should open the country to foreign trade. With their primitive weapons and organisation, and terrified by the 'black ships' which they had not seen before, the Japanese signed a trade treaty with the USA. Within a few years eighteen other countries had trade treaties, all of them unfair to Japan.

In the next 50 years Japan industrialised itself rapidly. It employed western engineers and architects to build factories, dockyards, railways and roads. Foreign military and naval officers showed it how to build ships and weapons, and trained the armed forces. Doctors, teachers and other professional people helped Japan to catch up with the west. But Japan quickly learned to try some of the other ideas it had learned. When in 1898 the Koreans rebelled against their Chinese masters, Japan, without warning, invaded the country and quickly defeated the Chinese. Though Korea was now supposed to be independent, it was really a Japanese colony. Japan also took Taiwan from China and had a lease on the Liaotung peninsula, which was near the Russian naval base of Port Arthur. The western nations made Japan give up this lease, which was immediately taken by Russia. Japan wanted revenge — and the Liaotung peninsula.

The Japanese writing says this is a painting of a train on the Takanawa to Japan railway, 1880.

In 1904 the expected war between Japan and Russia broke out as both were trying to expand into north-eastern China. Again without warning the Japanese fleet crept into Port Arthur at night and sank three Russian warships, and Japanese soldiers captured the port itself (1905). Another Russian fleet sailed from Europe to Japan, where 48 out of its 50 ships were sunk with a loss to the Japanese navy of only three. But the war had brought Japan almost to collapse and it was glad when the USA got the two sides to a peace conference. Japan took the lease of the peninsula, the Russian railway that ran through that part of China, and half of the Russian island of Sakhalin to the north of Japan.

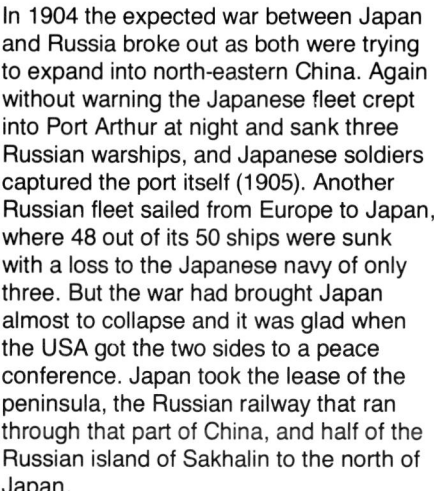

A painting of the naval battle of Tsoushima, 1905. The Japanese have destroyed the Russian fleet.

In World War 1 Japan was on the side of Britain and France, but took little part in any fighting except to seize the German sphere in China (see page 7) and the German islands in the Pacific Ocean. At the Versailles conference it demanded and was given these islands, which were to be invaluable to it twenty years later as naval bases in World War 2. Japanese industry made immense advances in World War 1 supplying goods for the allied forces. In addition, while the European factories were busy making weapons and equipment they could not keep up the supply of goods for overseas markets, and the Japanese factories stepped in to capture many of the very profitable markets in Asia (in India, for example) with goods of all kinds — clothing, engineering, chemicals.

The revolutionary Fidel Castro who overthrew the dictator Batista in Cuba in 1959 and set up the first communist state in the Americas.

West Indian immigrants arriving at Southampton Docks to find work in Britain. 300 000 arrived in 1956 alone.

The Caribbean

This consists of thousands of islands, formerly all part of the Spanish empire. In wars against Spain in the eighteenth century Britain and France seized most of them. In 1898 the US fought and beat Spain, which then still owned Cuba, and gave the Cubans independence under American influence (1903). The US also seized Puerto Rico in 1898, and in 1917 it bought some of the Virgin Islands from Denmark.

·In the 1960s and 1970s the British colonies in the area all became fully independent or self-governing, and they have all remained within the Commonwealth. They are mainly very poor, and some are really too small to be independent countries. Antigua has a total population of only 75 000, and the largest, Jamaica, a population of 2 250 000.

The French possessions have not yet been given full independence.

A shanty town in Guyana with many families sharing one cold water tap. This is typical of many parts of the Caribbean.

Cuba

In 1959 the right-wing dictator was overthrown by the left-wing Fidel Castro, who established communism on the island. This worried the US, which did not want a communist state anywhere in or near the American continent. In 1961 the US helped in an invasion of Cuba by Cuban refugees, but this was a disaster. Shortly after this there was a crisis when the USSR tried to base Soviet missiles on the island (page 41). Recently trade with the US has begun again and there is less tension.

Central America

Guatemala, Honduras, El Salvador, Nicaragua, Costa Rica and Panama, together with Belize, formerly the colony of British Honduras, which gained independence within the Commonwealth in 1981. These were once called 'the banana republics' because their whole economy depended on fruit, especially bananas. They·are particularly unsettled, with left-wing guerilla movements in the right-wing states, and right-wing movements in the left-wing states. There are constant border disputes. The US is very concerned about this region too.

Not far from such shanty houses as the one on this page are luxury hotels and beaches for tourists mainly from the USA. This one is in Jamaica.

Communism and the Church in Latin-America

For the vast numbers of poor peasants in Latin-America communism seems to offer some hope. But in most countries the right-wing families or the army are so firmly in control of everything that it is difficult to establish socialism. Many people cannot read, and this makes fair elections difficult. Because so few poor people are educated, political leaders usually come from privileged families. In some countries, however, the Catholic Church has taken up the cause of the ordinary people, and has been very out-spoken against the more extreme dictators of both left and right. The Church is very important, and though most of its leaders come from the old ruling families it is becoming more and more involved in politics.

THE WEALTHY FAMILIES FROM WHICH THE HIGHER CLERGY COME

THE CHURCH

THE GUERILLA OPPOSITION—OFTEN ANTI-CHURCH, VIOLENT AND PERSECUTED

Sandinista guerillas in Nicaragua. Nicaragua is fairly typical of US involvement in central America. It was occupied by US marines until they were driven out in 1933. In 1936 it fell under the control of the right-wing Somoza family, who in turn were driven out by the left-wing Sandinistas in 1979. Today right-wing 'contras' backed by the US are the guerillas, fighting the Sandinista government.

US involvement in Latin-America

The US is very concerned with affairs in Latin-America, and wants the whole area to become more settled. It is particularly anxious that communism does not become firmly established on the American continent, because it might spread to the USA, especially among the poorer blacks. Communist countries might allow the Soviet Union to have military bases very near the USA.

America has helped the Caribbean with huge sums of money in order to prevent the islands from becoming communist or left-wing. In 1983 US troops invaded Grenada and overthrew the pro-Cuban government of Maurice Bishop. But the islands are still very poor because many jobs are provided by foreign businesses, especially American ones, and so the profits are not kept in the Caribbean.

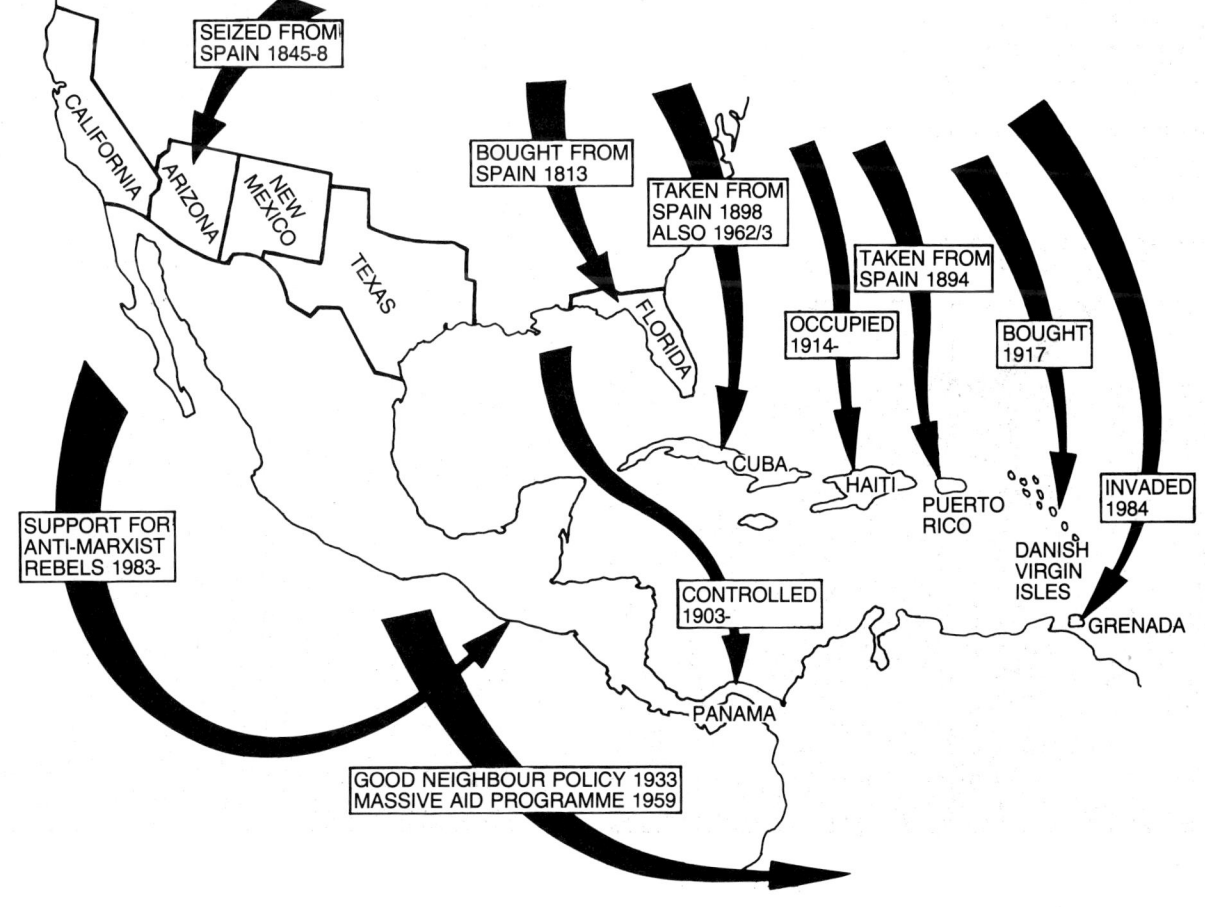

SEIZED FROM SPAIN 1845-8

CALIFORNIA

ARIZONA

NEW MEXICO

TEXAS

BOUGHT FROM SPAIN 1813

FLORIDA

TAKEN FROM SPAIN 1898 ALSO 1962/3

TAKEN FROM SPAIN 1894

OCCUPIED 1914-

BOUGHT 1917

CUBA

HAITI

PUERTO RICO

INVADED 1984

DANISH VIRGIN ISLES

GRENADA

SUPPORT FOR ANTI-MARXIST REBELS 1983-

CONTROLLED 1903-

PANAMA

GOOD NEIGHBOUR POLICY 1933 MASSIVE AID PROGRAMME 1959

Black Africa

1700 Slaves and coastal trade

Explorers and missionaries

1700

A century and a half ago Africa south of the Sahara was almost unknown to white people. There were slave trading settlements run by Britain, France, Holland, Portugal and Denmark round the coasts from the middle of the seventeenth century, and later settlements for such goods as ivory and timber. In the southern tip of the continent Dutch (Boer) farmers had been settling from the seventeenth century onwards in the rich farming lands, using the black people there as their slaves. The interior was mysterious to white people and ruled by powerful tribes who were often at war with one another. There were some mysterious civilisations which we still know very little about. On the eastern side a people left the great ruins of Zimbabwe shown below and on the western coasts there was an organised and educated society which produced the bronze figures of Benin.

In 1807 Britain banned the slave trade, and slavery itself in 1833 so that most of the trading stations were abandoned. It looked as if Africa would be left to itself again, apart from the southern tip (see page 84), but now missionaries and explorers began to take an interest in the interior.

Soon after the middle of the nineteenth century Britain, France, Holland, Portugal, Spain, Belgium and later Germany began a scramble to seize parts of Africa as colonies, but for the most part they left them totally undeveloped.

The continent was divided up more or less at random. Often the frontiers cut through the middle of tribal territory, so that one part of a tribe was ruled by one country and another part by another. There were not many white settlers, except in a few places, and a

Part of the ruined city of Zimbabwe (14th-15th century AD) The modern state of Zimbabwe was named after this ancient city when it became independent in 1980.

A 13th century bronze head from West Africa. It shows there must have been a very civilised culture there.

Land controlled by non-whites

Land controlled by white nations

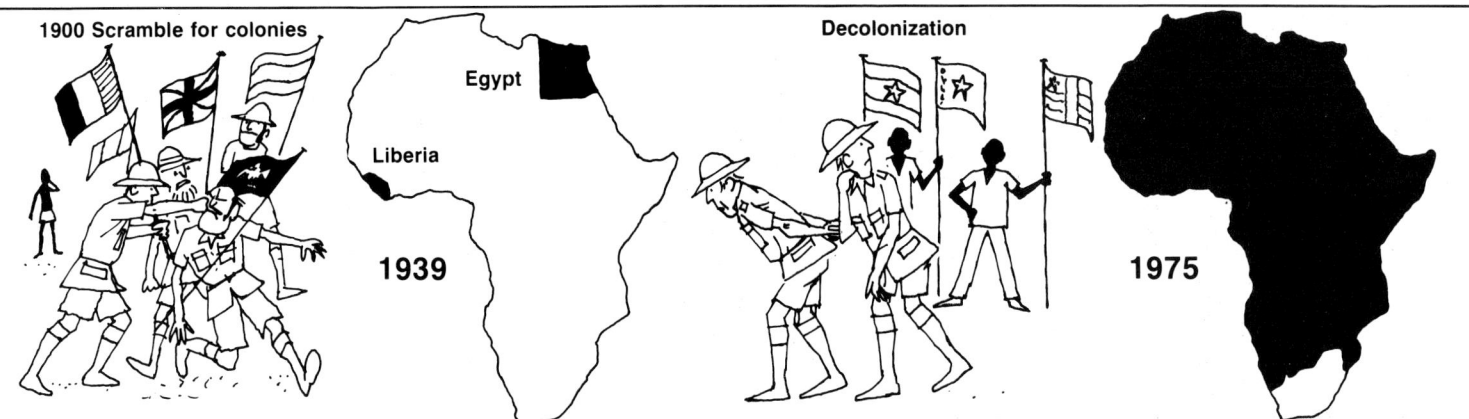

1900 Scramble for colonies
Egypt
Liberia
1939
Decolonization
1975

handful of colonial administrators tried to impose white men's ideas and laws on vast areas of land and on millions of people who did not understand them.

When World War 2 broke out the only independent black state south of the Sahara was Liberia, a small country on the west coast which had been set up in the nineteenth century as a refuge for black slaves from America who had escaped or been freed. The rest was in the hands of colonial powers.

The war was a turning point. Black soldiers fought together with whites, and saw the great differences in standards of living. When the war ended the returning blacks began to demand more for themselves. Britain and France, perhaps too late, began a big programme of modernisation in their colonies, building roads, power stations, irrigation projects, and most important of all, expanding the education programme, especially in higher and technical education. But for the black people this was not enough. They wanted not only higher standards, but independence also. They had seen how in the east the Japanese had easily driven out the colonial powers from south-east Asia, and how the countries there had achieved independence. The United Nations, the Soviet Union and the USA began to put pressure on the European states to give freedom to their colonies in Africa. So, in the 1950s and 1960s one state after another became independent, most of the British and French ones peacefully. The Belgians and Portuguese were reluctant to give up their possessions of the Congo and Angola, and there was bitter fighting, but by 1979 the whole of Southern Africa, with the exception of Boer South Africa, had become independent.

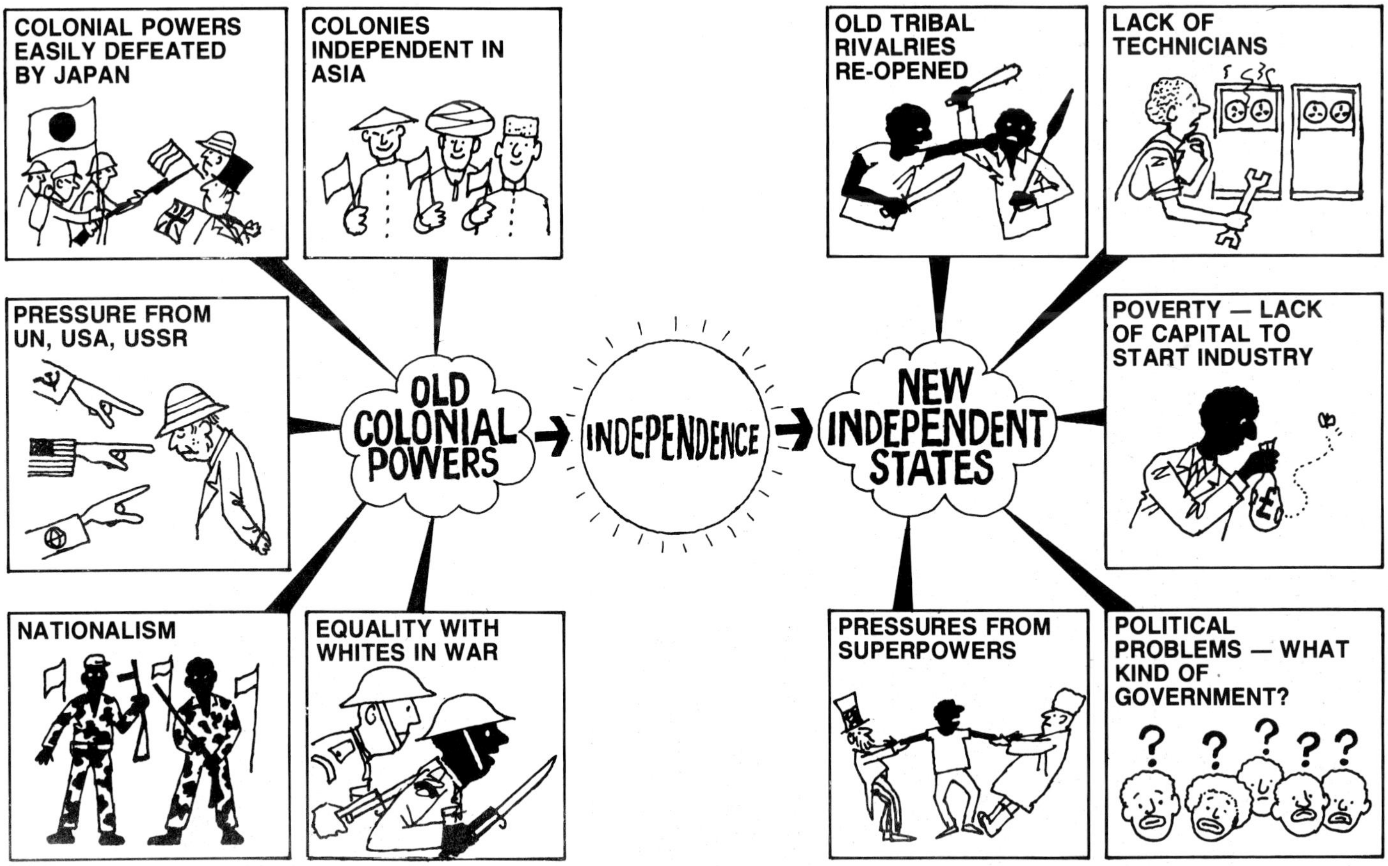

COLONIAL POWERS EASILY DEFEATED BY JAPAN
COLONIES INDEPENDENT IN ASIA
PRESSURE FROM UN, USA, USSR
NATIONALISM
EQUALITY WITH WHITES IN WAR
OLD COLONIAL POWERS
INDEPENDENCE
NEW INDEPENDENT STATES
OLD TRIBAL RIVALRIES RE-OPENED
LACK OF TECHNICIANS
POVERTY — LACK OF CAPITAL TO START INDUSTRY
PRESSURES FROM SUPERPOWERS
POLITICAL PROBLEMS — WHAT KIND OF GOVERNMENT?
? ? ? ? ?

South Africa

From the middle of the seventeenth century the Dutch, often known as the Boers or farmers, had been settling in the tip of South Africa, driving the black people from their lands, and making them slaves. In 1814 Britain compulsorily 'bought' the land from the Dutch and began to settle there too. The Boers and the Dutch Reformed Church believed the blacks to be an inferior race, fit only to be slaves. Quarrels soon developed between British and Boers. The British gave the black people rights of citizenship, abolished slavery and tried to protect the blacks from the harsh treatment of the Boers. In 1836 many Boers began the Great Trek. They moved further north into what is now Transvaal, Orange Free State and Natal, to be free of British restrictions.

A Boer commando before the Battle of Mafeking against the British.

Britain recognised the Transvaal and the Orange Free State as independent Boer states in 1881, but in 1899 war broke out between the Boers and Britain. The Boers were defeated. Four states (Orange Free State, Transvaal, Natal and the Cape) became the Union of South Africa in the British Empire in 1910. It was a self-governing dominion with a Boer prime minister, General Botha. Because he allowed children to be taught in their own language until they were 12, a section of his party broke away. They wanted Dutch (Afrikaans) to be the most important language and formed a new party called the Nationalists.

In 1924 the Nationalist Party came to power, and the 'white' policy was stepped up. In 1936 blacks lost all voting rights, though the 'coloureds' (people of mixed race and Indians)

retained some of theirs. In 1948 the Nationalist Party became more extreme and set out on its policy of apartheid (apartness). In theory this means 'separate but equal development' for all races, but you can see what happens in practice opposite.

The Nationalist Party is creating separate black tribal states which are supposed to be self-governing, but which are really totally under the control of the South African government. The black states will cover about 13% of South Africa, though their people form 70% of the population. Under a new constitution of 1984 the 3 million coloureds were allowed to vote for a kind of assembly which was almost powerless. Two-thirds of the people allowed to vote refused to do so. The 16 million blacks have not been allowed even this kind of assembly.

Because of its racist policies South Africa has been almost outlawed from the world community. It left the British Commonwealth in 1961; it has no international sporting links, and has been condemned again and again by the United Nations. Much of its trade has been cut off, but this has had the effect of forcing it to develop its own industries. South Africa is now surrounded by independent black states which are opposed to its racial policies. It is much richer than they are now, but how much longer can it hold out against them?

Victoria West in Karou, South Africa. The European township is in the foreground and the black one is in the background. Look at the differences.

APARTHEID

Pass laws
Until 1985 all blacks were forced to carry passes. If the police found a black without a pass, or one which was out of date or not signed, the person could be banished to the tribal homeland, or sent as a convict to a white farm.

Politics
3.5 million whites elect 165 MPs (all white). 13 million blacks were allowed 3 MPs (whites) until 1959, when they lost even these. Under the constitution of 1984 Indians and people of mixed race are allowed to elect representatives for a separate parliament with no real power.

Legal system
People can be arrested and held in prison without trial for 'activities against the state', especially for membership of the African National Congress (ANC), the blacks' political party, which was banned in the 1960s for terrorist activities.

Segregation
Some segregation has now gone, but it is still total in schools. Black schools have an average of one teacher for 80 pupils, white children of 1 for 12. There are 65,000 white students in universities, and 1,200 blacks, who are in segregated universities.

Townships
Blacks are not allowed to live in towns except with special permission — if they are servants, for example. They have to live in townships, often built out of sight of the cities, and travel to work each day. Some of the townships consist of rows of modern concrete one- or two-roomed huts, but most are shanty towns of plastic and tin.

Jobs
Blacks are normally banned from any skilled work, which is reserved for whites. Where blacks and whites are doing the same work — in the mines, for example — black wages are about one-eighth of the whites'.

CHEAP LABOUR

A funeral of one of the people killed in uprisings in South Africa in 1985.

The Third World

After World War 2 many nations joined one of two groups — the communist world of Russia and her allies, or the western world of America and western Europe. All of these were industrialised and fairly prosperous. Many countries in Africa and Asia, all poor and under-developed, did not want to belong to either group and perhaps get involved in another world war. 29 of these 'non-aligned' nations held a conference in Indonesia in 1955 and became known as the Third World. They were soon joined by countries in Latin-America and recently-independent states in Africa and Asia, all of which had similar problems.

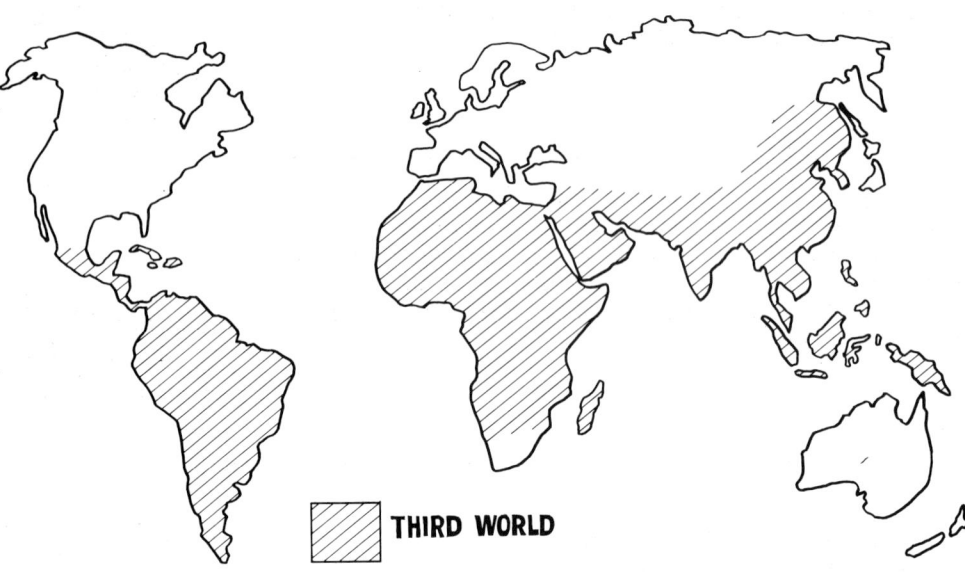

THIRD WORLD

This chart shows how some of the world's resources are shared out between the Third World and the rest. The two basic problems are poverty and a soaring birthrate. These present the countries of the Third World with terrible difficulties. First, they cannot become developed and prosperous unless they have more money, but they cannot get more money unless they become prosperous and developed. Secondly, the population increase races ahead more quickly than any improvement in agricultural or industrial production. Somehow the Third World has to break out of this vicious spiral.

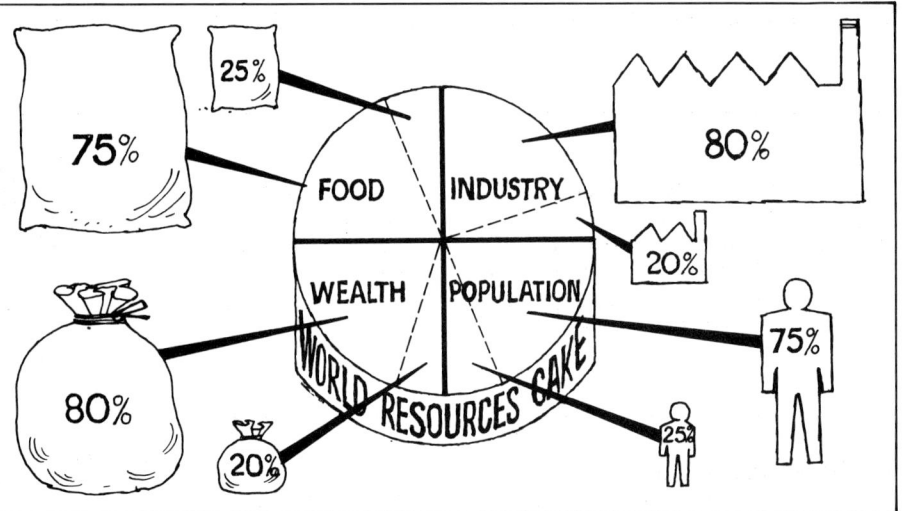

POVERTY
POOR AGRICULTURAL METHODS
OFTEN POOR LAND —DESERT, SWAMP, MOUNTAINS
LITTLE INDUSTRY

SOARING POPULATION TO FEED
POOR EDUCATION ESPECIALLY HIGHER TECHNICIANS
POOR MEDICAL HEALTH CARE
OFTEN POLITICALLY UNSTABLE AND MUCH CORRUPTION

Poor agriculture

Much of the Third World has poor agricultural land. On top of this farming methods are often primitive and low-yielding, partly because people cannot afford modern machinery. Often the crops and animals are poor varieties very subject to disease, and suitable only for local use, not for export.

Industry

There is little industry because it is very expensive to build factories and import machines. There is too a desperate shortage of people trained as technicians, engineers, sales staff and managers. Often communications such as railways and roads on which industry depends are poor.

Population

People in The Third World have large families to make up for the appalling death rate. Though medical care is still poor by western standards, it does keep more people alive, and populations are soaring. The increase is outstripping the very small improvement in food supplies, and in many countries the standard of living is actually falling. Fewer than 1% of the people in the Third World use contraception. As a result there are 200,000 births a day.

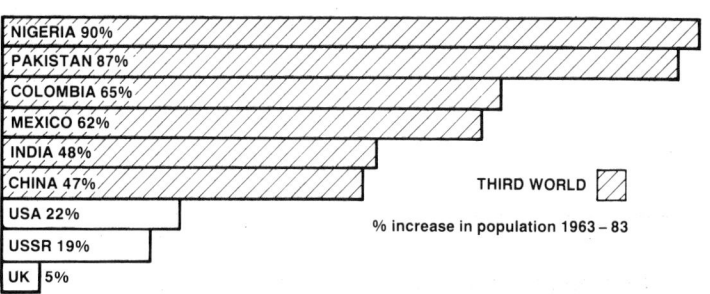

NIGERIA 90%
PAKISTAN 87%
COLOMBIA 65%
MEXICO 62%
INDIA 48%
CHINA 47%
USA 22%
USSR 19%
UK 5%

THIRD WORLD

% increase in population 1963 – 83

Education

Education is very expensive and most Third World countries have only compulsory primary schooling. In many countries only about 20% of the population can read and write. Secondary and higher education is for a very few, which means there is a terrible shortage of teachers, scientists, doctors, engineers and professional people of all kinds.

Medicine and health

Though more people are staying alive, medical care is generally very bad, with few doctors and hospitals, and poor treatment. Sanitation outside the chief cities often does not exist, and over half the Third World does not have any water supply except the local stream or pond, which is likely to dry up at any time.

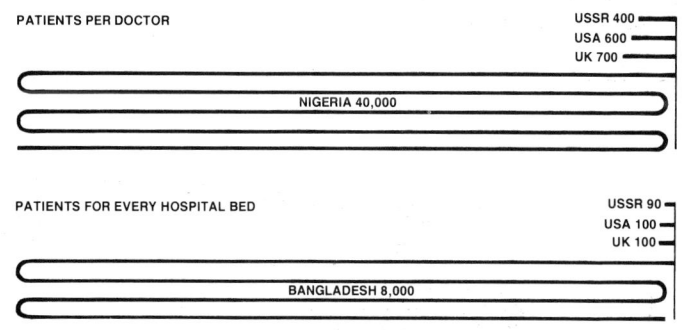

PATIENTS PER DOCTOR

USSR 400
USA 600
UK 700

NIGERIA 40,000

PATIENTS FOR EVERY HOSPITAL BED

USSR 90
USA 100
UK 100

BANGLADESH 8,000

Traditions

There are very strong traditions in the Third World countries which come from times when there were many fewer people and conditions were simpler, and which are a barrier to development today. These affect health, farming, government, education and social relations.

Helping the Third World

Developed nations must create industry in underdeveloped countries like this oil refinery in the Caribbean.

This health assistant in a Burmese village is showing the people how to chlorinate their wells to prevent the spread of diseases.

Money

Money to help Third World countries can come as gifts or loans from wealthier nations, or from international agencies such as the IMF (International Monetary Fund). Private businesses can also invest in the Third World by opening factories, mines and farms. They employ local workers and train local people to take over technical and senior posts. Much of the profit can be re-invested in the country.

Markets

There is no point in Third World countries setting up industries if they cannot sell their goods because the developed countries put up tariff barriers against them. The rest of the world must be prepared to offer markets for the goods on a fair basis. The developed world too must see that the Third World offers the right kind of goods, of acceptable quality and design.

Laying a pipeline in Sudan to improve the scarce water supply.

Education and expertise

Developed countries can send teachers, professional people and experts of all kinds under aid schemes, or they can be recruited by Third World governments on a normal commercial basis. The experts will both supervise agricultural, industrial and engineering projects and also train local people to take over when they have enough experience.

Political stability

A country cannot develop if there are constant changes of government, civil wars and rebellions, so developed countries should try to help to keep Third World countries politically stable. This does not mean that outside nations should try to impose their own form of government. The political systems of the developed world may not be suitable for the Third World.

A Third World tree nursery. Farmers buy seedlings here to promote regrowth of trees and stop soil erosion.

Sudan. Note how the grazing animals and people cutting wood for fuel have turned the land immediately round the village into desert. The large trees in the 'gardens' are kept for shade.

An Oxfam veterinary specialist teaching farmers in Sudan how to take care of the cattle on which they depend. Animals here suffer terribly from parasites, insects and diseases.

Voluntary organisations

As well as separate governments and the United Nations there are many voluntary organisations that try to help the Third World. They do not have vast amounts of money and concentrate on small, important areas where the results are out of proportion with the cash spent on them. These include digging wells, setting up schools, clinics and hospitals, advising on farming, providing immunisation and community health services, training local people for simple medical care, providing food, shelter and clothing in emergencies. The voluntary organisations include many religious bodies, the Save the Children Fund, Oxfam, War on Want and many others.

The Catholic missionary, Mother Theresa, who has spent most of her life working among the desperately poor in Calcutta, India. She was awarded the Nobel Peace prize for her work.

A school for poor children in Africa. They have no pens, paper or books, let alone a classroom and desk. With the best will possible, they cannot really become educated in conditions like these, and education is essential if they are to raise their standard of living.

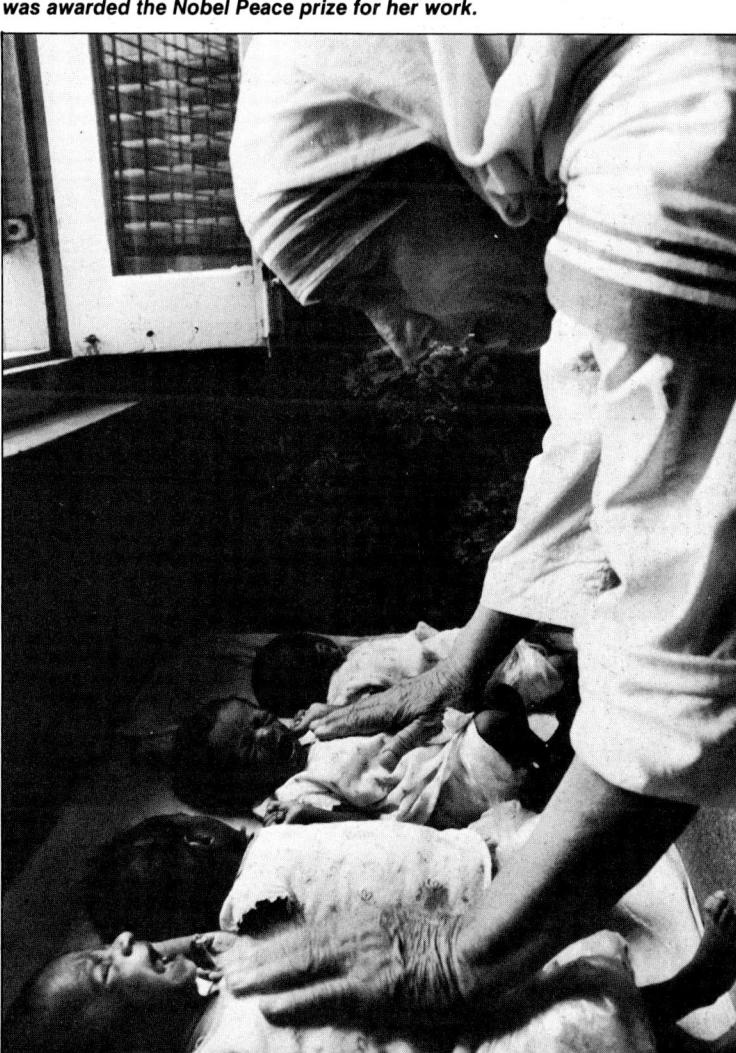

Race, religion and nationalism

Racism

Racism is the belief that one race is better than another. People usually think of race as colour — black, brown, yellow or white — though sometimes religious differences seem important: between Jews and non-Jews, for example.

Some scientists believe that there are three main racial groups: negroid — black people from Africa; mongoloid — yellow-skinned people from China and Japan, and caucasoid — Indo-Europeans with brown or white skins. No one has ever proved that any one group is naturally better or worse than any other. Pupils from Asian or black families in European schools may have different attitudes because of their home backgrounds. Their parents or grandparents may have been born in another country where ideas and customs are different from European ones.

In the twentieth century racism has been linked with political ideas. Left-wing parties often wish to bring races together, extreme right-wing parties favour segregation. In modern times the most frightening examples of racism are apartheid in South Africa (pages 84-85) and anti-semitism in Nazi Germany between 1933 and 1945.

Anti-semitism

For almost 2000 years some Europeans have hated Jews. Why is this? There are many theories about it but no one can be quite sure of the reasons. Jews have been persecuted for centuries, but the horrifying climax came under the Nazi government in Germany. The Nazis blamed the Jews for many of Germany's problems after World War 1. They said that people of 'pure' German blood were a nobler and better race than the Jews. At first Jews were laughed at and made to wear badges on their clothing so that they could be recognised, later they were brutally treated and finally murdered in millions.

The Nazi 'final solution' meant that Jewish people in Germany and the occupied countries were to be rounded up and slaughtered in special extermination camps. They were gassed, shot, beaten or starved to death, or used in horrifying medical experiments. It is thought that 6 million Jews died in what is known as The Holocaust. When the Jewish state of Israel was set up in 1948 (page 65) many people saw it as a way of helping the Jewish people after their terrible sufferings .

A heap of Jewish corpses at the Buchenwald concentration camp.

This sign shows both the English and Welsh for 'Welcome to Wales'.

Racism displayed by National Front graffiti.

Nationalism

Nationalism is the feeling that people of the same background — language, race, religion, tradition, customs, etc. — should be allowed to choose their own government, rather than be ruled by people of a different race or background. Until World War 2, for example, at least a quarter of the people in the world — blacks in Africa and the people of India and south-east Asia — were governed by white European colonial powers. After the war nationalist movements among the peoples of those countries forced the whites to give them independence.

Today there are a number of minority groups who for various reasons now find themselves ruled by people of a different background. Some of these groups, for example, have been in a country of their own in the past but international treaties have made them part of another state.

When India became independent, it was split into Pakistan (mainly Muslims) and India (mainly Hindus). East Pakistan was ruled from West Pakistan. In 1971 East Pakistan broke away from West Pakistan and became the state of Bangladesh. The Bangladeshis feel that they are a separate people who should rule themselves. There is a movement for a separate kingdom for Sikhs, who wish to break away from India. The Kurds, a people who live in the region where Iraq, Iran and Russia meet, are constantly fighting a guerilla war to establish their own state. Although in Europe it is difficult for any nationalist group to break away to form its own state, there are a number who are struggling, sometimes with terrorist methods, to be given more freedom to run their own affairs within the state in which they are living. In Britain many Scots and Welsh people want their own parliamentary assemblies; Bretons in France and Basques in Spain want more independence.

These Sikhs are outraged by the storming of their sacred Golden Temple of Amritsar by Indian soldiers in which many Sikhs were killed.

India's path to independence

At the beginning of the twentieth century the sub-continent of India was ruled by the British. Eleven provinces, containing three-fifths of the population, were ruled directly, and the rest, consisting of over 500 states, were governed by Indian princes, who were largely under the control of the British. As the century wore on, many Indians longed to be independent, but they were deeply divided by race, language, caste, and above all, religion. It was only the presence of the British army that stopped massacres between the two largest religious groups, Hindus and Muslims.

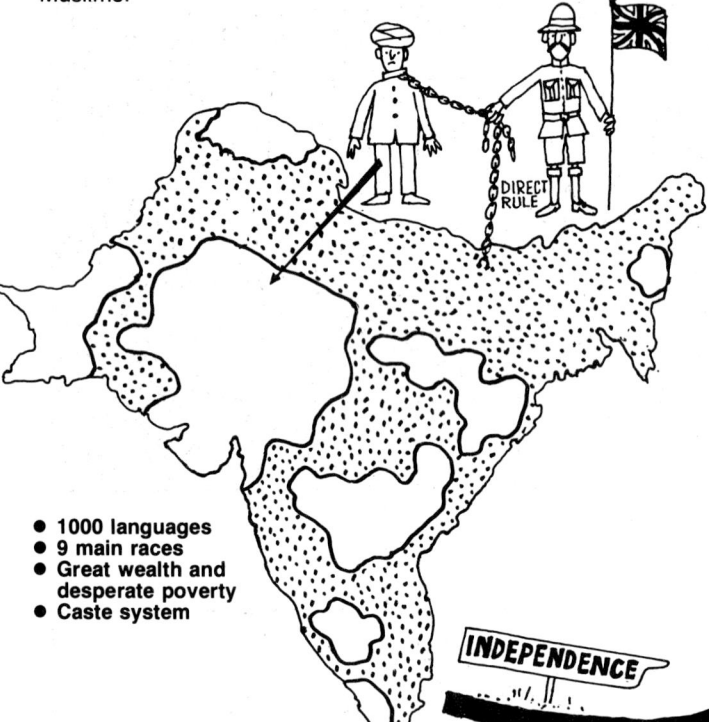

- 1000 languages
- 9 main races
- Great wealth and desperate poverty
- Caste system

INDEPENDENCE

Gandhi's followers getting ready to march to the coast to make their own salt from sea water. This was illegal because salt manufacture was a government monopoly.

Through the 1920s and the early 1930s little progress towards independence was made, and Congress under Gandhi began a great campaign of civil disobedience — protest rallies, demonstrations and strikes. By the India Act of 1935 the British gave self-government to the eleven provinces — the princes could join if they wanted to. In the elections which followed Congress won control of eight provincial governments, and formed coalitions with the Muslim League in others. This meant that if India did become a single country with one government the Muslims would always be a minority. The movement for a separate Muslim state with its own government grew.

Towards the end of the nineteenth century two political parties were founded to try to gain independence for India. They were the Indian National Congress (today's Congress Party), which soon became all-Hindu, and the Muslim League. In World War 1 many Indian soldiers fought for the allies, and though more power was given to Indians in 1919 they felt it was not enough. Three leaders emerged: Gandhi and Nehru in the Congress party, and Jinnah in the Muslim League. These three men were to be the main political figures in India for the next 40 years.

Gandhi, the Hindu lawyer who lead the Indian nationalist movement. Gandhi believed in home industries and is here spinning thread.

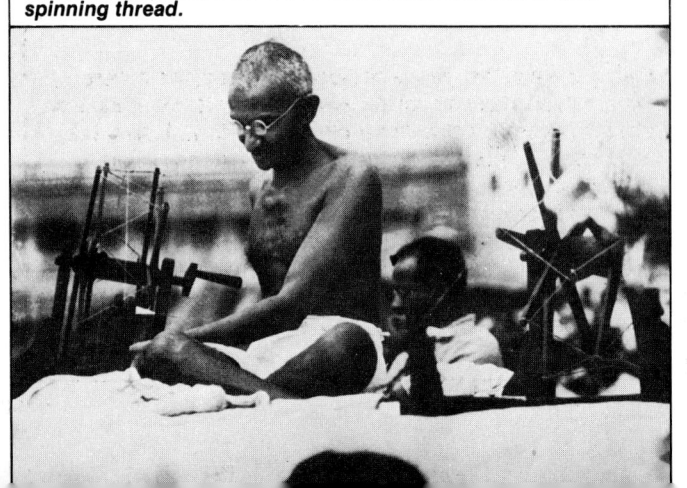

In World War 2 India was a great supply depot for the Pacific War, but Congress called for non-co-operation with the British because India did not have full independence. Most of the Congress leaders were imprisoned. Meanwhile the Japanese armies conquered Burma and it seemed certain that India would be captured too. The Japanese encouraged Congress to believe that Japan would hand over the government to them. As the position was desperate the British government offered India full independence as soon as the war was over, with complete freedom to do as it liked. But this freedom also meant that Muslims could form their own country, which was the last thing Congress wanted.

As Japan surrendered India was offered independence but Congress and the League quarrelled about a separate Muslim state. There were terrible massacres of both Hindus and Muslims, and the British army was brought in to keep the sides apart. At last the decision could be delayed no longer, and in 1947, to try to prevent a civil war, the great country divided itself into two separate and independent states — mainly Hindu India, and mainly Muslim Pakistan. The two main Muslim areas were in the west and the east so that Pakistan was split into two parts, the West, where the government was, and the East, 1,800 kilometres away. Thousands of Hindus and Muslims caught in each others' territory were killed. Millions fled from Pakistan to India and from India to Pakistan.

Below: in Hindu-Moslem riots after partition tens of thousands of people were killed. This Hindu was one of more than 2 000 murdered in five days in Calcutta.

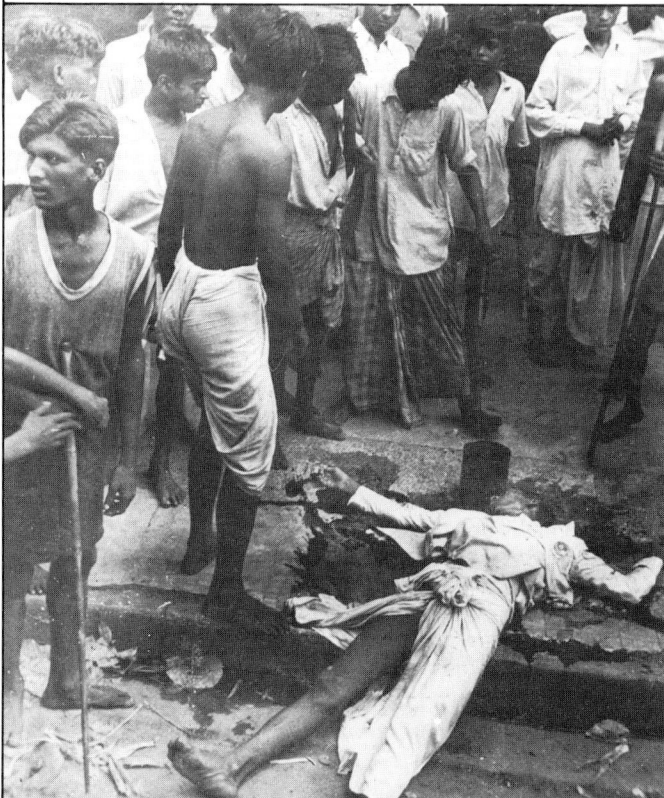

The two halves of Pakistan were both mainly Muslim, but they were very different peoples — different ways, different languages — and they were separated by unfriendly Indian territory which made communications difficult. East Pakistan demanded more independence, and in 1971 war broke out between the two. The Indian army crossed into East Pakistan and defeated the West Pakistan army. East Pakistan now became a separate independent country called Bangladesh.

Refugees from East Pakistan making their way to India.

When it seemed that peace had been restored, there were more troubles. Kashmir could have belonged to either India or Pakistan geographically. Its people were mainly Muslim, but were ruled by Hindus. It is in a very sensitive area, where China, USSR, Afghanistan, India and Pakistan all meet. In 1948-9 and again in 1965 India and Pakistan fought over Kashmir, and each occupied half of the country. The Chinese swept across the border in 1962, and before a cease-fire was arranged, threw back the Indian army. Although India and Pakistan have agreed not to fight over Kashmir again, it is still a danger spot.

South east Asia's road to independence

COLONIES
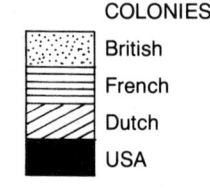
British
French
Dutch
USA

INDIA

CHINA

BURMA

THAILAND

FRENCH INDO-CHINA

HONG KONG

PHILIPINES (USA)

MALAY

DUTCH EAST INDIES

PAPUA

AUSTRALIA

In 1941 the Japanese swept through south-east Asia, defeating the weak colonial armies, and capturing every country except Thailand, which became an ally. Nationalists in the colonies were very impressed by the way a small Asian army had beaten the Europeans.

When Japan was defeated in 1945 the European colonial powers were not ready or able to return to south-east Asia immediately. In most countries the nationalists, who had often been waging guerilla wars against the Japanese, came out of hiding and took over control. They set up national governments.

By 1946 the French and Dutch forces returned to try to take over again, but the nationalists were in no mood to return to colonial rule. Bitter wars broke out in the Dutch East Indies and in French Indo-China. The Dutch gave in in 1949 and their empire became independent Indonesia. The French fought on until 1954, when they too were defeated.

Almost all of the British colonies in the region (Burma, Malaya, Singapore and later Borneo) were given independence by agreement between 1947 and 1957. All except Burma remained within the Commonwealth. In 1946 the USA gave independence to the Philippines.

COMMONWEALTH

GENEVA CONFERENCE 1954

END OF THE ROAD

In 1954 an international conference was convened at Geneva and the French colonies were given independence as North Vietnam, South Vietnam, Laos and Cambodia. The European empires in Asia had ended, but a terrible war was to start in the region (page 97).

Dutch troops return to Indonesia, 1947.

Burmese soldiers fighting Communist rebels, 1949.

Guerillas interrogate Indonesian civilians as the Dutch occupation troops withdraw, 1949.

Signing of the Indo-China truce agreement, Geneva 1954.

The Korean and Vietnam Wars

In the Cold War after World War 2 the USA in particular wanted to stop the spread of communism. In Europe it seemed as far as possible under control, but not in the far east, where the colonial states were becoming independent.

When the war against Japan ended, the Soviet armies occupied the northern half of Korea, which had been a Japanese colony. The US forces occupied the southern half, but the Potsdam conference decided that elections should be held to unite the country. The north refused to allow the elections to take place and the US and Soviet troops withdrew, leaving the country divided into a communist north and a non-communist south.

The Korean War 1950-1953

When China became communist in 1949 the whole picture changed. Northern Korea now had a powerful friendly ally just across the Yalu river which divided China from North Korea, while the south's nearest allies were the US forces in Japan, 650 km away.

The northern armies invaded the south, and drove the south Koreans back to the southern tip of the Korean peninsula. America was afraid of what it called the domino effect — one country would fall to the communists, and this would push the next, and the next, and so on until the whole of south-east Asia and perhaps even India, the Middle East and Africa were under communist rule.

The United States armies entered the war, backed by the United Nations. Soldiers from a dozen countries, including Britain, fought in Korea, but the majority were from America. The war raged from 1950 to 1953 but at last settled down along the line originally dividing the two halves. A cease-fire was eventually arranged, and this still holds, with nothing settled. Northern Korea is still communist, and the south still non-communist. But the point had been made that communism could not expand without being challenged.

United Nations troops pinned down by fire from Chinese troops in the ruins of a Korean town.

The Vietnam War 1957-1973

There was a very similar situation in Vietnam. When the French had been defeated there in 1954 the Geneva conference divided the country in half — a communist north, and a non-communist south. Backed by China, the north invaded the south in 1958. This time the United States intervened, not on behalf of the United Nations, but on its own account. Its tanks, aeroplanes, helicopters, warships, as well as chemical weapons such as napalm, were of little use against the lightly-armed Viet Cong soldiers from the north, led by General Giap. A few square kilometres gained in the day were lost in the night, and no matter how many billions of dollars and thousands of men the Americans poured in, they had little effect. At last the American public was so shocked by the loss of 46,000 killed and 304,000 wounded American soldiers (more than in World War 1), that it forced the government to seek a cease-fire in 1973.

Vietnam was now back where it had been in 1958 — divided in half. Then in 1975 the north swept over the frontier again, and in a few weeks had conquered the whole of Vietnam, setting up a communist government for the whole country. For the United States the dreadful war had been for absolutely nothing.

Civilians suffered terribly in the Vietnam war. Here a mother and her family struggle across a river to escape from a US air strike.
Below: a baby horribly burned by a napalm bomb dropped by the US Air Force.

Above: US planes spray 'agent orange' on the Vietnamese jungle, and, below, the result on the forest.

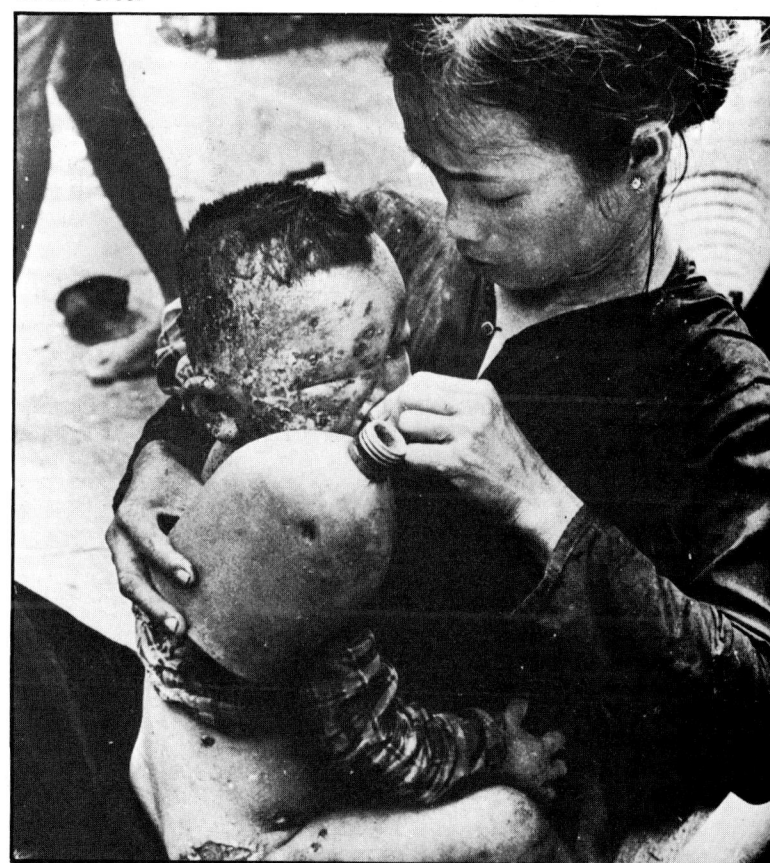

Right: an anti-war demonstration in Washington.

The Commonwealth

The Commonwealth, which includes 48 countries and a quarter of the world's population, is a puzzle to the rest of the world. There seems no reason why such a mixture of different states should work together as a unit, yet they do.

The old British empire of the nineteenth century gradually changed. First the white colonies of Canada, Australia, New Zealand and South Africa became self-governing dominions. The other parts of the empire were at different times given more power, until after World War 2 all of them, except a few tiny islands too small to stand completely on their own, became totally independent. Only three countries — Eire, Pakistan and South Africa, which was driven out — have left the Commonwealth so far (1986).

Factors which might break up the Commonwealth

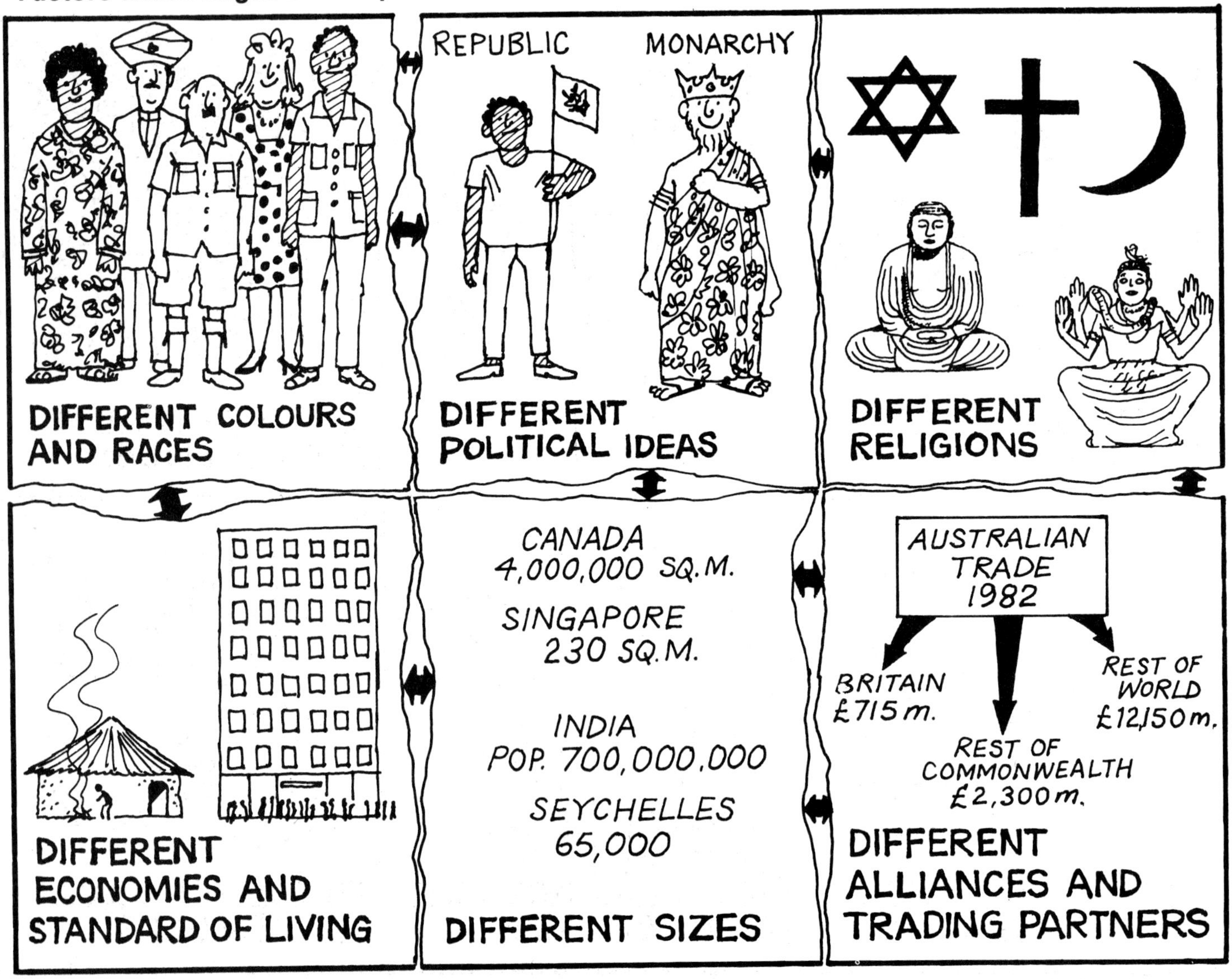

DIFFERENT COLOURS AND RACES

REPUBLIC   MONARCHY

DIFFERENT POLITICAL IDEAS

DIFFERENT RELIGIONS

DIFFERENT ECONOMIES AND STANDARD OF LIVING

CANADA 4,000,000 SQ. M.

SINGAPORE 230 SQ. M.

INDIA POP. 700,000,000

SEYCHELLES 65,000

DIFFERENT SIZES

AUSTRALIAN TRADE 1982

BRITAIN £715 m.

REST OF COMMONWEALTH £2,300 m.

REST OF WORLD £12,150 m.

DIFFERENT ALLIANCES AND TRADING PARTNERS

The Queen and Commonwealth leaders aboard the royal yacht Britannia during the 1985 Commonwealth Conference in Nassau.

Factors which hold the Commonwealth together

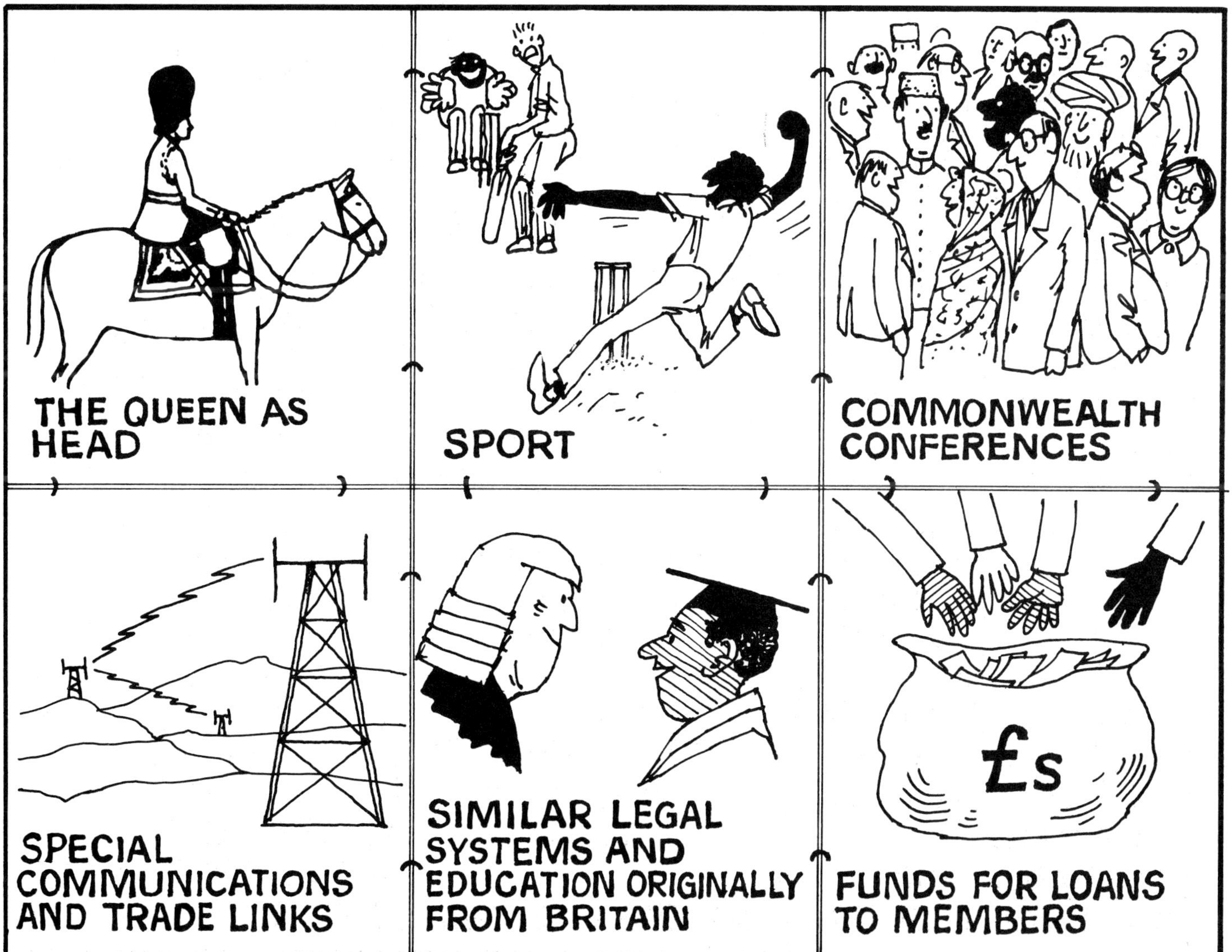

THE QUEEN AS HEAD

SPORT

COMMONWEALTH CONFERENCES

SPECIAL COMMUNICATIONS AND TRADE LINKS

SIMILAR LEGAL SYSTEMS AND EDUCATION ORIGINALLY FROM BRITAIN

FUNDS FOR LOANS TO MEMBERS

£s

As early as 1167 an English-Norman army invaded Ireland to seize land, and expeditions continued through the middle ages. Wars were frequent through the reign of Elizabeth I and died down only in 1607 when two Irish leaders, the earls of Tyrconnel and Tyrone, fled the country. James I gave lands in Ireland to English and Scottish people on condition that they settled English and Scottish Protestant farmers on the farms. The Scottish settlers, who were presbyterians, remained mainly in the north of the island — what is now Ulster. Most of the rest of Ireland was Catholic, so religious problems were added to the problems of land ownership.

Mac William Burke, a prosperous medieval steward, who died in 1580.

Ireland
1200 - 1850

For almost 800 years relations between Ireland and England have been a story of violence and bloodshed. For the first 400 years the quarrels were about power and land; for the next 400, religious differences were added to the fires of hatred.

The Irish rebelled in the 1640s and terrible cruelties were committed by both English and Irish. Cromwell's armies put down the rising savagely, and more Irish land was given to Protestants, increasing the bitterness. Ireland was becoming divided into rich, ruling Protestants from England and Scotland, and poor Irish peasant tenants who were Catholic.

Violence has been part of the Irish scene on both sides for centuries. This drawing is what a (Protestant) artist thought the Catholics did to prisoners they took.

Catholic James II was driven from the throne of England in 1688 and in 1689 went to Ireland to raise an Irish army to help him regain his crown. Protestant William of Orange, now William III of England, crossed to Ireland with a large army and by 1691 the defeat of both James and the Irish was total. More land went to Protestants. Catholics were forbidden to carry arms or buy land, and were barred from becoming army officers, government officials or lawyers. The Irish parliament in Dublin, made up entirely of Protestants, governed the country, but the real power was in the hands of the Lord Lieutenant, who was appointed by the English government.

King William III of England at the Battle of the Boyne. This victory of the protestant forces over James II is still celebrated in Ulster today.

The English government kept the Irish down for most of the eighteenth century, but the revolutions in America (1776) and France (1789) made the Irish realise that people could overthrow their masters. In 1791 an Irishman from Ulster founded the Society of United Irishmen, made up of both Catholics and Protestants, to reform the government of Ireland. When peaceful methods failed to bring reform, the more revolutionary members of the society began to work secretly for an uprising in favour of an Irish republic.

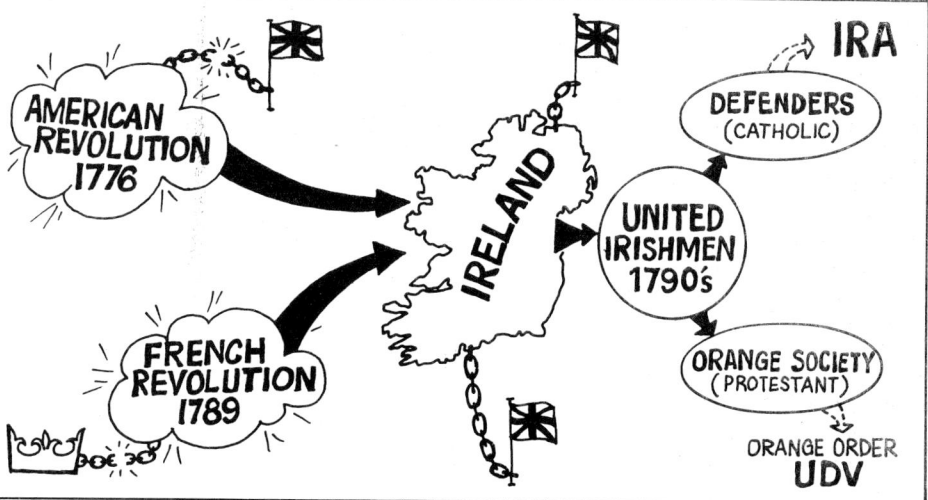

The rebellion broke out in 1798. After much cruelty on both sides the rising was put down. To overcome the problem that all MPs in the Dublin parliament were Protestant landowners, the Act of Union (1801) abolished the Irish parliament, and all Irish MPs came to parliament in London. But power in Ireland still lay with the Lord Lieutenant in Dublin.

The rebels executing their prisoners on the bridge at Wexford, June 1798.

Ireland, always poor, had even greater disasters to suffer. During 1845-1849 the potato crops, on which most peasants depended for food, were destroyed by disease. To its disgrace the English government did little to relieve the terrible suffering, and bodies of people who had died of starvation often lay in the roads for days because there was no one to bury them. By the time the famine eased a little in 1850 a million Irish had died of starvation or disease, and another million had emigrated, mainly to the USA. They took nothing with them except their rags and a burning hatred of England which survives among many Irish-Americans to this day. Ireland has never really recovered from the famine and the emigration, which continued for the rest of the nineteenth century. The population today is only a half of that of 1841. The population of the rest of Britain has trebled.

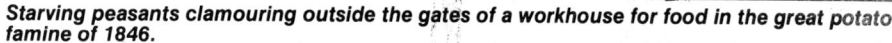

Starving peasants clamouring outside the gates of a workhouse for food in the great potato famine of 1846.

The desperation of the famine years led to the founding of the Fenian movement, which wanted to free Ireland of the English and found a republic. Strong branches were set up in the USA. By 1867 the Fenians had 80 000 men in Ireland under arms, supplied largely by American funds and equipment, and commanded by Irish-Americans who had fought in the American civil war. The Fenian rising of 1867 was easily defeated. The leader escaped to England, where he was arrested in Manchester. A group of Fenians ambushed the police van taking him and his assistant to prison, shot the guard and freed the prisoners.

Tens of thousands of Irish peasants lived in appalling conditions like this house, drawn in 1854.

Irish peasants being evicted from their cottage — probably by an English landlord — for not paying the rent in the late 19th century. Note the barefooted boy and the house without windows.

The great famine also brought the land-ownership question to a head. In those dreadful times many tenants could not pay their rent and were often evicted by greedy landlords. The Land League of Mayo, founded in 1879 by a former Fenian, tried to persuade tenants not to rent the farms from which occupiers had been evicted, and was very successful, so that many landowners were left with empty farms. Gradually English governments made reforms so that more tenants were able to buy their land.

In 1886 the Liberal prime minister, W E Gladstone, introduced a home rule bill for Ireland. Under this an Irish parliament would have had complete freedom for Irish affairs, but would still have been subject to London for such things as defence and foreign affairs. The Liberal party was divided over the bill. Many of its MPs thought that Gladstone was splitting up the British empire, giving in to rebellion and deserting the Protestants. So the bill was defeated. In 1893 another home rule bill was also defeated, but in 1914 yet another was passed by the House of Commons.

The six counties which made up Ulster were strongly against home rule because they felt that as Protestants they would be dominated by the Catholics of the rest of Ireland. In 1912 the Orange Order and the Ulster Unionists had formed a private army, the Ulster Volunteer Force, to resist home rule by civil war if necessary. As it happened, World War 1 broke out and the problem was postponed for a few years.

Many Catholics did not like the idea of home rule either, because under the home rule bill England still controlled certain parts of government. They wanted total freedom — an Irish republic — and nothing less. Secret military groups, especially the Irish Volunteers (later to be called the Irish Republican Army or the IRA) and the Irish Citizen Army, were formed to fight as fiercely as the Ulster organisations. At Easter 1916 the Volunteers and the Citizen Army staged a rebellion in Dublin, seizing the Post Office and other buildings. They held out for a week against the British army, and there were many deaths among civilians and the English troops. The rebels were opposed by the majority of people in Dublin, who were prepared to accept home rule. When they surrendered they were treated leniently, apart from the leaders, 16 of whom were shot.

THE LIVE SHELL.

(WHICH OF 'EM WILL THROW IT OVERBOARD?)

The political problems of Britain and Ireland were as difficult a century ago as they are today, as this Punch cartoon shows.

In the election after World War 1, the Irish republicans, called Sinn Fein (ourselves alone) won 73 seats. They refused to go to London and made themselves into an Irish parliament in Dublin for a republican Ireland. Eamon de Valera became their president. Civil war broke out and the IRA (the Sinn Fein army) fought British police and troops for three years.

In 1920 there was a government of Ireland bill which allowed for two parliaments, one in Dublin for the south and one in Belfast for the north (Ulster). Both were to have allegiance to the British monarch. The Dublin parliament accepted the bill in 1921 and the Irish Free State was created. But de Valera and a small number of followers refused to accept anything but a republic and fought a civil war with Sinn Fein, their own party, until 1923. By this time de Valera had been defeated and entered the Irish parliament. He led southern Ireland to complete independence as the Irish Republic in 1937.

In the south a Protestant minority lived quite happily with a Catholic majority, but all the old arguments were kept up in Ulster, where the Protestants had a majority of about two to one. They also had a permanent majority in the Ulster parliament, and Catholics were in some ways unjustly treated. In general they had the lower-paid jobs and lived in the worst housing. The police, the Royal Ulster Constabulary, were almost all Protestants and were accused of being against Catholics. It was easy for the IRA to play on the feelings of the Catholics and to demand that Ulster should be joined with the south, where things seemed much better for Catholics. Protestants wanted to remain part of Britain.

Although governments tried to improve matters for Catholics, tension increased and violence broke out. In 1969 the British government sent in the army to protect the Catholics from Protestant mobs. From then on the violence which has been part of Irish history for so long once more began its terrible and destructive cycle.

Top: the Post Office in Dublin, recaptured by the British army after the Easter Rising of 1916. The Post Office is still regarded as a shrine by the IRA.

Centre: violence in Belfast, 1972. The main raliway station and a train are severely damaged by an IRA bomb.

Bottom: violence in Belfast, 1979. Police with riot gear are attacked after a protest march. Since the latest series of troubles began in 1969 over 2 000 people out of a total population of about 2 million have been killed. Ulster costs the British government over £500 000 000 a year.

Nuclear weapons

Ever since scientists discovered that atoms were made of minute electrical particles, they dreamed of breaking them up to get what seemed unlimited energy from the nucleus. The dream — or nightmare — did not come true until World War 2, when a group of international scientists in the USA created the first atom bombs. These were dropped on Japan to end the Pacific War, and though they were very small bombs compared with modern nuclear weapons, each had more explosive power than all the conventional bombs dropped on Germany in World War 2 put together. At first the nuclear bomb, which is exploded high in the air, gives a searing heat (80,000 people were turned to ashes at Hiroshima within a fraction of a second). The heat is followed by a blast which destroys buildings for miles, and then by radiation, which can take weeks, months or even years to kill its victims. And if they do not die they can suffer from horrible forms of cancer, become sterile, or else produce terribly deformed children.

Below left: this woman has had the pattern of her kimono burned on to her skin by the atom bomb dropped on Hiroshima.

Below right: you can see a shadow on these steps 200 yards from the centre of damage in Hiroshima. The heat was so intense that it burnt the polish from the granite steps, except where a man was sitting.

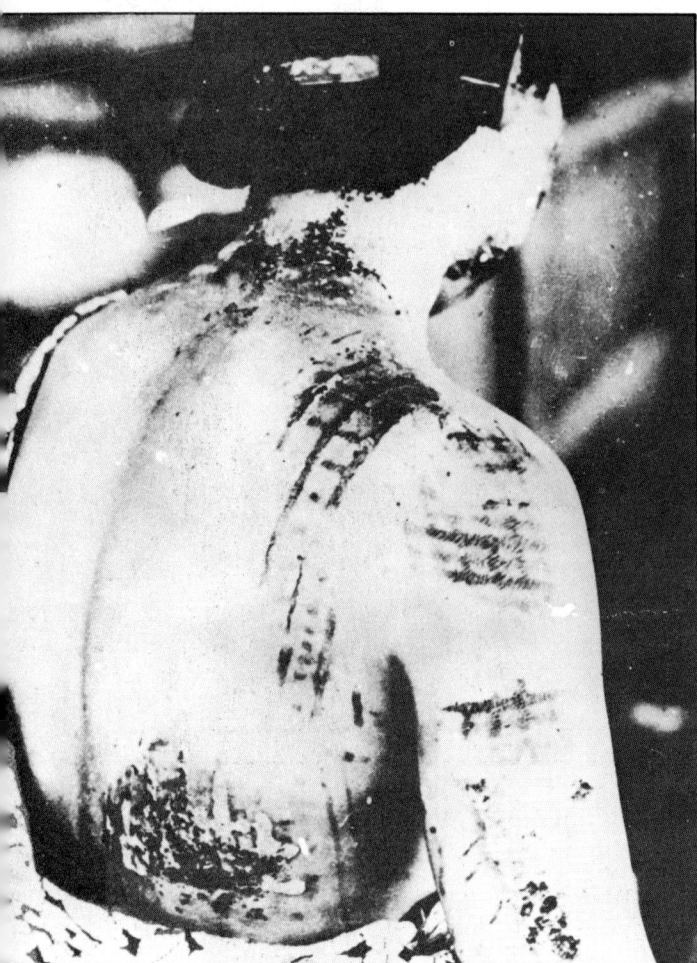

Partly because of scientist-spies in Britain and the USA, Russia developed the atom bomb soon after the Americans. Britain and France also made nuclear weapons in a very limited way, but did not have the resources to develop them fully. The fact that the two great powers, the USA and the USSR alone had practical nuclear bombs and the means of delivering them was a great danger, but also a great strength. The danger was that they would destroy one another (and many other nations as well), but the strength was that both knew this, and would be most reluctant to use the bombs because both knew that neither could survive. This became even more obvious when the hydrogen bomb (a completely different type of nuclear bomb and hundreds of times more powerful) was invented on both sides. Hydrogen (or fusion) bombs are so powerful that they are measured in mega-tonnes, that is, the explosive power of a million tonnes of TNT. Today there are 100 + mega-tonne bombs. The biggest conventional bomb in World War 2 was 10 tonnes.

Many countries now are capable of making nuclear weapons — China, India, Israel, South Africa and probably others already have them. The more developed countries have a great deal to lose in a nuclear war but some of the smaller states do not, and might be prepared to use nuclear weapons to get their own way or to hold the world to ransom. There is a danger that if two major powers became involved in a war with conventional weapons such as tanks and guns and one side looked like losing, that side would be tempted to use tactical nuclear weapons. These are small atomic weapons used in battle to knock out the enemy forces. This would almost certainly lead to the use of strategic nuclear weapons — the great 100-megatonne rockets that would wipe out whole cities and probably destroy civilisation.

A Polaris missile after being launched from a submarine.

Some of the bombs used in World War II. Their capacity for destruction is only a fraction of that of a single nuclear bomb.

The probable results of a nuclear war are so horrifying that everyone wants to prevent one. But the great powers cannot agree. Each is afraid that if they stop making the weapons someone else will go on doing so. The problem is to check what others are doing, and though some things can be detected from satellites, it is still possible for weapons to be made in secret. There have been many conferences between east and west over limiting nuclear weapons but so far all have broken down over the question of inspection.

In the 1960s, however, so many nuclear bombs were being tested that the amount of radiation fall-out was increasing to very serious levels all over the world. The great powers (except France and China) signed a treaty under which they agreed not to test any more nuclear weapons in the air or under water. They are now all exploded deep underground, where little radiation escapes.

The exploration of space has made the problems worse. Missiles loaded with nuclear bombs can circle the earth for years, waiting for a signal to fall on a certain target. These are followed by anti-missile 'hunter' missiles waiting for a signal to attack the missiles. These too are probably followed by anti-anti-missile missiles. These and other 'defence' systems are so expensive that they can take a very large proportion of a country's budget. A single missile can cost £13 million enough to build 500 new hospitals or 10 000 new schools. The two great unsolved questions are: 1. Can we afford nuclear weapons? and 2. Can we afford NOT to have them?

Space

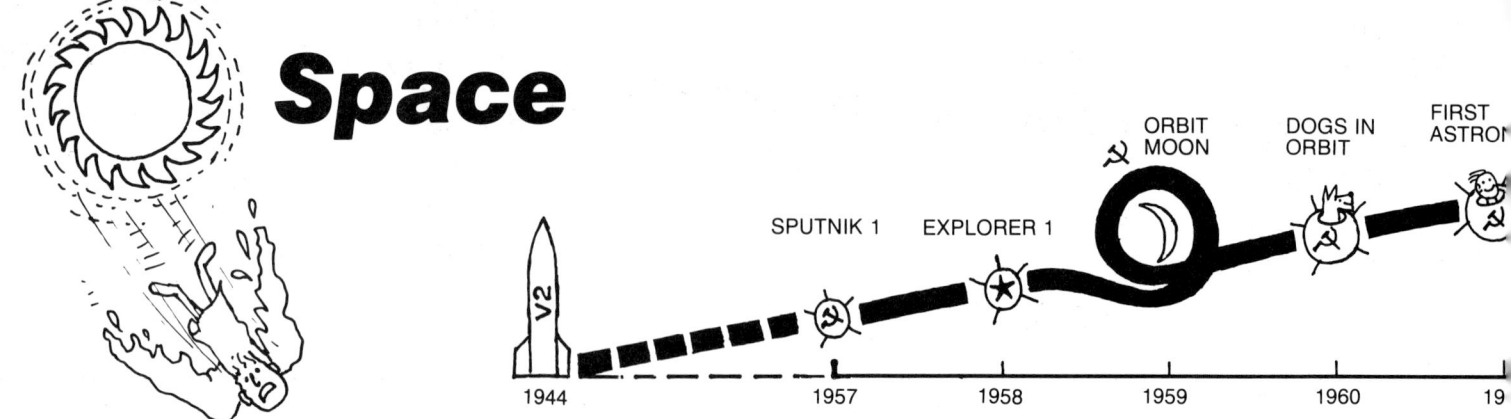

SPUTNIK 1   EXPLORER 1   ORBIT MOON   DOGS IN ORBIT   FIRST ASTRON

1944   1957   1958   1959   1960   19

The first attempt to conquer space was something of a disaster. According to ancient Greek legends Icarus used wings of wax, but flew so close to the sun that they melted and he crashed into the sea, where he drowned. Whatever the truth of that, the Chinese did use rockets both as fireworks and as weapons more than 2000 years ago. Experiments were made, particularly in Germany between the two world wars, to send mail by small rockets, but these were not very successful. These experiments, however, led Germany to produce the V2, the first high-altitude rocket, which they used to bombard London in 1944. Had this come into service in large numbers, before the war was in its final stages, it might have meant a defeat for Britain.

When the war ended both the USA and the USSR took the German rocket technology and scientists to their own countries and began a race to develop rockets for use in space. The Russians were the most successful at first, and launched the world's first satellite, Sputnik 1, in 1957. The Americans followed with Explorer 1 in 1958. But then the USSR made several major

Space exploration —

A Pershing II missile.

Space could be the next and very expensive battlefield for World War 3. Enough Inter-Continental Ballistic Missiles (ICBMs) with nuclear warheads already exist to destroy civilisation, but if these are launched from earth, they can be detected and perhaps some defensive action taken. If the missiles are already in orbit, flying round the world year after year, they can be given a message when necessary, and dive straight to their target. It would be very difficult to find a defence against them.

Nations could have anti-missile missiles also in space following the nuclear missiles, and ready to attack them the moment they moved out of orbit. And then there would be anti-anti-missile missiles hunting the hunters. And so the whole thing would grow into what is called a 'star-wars' programme, the cost of which would be as damaging as the programme itself. This is why the great powers are trying — unsuccessfully at the moment — to come to an agreement not to continue with such programmes.

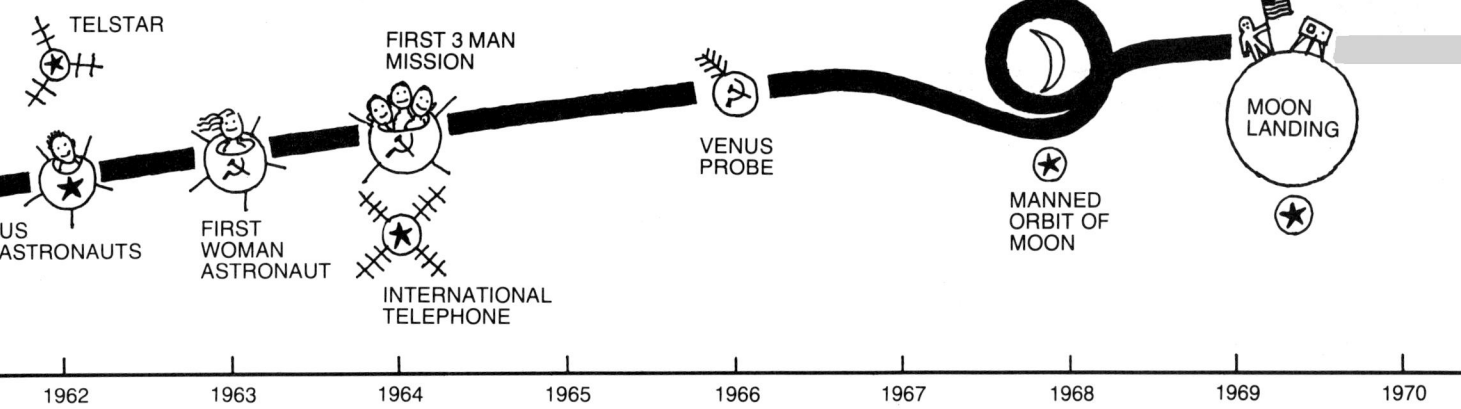

TELSTAR

US ASTRONAUTS

FIRST WOMAN ASTRONAUT

FIRST 3 MAN MISSION

INTERNATIONAL TELEPHONE

VENUS PROBE

MANNED ORBIT OF MOON

MOON LANDING

| 1962 | 1963 | 1964 | 1965 | 1966 | 1967 | 1968 | 1969 | 1970 |

steps. In 1959 Russian satellites reached the moon and sent back pictures of the other side, and also went round the sun. In 1960 a Soviet rocket carried two dogs into space and brought them back safely, and then in 1961 Yuri Gagarin became the first man to be put into orbit round the world.

The USA was now seriously worried because the USSR seemed so far ahead, and began a very big space programme. It put its first astronaut, Colonel Glenn, into orbit in 1962. The US also launched the first communications satellite, Telstar. In 1963 the

Russians put the first woman in space, and the following year a 3-man satellite. By 1965 the Russians had put eight manned flights into space, and the Americans seven. Developments now came more quickly. The USSR sent a probe to Venus, and in 1968 the USA sent a manned flight round the moon. Then came the moon landing by the American Apollo mission in 1969. And all the time more and more communications and spy satellites, as well as more dangerous pieces of equipment were being put into orbit round the earth.

curse or blessing?

Spy-satellites can pick out tiny details anywhere on the earth's surface, so that it is difficult for any nation to keep major military secrets.

Space travel helps pure science and helps people to find out much more about the earth and the universe.

Space has opened up a completely new world of communications, so that any place in the world can send and receive live pictures and speech. Before long we shall be able to tune in to any TV programme broadcast anywhere on earth.

Certain delicate technical processes, such as making very pure electronic chips, can be done only where there is no force of gravity. In the future we may have small orbiting space factories for these processes.

In developing space equipment scientists and engineers have invented materials and equipment that are now used in everyday life. Two examples are solar-power calculators and metallic blankets.

Space travel may eventually be necessary to take people to other planets, either for raw materials, or if there were a disaster on earth, to start a colony on another planet.

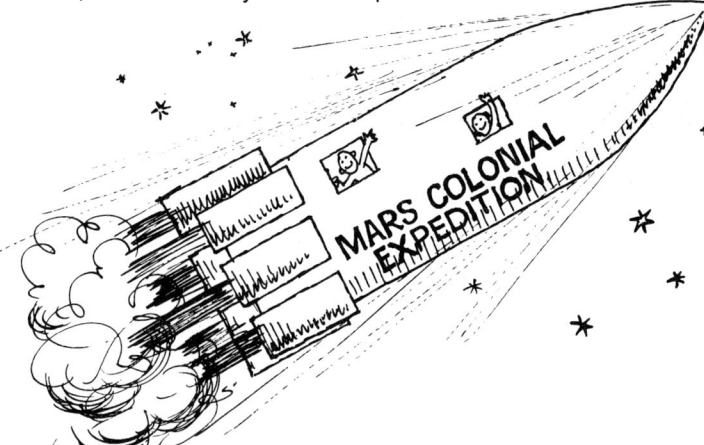

An astronaut on a manned manoeuvring unit prepares to dock with a spinning satellite.

Energy

From the very earliest times people have looked for sources of power or energy. Animals, wind and water were used for hundreds of thousands of years to make life easier for human beings. Then in the eighteenth century the steam engine was invented, and with plenty of cheap coal, steam power was supreme in industry and for rail transport for over a century. In the late nineteenth century came electricity, obtained from coal-fired power stations, and then oil for heating boilers, and driving vehicles. Coal and oil were cheap, and vast amounts have been wasted — unnecessary heating and lighting, unnecessarily large and extravagant cars used for the shortest journeys, transport systems of all kinds running with very few passengers, buildings which allowed most of the heat to escape through the roof and walls. Energy seemed cheap and inexhaustible.

This comfortable idea was shattered when in the 1960s the price of coal began to rise and when the Arab-Israeli war of 1973 sent the price of oil soaring. Energy became much more expensive, and the world suddenly realised that fossil fuels (coal, oil, natural gas) might soon be gone for ever, and could never be replaced. People began to search for alternative sources of energy, and also to look for ways of using energy less wastefully.

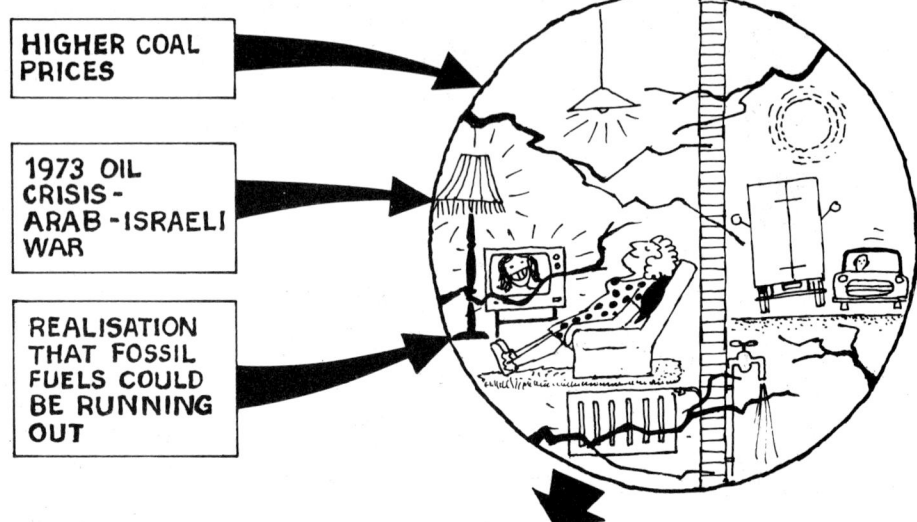

HIGHER COAL PRICES

1973 OIL CRISIS – ARAB-ISRAELI WAR

REALISATION THAT FOSSIL FUELS COULD BE RUNNING OUT

A solar-powered TV set in West Africa. This enables people where there will be no mains electricity for many years to have radio and TV. The power comes from the solar panel on the right.

We are trying to solve the energy crisis by making electricity from nuclear fuels instead of coal and oil, and by using natural sources of power such as wind, water and the sun. We are trying to save fossil fuels by designing smaller and more efficient petrol engines, electricity-powered vehicles and more economic trains and aeroplanes. Good insulation in buildings can reduce by a third the amount of fuel needed to keep the temperature comfortable.

The Central Electricity Generating Board's nuclear power station at Oldbury on Severn in Gloucestershire, opened in 1969.

OIL *KNOWN RESERVES 80,000 m TONNES*

ANNUAL CONSUMPTION 3,000 m TONNES (5% OF RESERVE)

COAL *KNOWN RESERVES 7000,000 m TONNES*

ANNUAL CONSUMPTION 2,500 m TONNES (.036% OF RESERVE).

NATURAL GAS *KNOWN RESERVES 55 billion cu.m.*

ANNUAL CONSUMPTION 1·5 billion cu.m. (3% OF RESERVE)

In almost all countries most of the energy comes from fossil fuels. There are only limited amounts of all of these under the earth, and when they have been used up they cannot be replaced. No one can be sure how long they will last — but in any case prices will rise as supplies become more difficult to obtain.

Every year the world demands more and more energy, and while solar, water and wind power can supply some, it is only a very small part. Many countries do not have enough sun or running water to make energy in this way.

The answer seems to be nuclear power. This is rather like a nuclear weapon which has been slowed down so that instead of making a tremendous explosion lasting a second or two, it burns slowly at a relatively lower temperature for many, many years. The heat is used to turn water into steam to drive turbines and dynamos.

SOURCE OF MATERIAL FOR NUCLEAR WEAPONS

DANGER

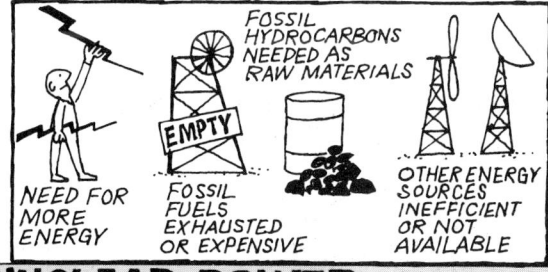

NEED FOR MORE ENERGY — FOSSIL FUELS EXHAUSTED OR EXPENSIVE — EMPTY — FOSSIL HYDROCARBONS NEEDED AS RAW MATERIALS — OTHER ENERGY SOURCES INEFFICIENT OR NOT AVAILABLE

NUCLEAR POWER OR NO NUCLEAR POWER

Unfortunately even the slow burning of the nuclear fuel causes dangerous radiation, and great care is needed to prevent this leaking out. It is possible to build shielding to stop radiation escaping, but this is very expensive. However, once the power station has been constructed, the running costs in nuclear material are very low indeed. But there is always a danger that radiation might leak out, or even that a nuclear power station might be damaged because of a failure in the safety system.

There would be no major explosion, but radio-active material could be scattered over a wide area, making it uninhabitable. Many people object to nuclear power because of the possible dangers. 150 years ago thousands refused to travel on the newly-invented railways because they believed the speed, 30 mph, would damage their health, or even kill them. Are we reacting in a similar way? Should we take the risk with nuclear power, which scientists say is very slight?

Pollution and conservation

Pollution and the modern way of living sometimes seem like the two sides of a coin — you cannot have one without the other. Pollution takes two main forms: (1) chemical pollution, which makes life unpleasant and can be very dangerous to health, and (2) visual and aural pollution — sights and noises which make life unpleasant and can even cause mental problems.

We all want cheap and convenient transport — cars. We want cheap distribution of food and other goods — lorries. We want fast travel over long distances by air.	All motor vehicles produce highly-poisonous exhaust fumes, which are unpleasant and dangerous, especially the lead content. Motor vehicles and aircraft create serious noise pollution, and sometimes visual pollution.
We all want cheap and widely available energy in our homes and in industry. Our whole way of life would grind to a stop without a plentiful supply of cheap power.	Energy means fumes from coal or oil-fired power stations, possible radiation dangers from nuclear ones, and visual pollution from the buildings and from the pylons and power cables.
We all want a wide range of cheap foods — meat, fruit, vegetables, cereals and dairy products.	To increase yields chemical fertilisers, weed and insect killers are used. Many of these find their way into rivers and water supplies which can become heavily and dangerously polluted.
We all want entertainment — and this includes music of various kinds, or noisy sports. Companies need to sell their products through advertisements, and often do so at sports events and in other public places.	People's tastes differ, and one person's pleasure is another's pollution. Music played loudly out of doors or in flats or at sports events can become a noise pollution. Large advertising hoardings can be a visual pollution.

Forests all over Europe, like this one in Czechoslovakia, are dying. It is thought that air pollution is the cause.

Pollution on beaches is common throughout the world. This one is in southern Portugal.

Conservation

60 years ago this land was rich agricultural country. Today, because over-greedy or inefficient farmers tried to squeeze every scrap of profit from the soil, it has turned into a barren desert, with no hope of recovery. It is lost for ever. Many people think that we are treating the whole earth in this way. We are taking everything we can from it now, for our own pleasure and profit, and risk leaving a dying planet for future generations. We need conservation policies to preserve things which we enjoy now for those who will come after us.

Soils

All life depends on vegetation, so we must take care not to destroy the soil in which plants grow. Soil can be 'killed' by over-cropping and over-grazing, and by chopping down vegetation so that erosion takes place. All of these are common in third-world countries where very poor nations are struggling to produce enough for soaring populations. The answers are education in agriculture, and government action to stop farmers from exhausting the soil for ever. But education takes a long time and people are hungry now.

Fuels and minerals

The world has a limited stock of oil and minerals and when they have gone they cannot be replaced. Every year the world uses about 2,500,000,000 tonnes of coal, 3,000,000,000 tonnes of oil and 5,000,000,000 tonnes of iron ore. This cannot go on for ever, especially as consumption is still rising. No one knows how long the reserves will last — some minerals are already difficult and expensive to mine. Oil and coal are our main sources of energy and also the raw materials of vital products such as drugs and plastics. Many people think we should now be working harder on alternative forms of energy — from the sun, wind and water. We should be trying harder to save energy — insulating buildings and inventing forms of transport which do not use so much oil, for example.

International co-operation

While future generations may be able to live without giant pandas, or beautiful scenery, or great buildings, their world would be a much poorer place. It is up to us to make sure that we leave them a world worth living in. Often valuable or rare animals and plants can be saved only by international agreement and co-operation. We must have international policies to prevent over-fishing of the sea, for example, as fish are a valuable food. Individual countries need organisations like Britain's National Trust to help preserve beautiful areas of the country and famous buildings.

Above: an abandoned farm in Oklahoma, USA. Cutting down trees and overcropping the land has turned some of the richest farm land into a desert.

Below: solar panels being used in Africa to provide electricity to pump water from deep wells.

111

Politics in Britain

'First-past-the-post'

In Britain MPs are elected by the 'first-past-the-post' system. That is, the candidate who gets the most votes, even only one more than the nearest rival, becomes MP. In theory this could lead to the following:

Blobbs 11,003 votes
Dobbs 11,002 votes
Slobbs 11,001 votes

Blobbs would become the MP for that constituency even though two out of every three voters had voted against him.

In three other constituencies the following could be the results:

Grunge (Lab) 29,000   Trippe (Con) 3,000
Froop (Con) 23,200   Chunte (Lab) 21,300
Poggle (Con) 19,000   Flumpe (Lab) 18,500

The total Labour vote is 68,000; the total Conservative 45,200, yet the Conservatives have two out of three MPs. The system is particularly hard on smaller parties such as the Liberals and the SDP. In the 1983 election it took an average of 32,777 votes to get one Conservative MP elected. 40,465 votes for one Labour MP, but 338,284 to get one Liberal/SDP member. The winning party always gets its MPs much more 'cheaply' than the others.

Proportional representation

Many people think that Britain should have proportional representation on the alternative vote system. Electors mark their voting paper in order of preference for each candidate. The votes are counted in the usual way, on the basis of first choices only. If one candidate gets more than 50% of the total votes cast, he or she is elected. If no one gets 50% the candidate with the lowest number is eliminated, and his votes are distributed among the remaining candidates on the basis of the second choice. This continues until one emerges with more than half of the votes cast. The table below shows the actual number of MPs for each party in the 1983 election, and in brackets what the number would have been if MPs had been allocated in proportion to the total number of votes cast for each party.

Conservative 387 (276)
Labour 209 (179)
Lib/SDP Alliance 23 (167)

Proportional representation however does not usually give one party a clear majority over the others together, so that the largest single party has to form a coalition with one of the others. This can lead to frequent elections and weak governments as the coalition partners quarrel. 'First-past-the-post' usually gives one party a clear majority, even if it does produce unfairness.

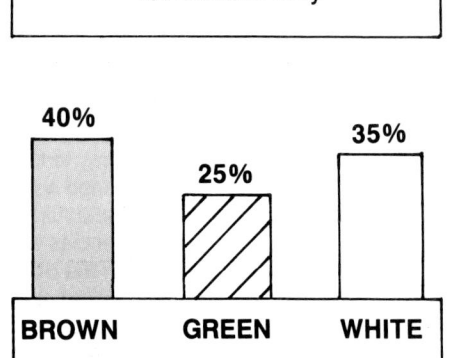

FIRST COUNT
1st choices only

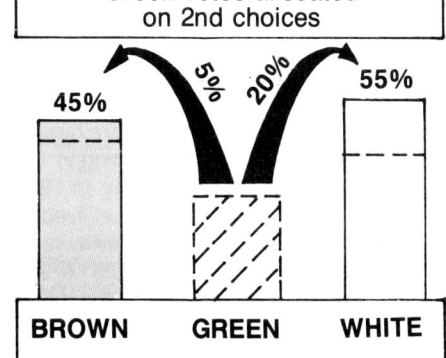

SECOND COUNT
Green votes allocated on 2nd choices

Counting votes at Camden South during a general election.

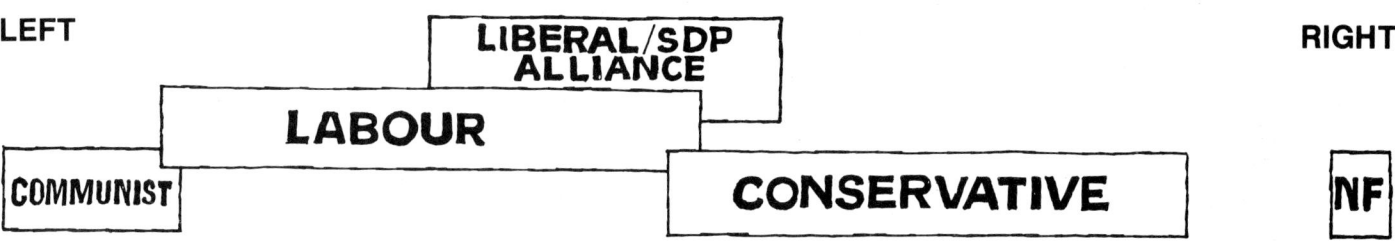

LEFT   LIBERAL/SDP ALLIANCE   RIGHT

LABOUR

COMMUNIST   CONSERVATIVE   NF

British political parties

The main parties in British politics are the Labour Party, the Conservative Party and the Liberal/SDP Alliance, though it is not yet clear how much effect the Alliance will have in the future. In Scotland and Wales there are small nationalist parties, the Scottish Nationalist Party and Plaid Cymru, which seek more, if not complete independence for those countries. In Ulster there are a number of political parties, divided largely on religious lines, though mostly their aims are more political than religious. There are communist and other very small parties, but these rarely have a single MP.

There is such a wide range of attitudes inside each of the main parties that it is difficult to say exactly where each stands on any issue. The examples here give a broad idea of the main Labour and Conservative policies — the ideas a government of those parties would probably follow. The Alliance parties are very much in the centre on most issues, with perhaps a slight leaning in most things towards Labour. (The founder members of the SDP came from the Labour party.)

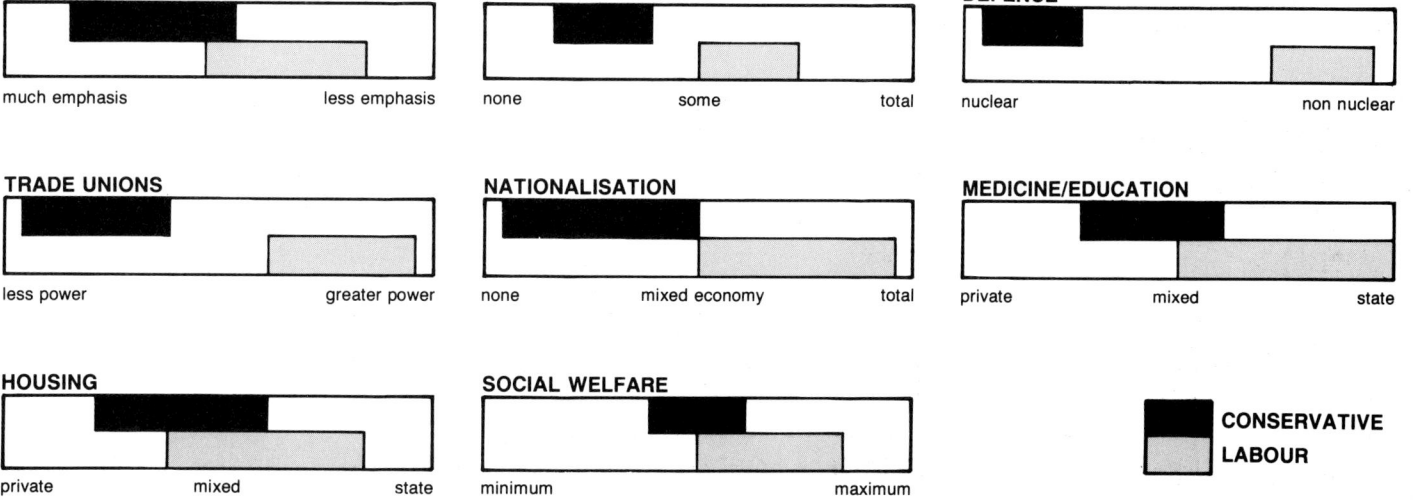

FOREIGN AFFAIRS

much emphasis   less emphasis

STATE CONTROL

none   some   total

DEFENCE

nuclear   non nuclear

TRADE UNIONS

less power   greater power

NATIONALISATION

none   mixed economy   total

MEDICINE/EDUCATION

private   mixed   state

HOUSING

private   mixed   state

SOCIAL WELFARE

minimum   maximum

■ CONSERVATIVE
▨ LABOUR

Nationalisation and devolution

Nationalisation means that the government takes over an industry or a service from private ownership and runs it on behalf of the state. There are various arguments for nationalisation.

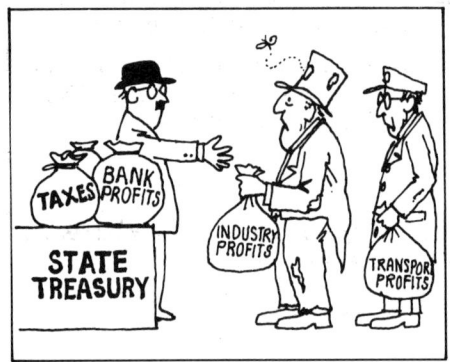

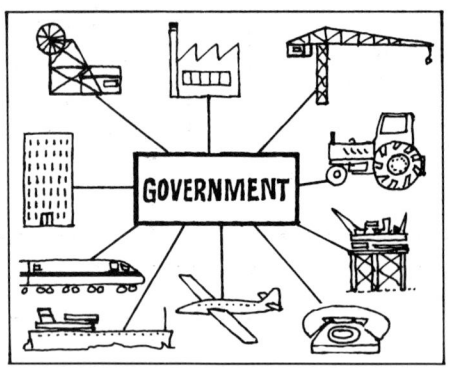

Political principles

1. Left-wing parties believe that if the state runs industries the profits can be used for state purposes. For example, the profits made in a year by the major banks are the equivalent of all VAT and customs and excise duties together. If the banks were nationalised, much of this money could be used to improve things which we all need, such as health services or education, or it might be invested in industries to provide employment where there are few jobs.

2. State-controlled industry can be directed to provide things which the country as a whole needs, which are not always what gives private companies the most profit.

3. State control means that at least in theory 'the people' have some say in the running of industry and services by electing different governments with different views.

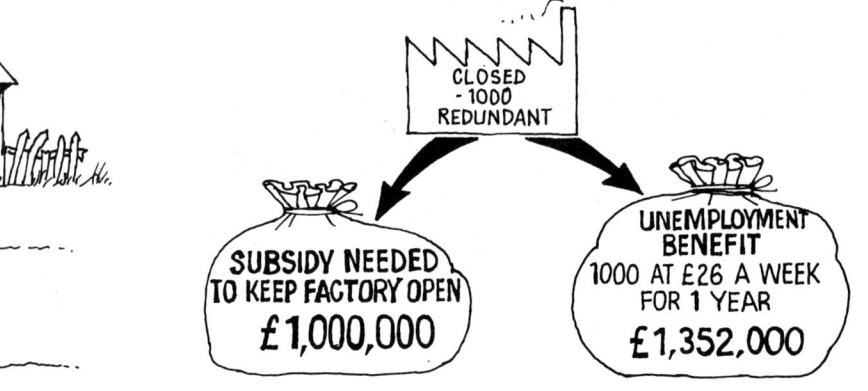

Practical reasons

1. Private businesses must make a profit. If they do not they close down, or offer poorer goods and services to reduce costs. Some industries and organisations are too important to the public and the country to be left to private companies. Railways, for example, are very expensive to run and often make huge losses, but they must be kept going or the whole country would be very badly affected. This means state ownership.

2. Some industries which are now unprofitable, shipbuilding, for example, should be kept going for defence reasons; they also provide jobs. It may well be cheaper to subsidise unprofitable companies than to pay unemployment benefit to people who would otherwise be unemployed.

Nationalised industries	Denationalised or partly denationalised in 1986	Industries which could be nationalised under a left-wing government
National Coal Board	British Telecom	Banking
Post Office	British National Oil Corporation	Land
British Shipbuilders	British Aerospace	Insurance
British National Bus Corporation	Cable and Wireless	Electronics
British Steel	Britoil	
Electricity industry	British Rail subsidiaries	
British Rail	British Gas	
	British Airports Authority	

Nationalisation or private enterprise?

1. Profits should go to the state where they will benefit everyone, and not into the pockets of private people.

2. Some industries, such as railways and gas and electricity, are better organised on a national basis, because they have to link up in all parts of the country. Private enterprise might select only the parts that offered most profit and leave out the others.

3. 'The people', through voting for different governments, can have some control over important industries and services.

4. Some industries and services are essential for social or defence reasons and must be maintained even if they cost the government large amounts in subsidy.

1. Private industries are more efficient. They are run by experts who must make profits instead of by people who get their salary whatever happens.

2. If a nationalised industry loses money, everyone is taxed to pay.

3. Private industry supplies people with what they really want and not what the government planners decide they want.

4. Nationalised industries often have no competitors and can fix their own prices. Private enterprise has to be competitive or it goes out of business. This keeps prices down.

Central control or devolution?

All governments face the problem of deciding how much power in running the country should be given to regional authorities, and how much should be kept by the central government. Some aspects of government — defence, foreign relations, for example, must be organised nationally, but others might be devolved to local authorities.

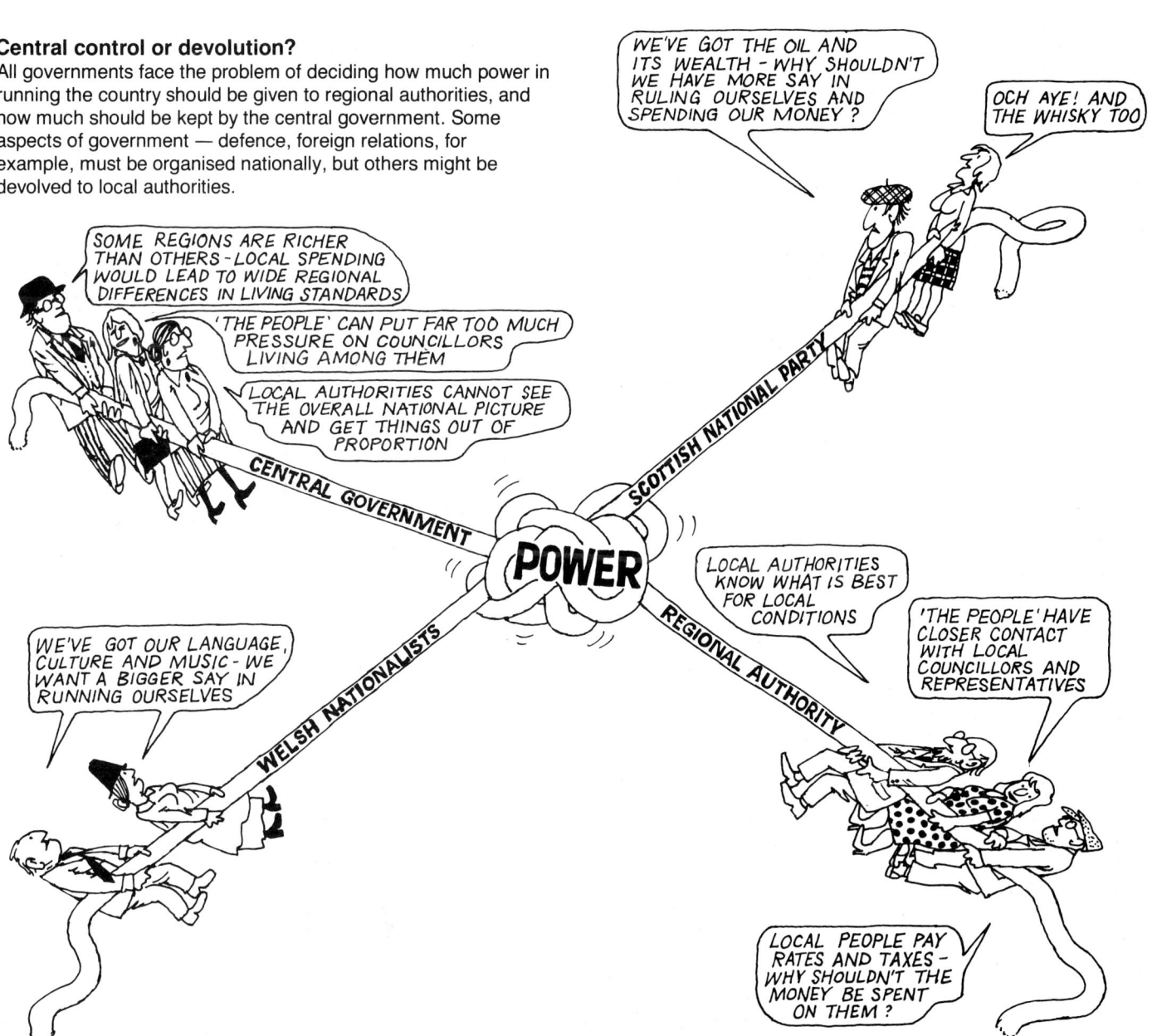

Unemployment

Unemployment in non-communist countries depends on the amount of goods a firm or nation can sell. If the product is not very good, or unreliable, or too expensive, or unsuitable for the market, people will not buy it. The factory will make less, need fewer workers, and so there will be unemployment. Britain has to buy most of its raw materials from overseas, so that it has to sell the finished goods overseas to pay for them. Many other countries are trying to sell in the international market so that there is fierce competition, and those that fail can have serious unemployment problems at home.

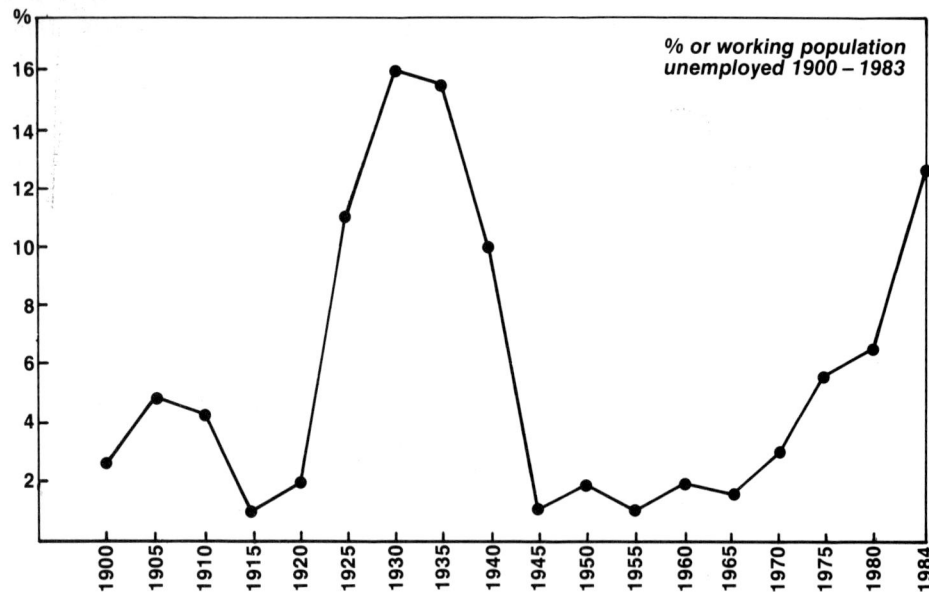

% or working population unemployed 1900 – 1983

Technology. Technical advances and automation mean that one person — or even a machine — can now do the work that formerly needed many employees. Whole factories can be run by a handful of workpeople. (See also pages 126-127.)

Management and unions. In times of advances in technology both management and unions need imagination and understanding. Unions may have to be prepared to accept redundancies and share jobs with other unions; managements must understand that union members will not willingly give up their jobs. In addition, management must put more money into training. In Britain management and unions have too often failed to work together, and this has slowed down production or resulted in high prices. In the long run more jobs are lost because British goods cannot compete in world markets.

World economy. When the world economy is in a slump, countries cannot buy so many goods, which means unemployment, especially in countries where manufacturing costs are high.

New producers. Newly industrialised countries such as India, Taiwan and Korea are competing in world markets. Their equipment is often very modern and their costs lower, so that they can take trade from older industrialised countries.

Ideas for reducing unemployment

In Britain people often feel ashamed if they are out of work. A job gives us a value. Most people would prefer to earn their own living and not be dependent on the welfare state. Although we may one day come to accept that not everyone can have a job, we have not reached that stage yet, and we need to consider ways of increasing the jobs available.

Sharing jobs. Instead of each employee working about 8 hours a day, two people could do 4 each. This would increase employers' costs, but employed people are not claiming unemployment benefit from the state.

Earlier retirement. If people retired at 50 or 55 a large number of people would be taken out of the job market, and this would allow younger unemployed people to work.

Public works. The state could employ large numbers of people building and repairing roads, houses and doing other jobs which would be for the benefit of everyone. This would mean that the state would have to find large sums of money to pay them, but such things as better roads and railways, for example, would mean that our industry could be more efficient.

Trade Unions

In the first half of the nineteenth century working men had to fight to form trade unions to protect themselves against greedy employers. The governments — largely representing the upper and middle classes — were afraid of workers combining for better wages and conditions. However, after about the middle of the century things began to improve. In 1867 working men in towns were given the vote, and in 1884 male farm workers. In 1870 education was made compulsory, and in 1871 trade unions were made legal and given the right to picket to help their strikes. The unions of skilled and better-paid craftsmen such as the engineers were becoming quite powerful, because their members could pay quite high subscriptions, and if they went on strike they could not be replaced as easily as unskilled labourers could.

1832 REFORM ACT

1867 WORKING MEN IN TOWNS GIVEN THE VOTE

1870 COMPULSORY EDUCATION

1871 UNIONS GIVEN LEGAL RIGHTS

1884 MALE FARM WORKERS GIVEN THE VOTE

1880s GROWTH OF MANUAL LABOUR UNIONS

TO 20TH CENTURY

RISE OF TRADE UNIONS

In the 1880s some unions for unskilled workers were formed and began to show their strength. In 1888, led by the formidable Mrs Annie Besant, the girls who made matches under terrible conditions struck for better wages — and got them. In 1889 the gasworkers formed a union, threatened a strike for an eight-hour day — and the employers gave in. Three months later a dockworkers' union was formed, and struck for sixpence an hour (2½p). Wealthy Londoners were shocked as the ragged, half-starved dockers marched through the city, and the men got most of what they were demanding.

The strike committee of the matchmakers in 1888, probably the first time in Britain that women took organised industrial action. Although there was no union for women, seven hundred girls suddenly went on strike against the terrible conditions in Bryant and May's match factory — and won their demands.

The ups and downs of the Trade Unio

1893 Instead of fighting employers one by one the trade unions helped to found the Labour party, which they hoped would eventually win their battles in parliament by getting laws changed. However, as yet they had no MPs.

1906 41 Labour MPs (and some others sympathetic to the Labour party) were elected. With the help of the Liberal government the Taff Vale decision was reversed. Unions could no longer be sued in the courts for damages resulting from a strike.

> **UNION FEES 11/-**
> INCLUDES 1/- POLITICAL LEVY
>
> ** YOU MAY CONTRACT OUT OF THE LEVY = FEES 10/-*

> **UNION FEES 10/-**
> YOU ARE INVITED TO PAY 1/- POLITICAL LEVY TOTAL 11/-

1911 The Liberal government introduced the payment of MPs — £400 a year. This gave Labour MPs a breathing space, and in 1913 a Trade Disputes Act allowed unions to spend funds for political purposes. Union members however had to be given the chance of 'contracting out', that is, not paying the political levy as part of their subscription.

1900 The owners of the Taff Vale railway in Wales sued the railwaymen's union for damages because of a strike. The court ordered the union to pay the owners £23,000. This meant that in any strike the union funds could be seized for compensation.

1909 The unions now faced another problem. They spent some of the money collected from members on political matters — supporting MPs, for example, who were not then paid any salary. A railway worker, Mr Osborne, won a case in the high court preventing the union from using any money for political purposes.

1919-1926 A sharp rise in union membership, which doubled to 8 million between 1914 and 1920. There was a wave of major strikes in railways, transport and mining, but they met with little success.

A bus leaving the General Omnibus Garage under police escort, 1926.

movement 1900 - 1982

1926 The mines were still privately owned. The owners were trying to force the miners' union to accept longer hours and a cut in wages. Although leaders of other unions were not very anxious to help the miners, they did agree to support them and a general strike was declared. Troops and volunteers were used to keep the country going, and after a few weeks the general strike collapsed, though the miners themselves remained on strike for some time longer. The government passed the 1927 Trade Disputes Act which made it illegal for one union to strike in support of another.

1945 In the election the Labour party was returned with a large majority, and formed its first strong government. One of its first acts was to repeal the 1927 Trade Disputes Act, so that strikes could be used for political aims. Under Ernest Bevin trade unionism began to move forward again, and increase its membership.

Pickets clash with police at the Grunwick factory, 1977.

Late 1970s-1980s The new technology and worldwide recession meant massive unemployment, especially in the older heavy industries — steel, coal, docks and transport. Union membership fell again, partly because many of the unemployed were no longer members. When managements wanted to cut jobs, industrial disputes became very bitter and violent, with massive picketing.

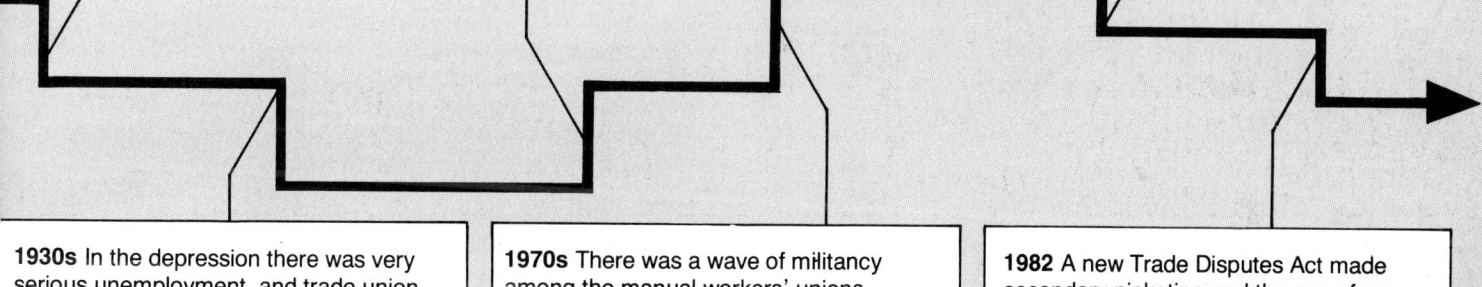

1930s In the depression there was very serious unemployment, and trade union membership fell sharply. Not only were many people out of work, but those who were employed were more concerned with keeping their jobs than with fighting union battles.

Jarrow marchers on their way to London to protest at unemployment in the 1930s.

1970s There was a wave of militancy among the manual workers' unions — dockers, miners, transport and public sector workers. With the new technology and rising standards of living, fewer people wanted manual jobs, and these unions had great power. Manual workers' strikes brought down a Conservative government in 1974 and a Labour one in 1979. But the public were made to realise how important the work of such people as dustmen, sewage workers, and hospital porters was, and these people were able to get better wages.

1982 A new Trade Disputes Act made secondary picketing and the use of more than six pickets in any one place illegal. If a union told its members to disobey these laws, the courts could order its funds to be seized for contempt.

Inflation

Inflation means that prices of goods are gradually rising. Sometimes they rise very slowly, but at other times very fast. The effect is that the value of money goes down. Let us say that a pound will buy five 20p pencils; in a year the price has risen to 25p a pencil, and the pound will only buy four.

No government likes this sort of thing to happen. In times of inflation, as the value of people's money goes down, they react in various ways.

Workers insist on higher wages to maintain their standard of living.

This may cause firms to raise the prices of their products so that they can afford higher wages and still make the same amount of profit — prices have risen yet again, and again people will start asking for higher wages.

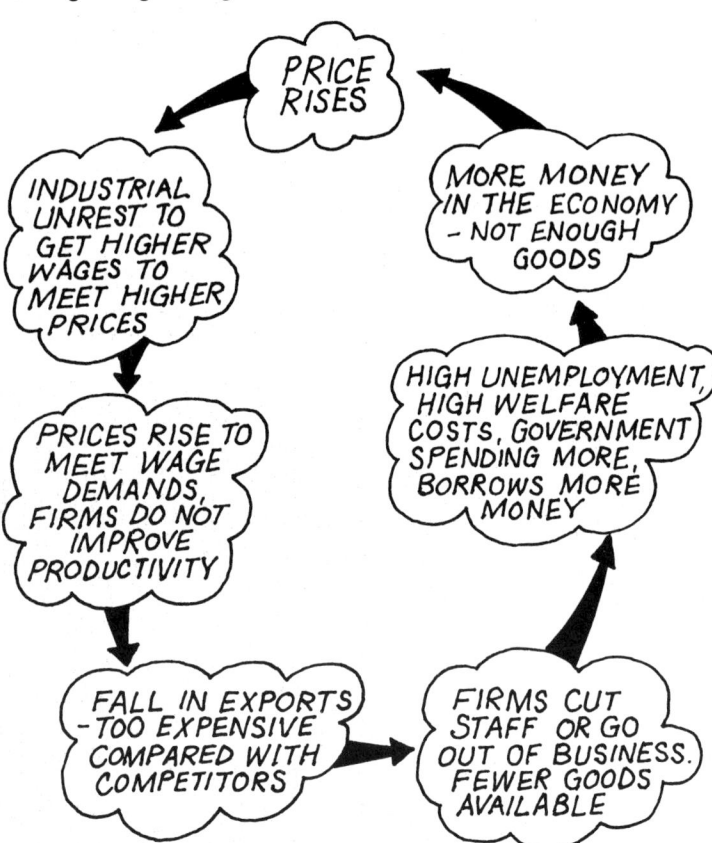

Firms which export their goods often become less competitive in times of inflation because their prices are too high in a world market. They sell less, so they produce less, their profits start to go down, they may have to make some of their staff redundant, they may even have to close down altogether. Unemployment gets worse.

If firms plan more efficient methods and their employees produce more goods in return for higher wages — increased productivity — matters may improve. They may be able to sell more and pay the higher wages without raising prices.

Some people say that inflation is 'too much money chasing too few goods'. When people have money over after they have paid for essentials like food, clothes and housing, they naturally spend it on things they want — perhaps a new car or a video recorder, for example. But if not enough of these are being produced — if productivity has not increased — firms can charge more for them. People have enough money to pay — prices are rising again.

Foreign goods may be imported to meet the demand. Their prices are lower than those of the home-produced variety, home companies may be put out of business as a result. Unemployment gets worse again.

A greengrocer's shop in 1907. Remember that the prices are in the old pounds, shillings and pence form of money.

Controlling inflation

No one really knows exactly how prices and wages get into the spiral of inflation, though there are various theories. Everyone agrees, however, that the results are bad for the whole country.

The secret of stopping inflation is one which every politician in the world would like to know. Here are some of the ideas that have been tried.

The government cuts the supply of money. It can do this in various ways. It may reduce the grants it makes to local government and raise the bank interest rate so that businesses do not borrow so much. Both of these mean that firms and local authorities have to cut back and raise production by using more efficient methods and perhaps by dismissing workers. Unemployment increases the government's social welfare costs.

Mass unemployment tends to reduce wage increases. Workers are more concerned about keeping a job of any sort than about striking for higher wages. They may also work more efficiently if there is a chance that the organisation they are working for may close down if they don't.

Prices and incomes policies. The government comes to an agreement with representatives of management and unions to control both prices and incomes. Managements keep prices steady and unions accept lower wage increases. Arrangements like this usually start off quite well, but sooner or later break down.

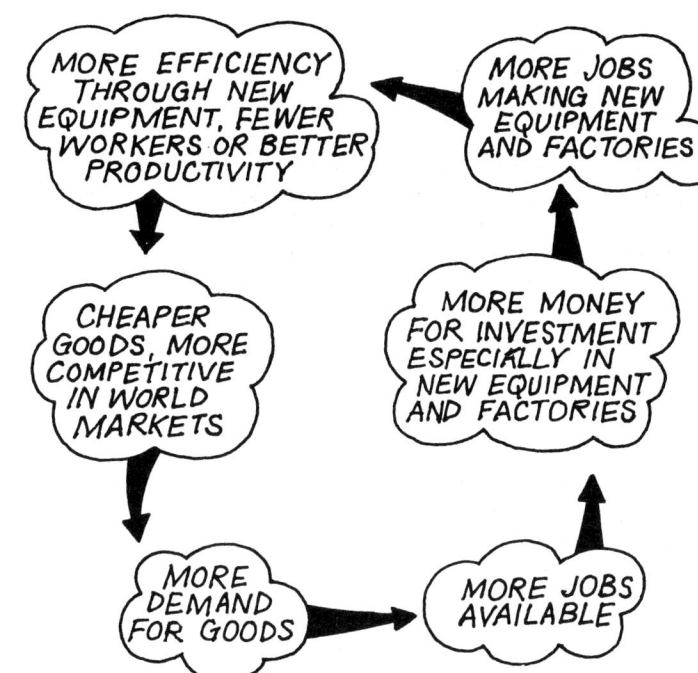

MORE EFFICIENCY THROUGH NEW EQUIPMENT, FEWER WORKERS OR BETTER PRODUCTIVITY
CHEAPER GOODS, MORE COMPETITIVE IN WORLD MARKETS
MORE DEMAND FOR GOODS
MORE JOBS AVAILABLE
MORE MONEY FOR INVESTMENT ESPECIALLY IN NEW EQUIPMENT AND FACTORIES
MORE JOBS MAKING NEW EQUIPMENT AND FACTORIES

***Real value of money** The price of grapes in the 1907 shop (left) was 8d per lb (about 3p in modern coins): in the 1980 shop they were 20p. They would seem to be much more expensive today, but if we relate them to the average wage we find that the prices are much lower. A person on the average wage of £2 in 1907 could buy 60 lb grapes if he spent his whole wages on them. In 1980 the person on the average wage of about £150 could buy a staggering 750 lb. The person in 1907 could buy 80 lb apples (bottom left) with his wages: in 1980 he could buy 833 lb. In practice the prices today are much lower.*

***A greengrocer's stall in 1986.** Note that little has changed in the kind of goods sold and the layout in eighty years. Only the prices are different.*

A MANCHEST
FRUITERER & FLORIST N
GOLDEN DELICIOUS
CHOICE EATING!
ALL SELECTED SALAD TOMATOES
CHOICE GRAPES
SWEET EATING!!
English
Phillips

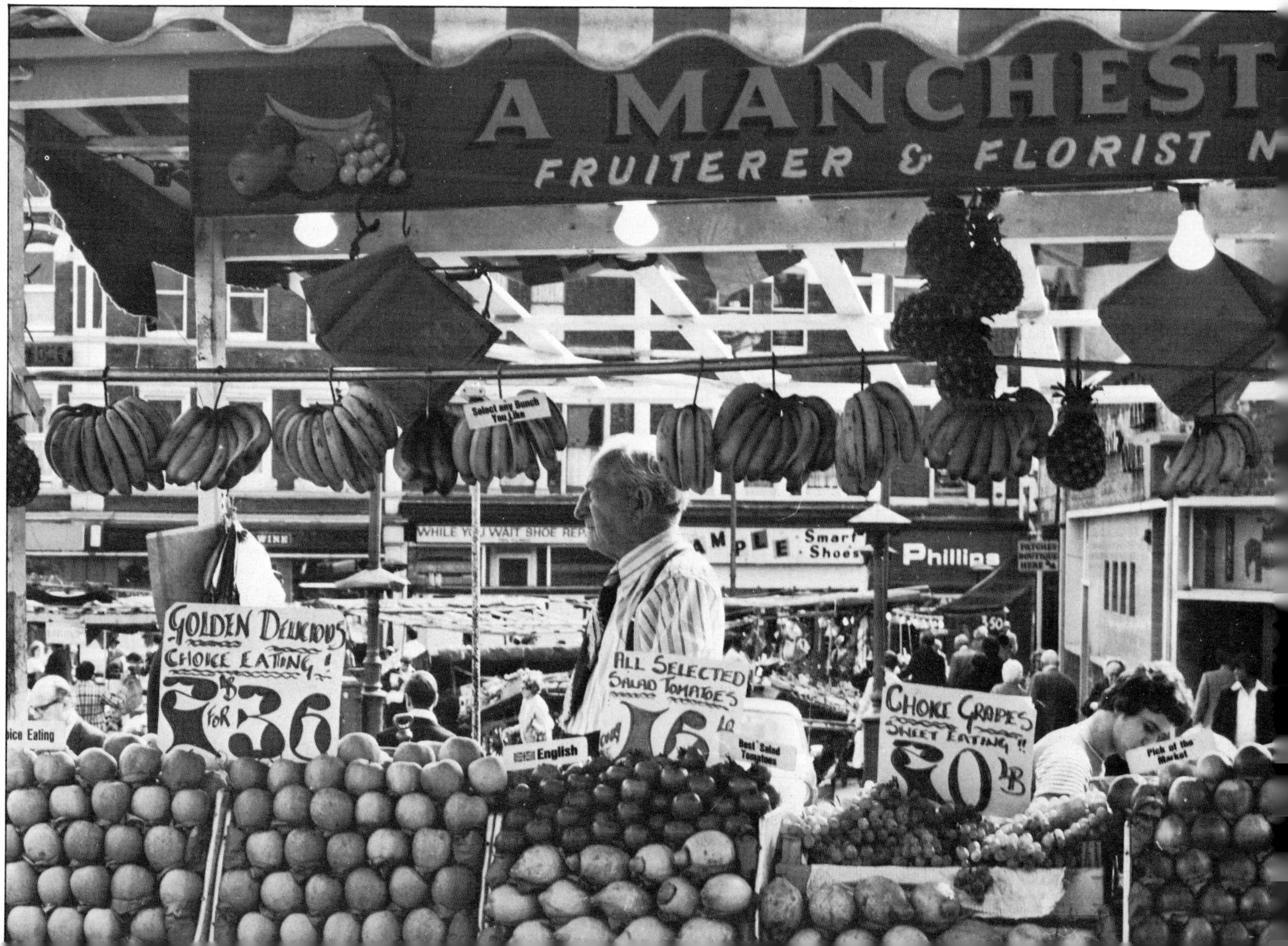

Science and technology

The twentieth century has seen more rapid and more dramatic advances in technology than any period in history. These have altered our whole way of life, and though many of our inventions and discoveries have been beneficial, some have produced serious problems.

The chart shows when some of the developments that we regard as essential parts of our lives took place. The drawings show when the inventions became widespread, even though the actual work of inventing may have taken place years earlier. Notice how the two great bursts in home equipment came after the two world wars.

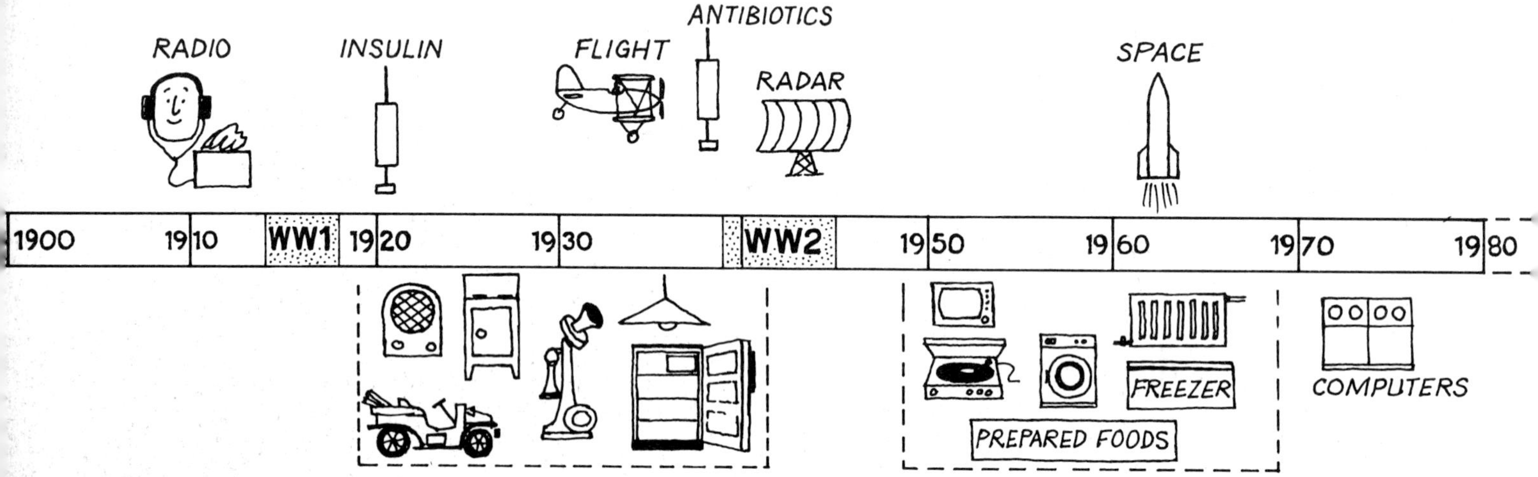

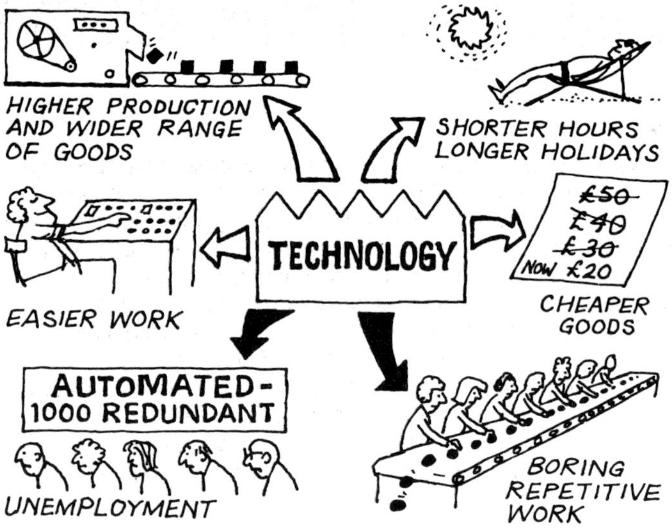

RADIO   INSULIN   FLIGHT   ANTIBIOTICS   RADAR   SPACE

| 1900 | 1910 | WW1 | 1920 | 1930 | WW2 | 1950 | 1960 | 1970 | 1980 |

PREPARED FOODS   FREEZER   COMPUTERS

HIGHER PRODUCTION AND WIDER RANGE OF GOODS

SHORTER HOURS LONGER HOLIDAYS

EASIER WORK

TECHNOLOGY

£50 £40 £30 NOW £20

CHEAPER GOODS

AUTOMATED – 1000 REDUNDANT

UNEMPLOYMENT

BORING REPETITIVE WORK

Work

Machines of constantly increasing complexity, and later on automation, electronics and robots, have taken much of the hard physical work out of industry. They allow much higher production from the same number of workers, which means shorter hours and longer holidays. They also mean cheaper goods and a much wider range of products, which enable more people to enjoy what were formerly luxuries. But technology in industry often means boring, repetitive work on production lines. It can also mean large-scale unemployment as fewer employees are needed.

A factory in 1909. Note the general air of confusion, and the dangerous machinery with unguarded belts (top left, bottom right).

A factory in 1980s. This is a completely automatic paint spraying shop in the British Leyland car factory.

The operations room in Sussex police communications centre.

Leisure

Technology has given us shorter working hours and much more leisure time. It has also given us many new ways of enjoying this leisure — private cars, radio, television, records, the ability to travel further afield on holidays. The cheaper industrial products enable people to enjoy a much higher standard of life in their homes — central heating, comfortable furniture, carpeting, a wide range of foodstuffs from all parts of the world available all the year, and plenty of clothing. Almost everything we use is cheaper today than it was fifty years ago if we relate the prices with the average wages then and now. For example, a typical new family car might cost £4,500 today. At the average industrial wage of £150 a week this represents 30 weeks' work. A similar car in the 1930s cost about £330, and the average wage was £3 — 110 weeks' work.

Equality

Technology and its products have meant a remarkable 'levelling-up' in society. The wealthy, leisured class of eighty years ago have almost gone. Foreign travel, sailing, motor cars, sports of all kinds, plenty of good food and clothing, bathrooms and running hot water, all of which were largely confined to the upper and middle classes, are now within the range of the majority of people. Most of the population have comfortable, warm homes, and the luxury of 'servants' in the form of labour-saving equipment, washing machines, freezers, vacuum cleaners, easy-care clothes, ready-prepared food, kitchen equipment and a whole range of preparations and chemicals to do many household tasks which once needed endless woman-power.

A typical kitchen in an ordinary house in the 1930s. Note the fold-down working surface and small coal-fired boiler.

About 1980 a family in the same circumstances would have a kitchen much like this one. Notice how much less cluttered it is.

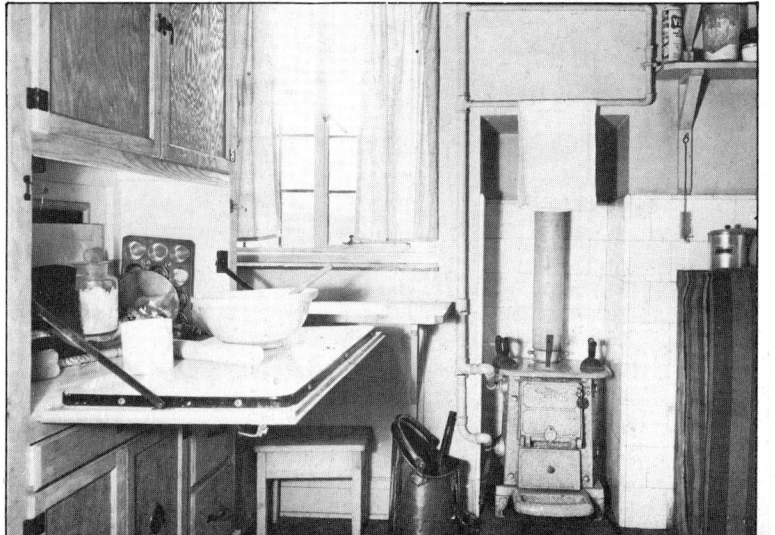

A battery-powered invalid vehicle which allows people who in other periods would have been completely house-bound, to enjoy a full, active life in the community.

The decrease in physical illnesses is partly counterbalanced by the increase in mental ones caused by modern life styles. There is the difficulty of coping with elderly people. When we are old most of us need pensions, special medical and general care, often special housing. Medical science is now keeping alive people who are very severely handicapped, mentally and physically. It is wonderful that we can give people longer and healthier lives, but we must also remember that the *quality* of life is as important as the *quantity*.

Health

Between 1900 and 1984 the expectation of life increased from 53 (men) and 56 (women) to 71 and 76. Infant deaths fell from 112 per 1,000 births to 15. Remarkable discoveries in drugs and advances in surgery allow conditions and diseases which were fatal a few years ago to be treated successfully. People are living longer, healthier lives, and while in almost everyway this seems an excellent thing, there are some problems.

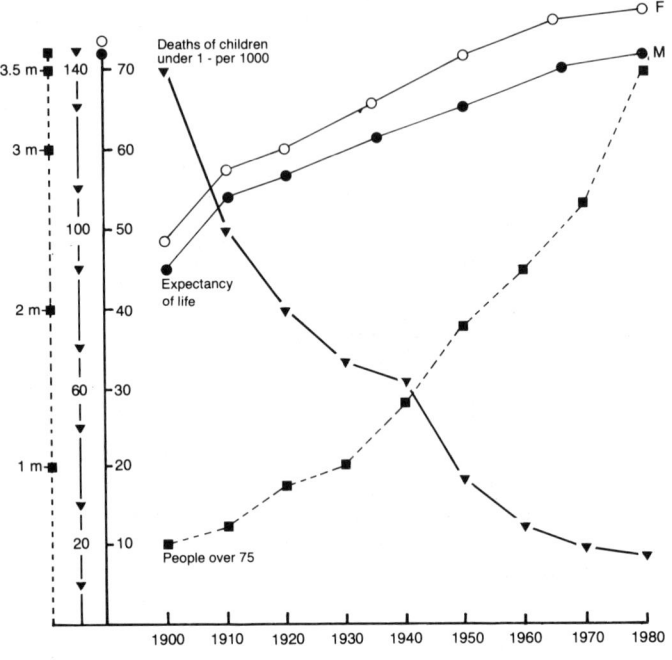

The destructive power of modern war is shown by this picture of Rotterdam destroyed by German bombers in 1940 as an act of revenge.

War

Two world wars have made a dramatic change in the technology of war — artillery, tanks, motor vehicles, aeroplanes, nuclear bombs, submarines, rockets, electronic and chemical weapons of all kinds. Modern technology has made it certain that a major war is no longer confined, but involves much of the world, directly or indirectly. No longer can wars be fought by armed forces alone. Civilians are in as much danger as the forces. Probably more people have been killed in wars in the twentieth century than in all the wars in the last 2,000 years put together.

Wars are evil, but as the chart on page 126 shows, they often produce technology useful for civil purposes. Today we can only hope that military technology has been too successful, and has created such terrible weapons that no country dare use them, as it could mean the end of civilisation, their own as well as the enemy's.

The impact of the motor vehicle

The motor vehicle is one of the most important influences on life in the twentieth century. In 1900 there were only about 10 000 in Britain — one for every 4 000 people. In 1982 there were 16 million private cars, 2 million goods vehicles, 1.4 million motor cycles and

120,000 buses. This is one vehicle for every three people in Great Britain. The cars alone, if placed bumper to bumper, would stretch for over 40,000 miles. If all the vehicles were on the road at the same time, there would be 85 on every mile of hard road in Britain. It is not surprising that they have such an influence on our lives.

Motor vehicles have helped to make a fairer society. In the past only the rich could move freely about the country, but today almost everyone can travel quickly and easily on pleasure or business on the spur of the moment. The car has liberated us and raised standards of living.

Motor vehicles have enabled people to live further away from their work. This gives them a much wider choice of jobs, and allows them to live in pleasant surroundings, away from the centres of large cities. With a car, shopping can be done in large stores further away from the customers' homes.

Motor vehicles have saved hundreds of thousands of lives in emergencies. Ambulances, fire engines are essential. Motor vehicles help in the fight against crime, though they have created new crimes of their own.

Motor vehicles have created a wide range of new jobs'— manufacturing; repairing; providing oil, petrol, tyres, spares and accessories; building roads and bridges and traffic control equipment; publishing books and magazines and maps etc.

Motor transport allows goods to be moved quickly and conveniently, especially over short distances. We can eat fresher food. Delivery of goods from factory to customer reduces the risk of damage.

BUT every year about 6,500 people are killed and 335,000 injured in road accidents. The cost of treating injured people is enormous. In addition, exhaust from motor vehicles pollutes the air. Heavy vehicles passing through towns and villages spoil them and make roads dangerous. Major roads often create ugly landscapes.

Social changes from 1900 onwards

Textiles and clothing

In 1900 synthetic materials such as nylon and terylene had not been invented and all clothes and household fabrics were made of cotton or wool, with linen and silk for the rich. These were all difficult to wash, especially as there was nothing except ordinary soap for laundry, and water had usually to be heated in kettles or coppers. All clothes and household linens had to be ironed, with solid flat irons heated in front of the fire or on a stove. Clothes were changed much less frequently — once a week for underclothes generally. Most clothes wore out more easily than those made of modern fabrics, so that there was constant mending to be done. In most working homes washing and ironing took up almost all of Monday and Tuesday each week.

Shopping

Shopping was usually done locally. Shops were almost always separate — butchers, greengrocers, bakers, fishmongers, tea and coffee merchants, and so on. Many people gave their orders to the shop assistants, and the goods were delivered to their homes. There was no question of serving yourself, as we often do today. There were some tinned and prepacked foods, though not nearly as many as today, but the majority were 'loose' — that is, the grocer would weigh out and wrap tea from a large chest, sugar from a sack, biscuits from a big tin, and so on. Ready-made clothes were becoming more popular, but many people bought material and made their own garments themselves, or paid a dressmaker.

A newspaper advertisement about 1912. What social differences are shown by the wearing of clothes like this in summer?

Below: a grocer's shop in December 1910. The boxes on the extreme right are loose biscuits. What differences in retailing are shown by this shop as compared with a modern one? Why should the shopkeeper choose this window display for December?

A fairly prosperous family in 1908 with their latest luxury, a phonograph. The boxes on the table (right) contain the cylindrical records. The girl holding the baby is one of the maids.

Sunday morning cycling in 1911. The bicycle was one of the greatest liberating movements of the late 19th century.

Leisure

The greatest difference in home entertainment in 1900 was that there was no radio or television, and only very crude and expensive 'gramophones'. People played cards and other games, read, talked and sang songs at the piano. (The housewife was usually busy cooking, cleaning or mending.) Men tended to drink heavily as beer was cheap. Outside the home there were some dances, roller skating, cycling, theatres in the towns, and sports of all kinds — though these were more for people to take part in rather than to watch. The cinema was still some years

Below: a working home about 1901. Note the five children — almost certainly one or two would have died and there would be more to come. Families of a dozen or more were fairly common among ordinary people, though the middle and upper classes were beginning to restrict the size of theirs by birth control. This family would have had at most two bedrooms.

away. There were only about 10,000 cars in the country, so that people had to walk, cycle or, for longer distances, travel by train.

Families

In 1900 families were much larger than today, especially among working people, though more middle and upper class people were beginning to practise effective birth control. In 1900 for every 1,000 of the population there were 28 births, in 1981 there were 11. Four or five children were quite usual, and sometimes there were ten or more. This often meant overcrowding in the small working class homes, with several children in one bed. Because there was no state social welfare, elderly relatives had to be taken care of. Families — parents, grandparents, uncles and aunts — often lived in the same district, or at least in nearby towns, especially in industrial areas. These 'extended' families sometimes helped one another in times of trouble, but also often quarrelled among themselves.

In terms of history 1900 is a very short time ago. There are still (1986) quite a lot of people in Britain who were alive in that year. But it was a very different world from our own. Society was much more sharply divided into the working class, the middle class and the upper class. There were much wider differences of income, and so there were wide differences in housing, leisure, possessions, mobility, food and drink, and almost everything else. Science, inventions, technology, two world wars and great political developments have meant that more changes have taken place in the world in this century than in any thousand years in the past. These pages show some of the ways people lived in 1900. Compare them with your own lifestyle.

1900

SCIENCE TECHNOLOGY INVENTION DISCOVERY

WORLD WARS SOCIAL CHANGE POLITICAL CHANGE

Houses

In 1900 perhaps more than half the population lived in small 4-5-roomed houses, the majority without bathrooms or inside lavatories. Families were often of 6 to 9 people, so that there was a lot of overcrowding. Perhaps 5% to 8% of the population lived in large houses of twenty or more rooms, managed by a number of servants. Almost all working people rented their homes and rents generally took a quarter to a half of their income.

Today the great majority of people live in houses of 6-8 rooms, usually in much smaller families, so that everyone has more space. Although there are still a few homes without inside lavatories, this is now unusual. In 1983 almost 6 houses out of every 10 were owner-occupied.

Above: this street in London was typical of the sort working people lived in.
Wealthier people lived in houses like the one on the left.

132

Comfort

Homes today are much more comfortable than those of 1900. Carpets, for example, were largely for the better off, and ordinary people had linoleum on floors and stairs, with perhaps a rug in the 'best' room. Furniture and bedding today are more comfortable and easier to manage. Modern homes are warmer and freer from draughts. In 1900 almost all houses were heated by coal fires, which needed constant attention and created much dust and dirt. Only a few houses had gas fires. Lighting was generally by gas — one light in the centre of the ceiling, or brackets round the walls. A few rich people living in town houses had electric lighting, but a very large number of ordinary homes still managed with oil lamps or even candles, especially in country districts.

Above: living room of a typical house in 1919.
Below: living room of a wealthy household of the same period.

Labour-saving equipment

In 1900 none of the equipment shown below right had been invented. The things shown below left had been invented, but were very crude and owned only by a few rich people. The work which these things do today was done by hand by servants in rich homes and by the housewife in ordinary homes. All of this equipment is now within the range of most families and makes life more comfortable than it was in the past.

CRUDE AND EXPENSIVE

TELEPHONE   VACUUM CLEANER
GAS COOKER   CENTRAL HEATING

NOT YET INVENTED

REFRIGERATOR   FREEZER   TELEVISION   RADIO   DISHWASHER
WASHING MACHINE   TUMBLE DRIER   ELECTRIC KITCHEN EQUIPMENT   DETERGENTS   ELECTRONIC EQUIPMENT

The beginnings of the welfare state

Today it seems natural that the state should help us when we are old or when we have misfortunes such as unemployment, sickness or injury. Yet it was only in the twentieth century that the government in Britain accepted any responsibility for social welfare. Before then people had to cope with their problems by themselves, or with the help of family and friends. There were some charities run by the churches or private people, but these were very uncertain, especially in the growing cities where they were most needed.

If a person was absolutely desperate, the parish might give a few pence a week as 'outdoor relief', but in the nineteenth century even this was stopped. Those who were without money or a job were forced into workhouses which were almost like prisons.

| GERMANY BEGINS SOCIAL WELFARE SCHEMES | BRITAIN 1908 — FIRST OLD AGE PENSION SCHEME (LLOYD GEORGE) | 1920 NATIONAL INSURANCE SCHEME EXTENDED TO SOME NON-MANUAL WORKERS |

1880   1890   1900   1910   1920

| FRANCE BEGINS SOME SOCIAL WELFARE SCHEMES | 1911 NATIONAL INSURANCE ACT (LLOYD GEORGE). UNEMPLOYMENT, SICKNESS, INJURY & MATERNITY BENEFIT FOR MANUAL WORKERS | 1926 NON-CONTRIBUTORY PENSION FOR WIDOWS, ORPHANS & OLD AGE PENSIONS EXTENDED |

The first step in Britain was the introduction by the Liberal government in 1908 of an old age pension of five shillings a week (perhaps the equivalent of £15-£20 today) for people over 70 if they had less than £21 a year. In 1909 labour exchanges, organised by a civil servant, William Beveridge, were set up to help people find jobs.

In 1911 the Liberal government passed Lloyd George's very important National Insurance Act. This gave sickness, injury and maternity benefit to some workers, and unemployment pay (later called the dole) to manual workers in such trades as building, where work was irregular. These benefits were contributory — that is, the workers, their employers and the government each paid a certain amount each week into the National Insurance Fund. In 1920 the early welfare schemes were extended to non-manual workers earning less than £250 a year.

In 1926 a Conservative government introduced non-contributory pensions for widows and orphans, and reduced the age for receiving the old age pension to 60 for women and 65 for men. In 1928 the pension was increased to ten shillings a week (about £25 today).

But after the terrible unemployment of the 1930s, it was obvious that much more needed to be done in state welfare, and a committee under William Beveridge was set up to make suggestions. The famous Beveridge Report was issued in 1942

The 'Two Nations' about 1900. An upper-class family in the West End of London take afternoon tea . . . and a family in the East End have none.

The excellent work of such men as General Booth with his Salvation Army, Dr Barnado and Robert Owen scarcely touched the surface of the terrible problems of poverty in the nineteenth century. A man who was later to become prime minister, Benjamin Disraeli, wrote in 1845 that Britain was 'Two Nations' — the rich and the poor.

Towards the end of the nineteenth century a few countries had begun to realise that some people were poor or unemployed or ill through no fault of their own, and that they should be helped by the state. Germany introduced old age, sickness and injury pensions between 1883 and 1889, and France followed a few years later.

1928 MAXIMUM OLD AGE PENSION DOUBLED TO 10/- WEEK	1942 DEVORIDGE REPORT — BASIS OF MODERN WELFARE STATE	1952 SOME CHARGES INTRODUCED TO HEALTH SERVICE

1940   **1950**   **1960**   **1970**   **1980**

1930s DEPRESSION. MASSIVE UNEMPLOYMENT. GREAT POVERTY & DISTRESS. COMMITTEE SET UP	1948 NATIONAL HEALTH SERVICE SET UP. ALL FREE	WELFARE SCHEMES EXTENDED IN MANY WAYS TO TRY TO MAKE SURE EVERYONE HAS JUST CARE & INCOME.

but little could be done at the time because Britain was in the middle of World War 2. However, it was acted upon by the Labour Government of Clement Attlee as soon as the war had ended, with, as the government said, 'state care from the cradle to the grave'.

The first great step was the setting up of the National Health Service in 1948. This gave free medical, dental and optical treatment for everyone, so that the poorest person in the country could have the most expensive operation possible if it were necessary. The Beveridge Report intended that all of this should be paid for by contributions from all working people, but the National Health Service was far more expensive than had been expected. In 1949 the Labour government passed a bill so that patients, with certain exceptions such as children and pensioners, should pay part of the cost of medicines, dentures and spectacles. The bill was not put into force, however, until 1952, when a Conservative government was in power.

The Beveridge Report remains the basis of the present welfare schemes in Britain although there have been many changes of detail, such as many more services and increased costs for prescriptions and equipment.

Left: Welsh miners (1926) being paid their first wages after being on strike.

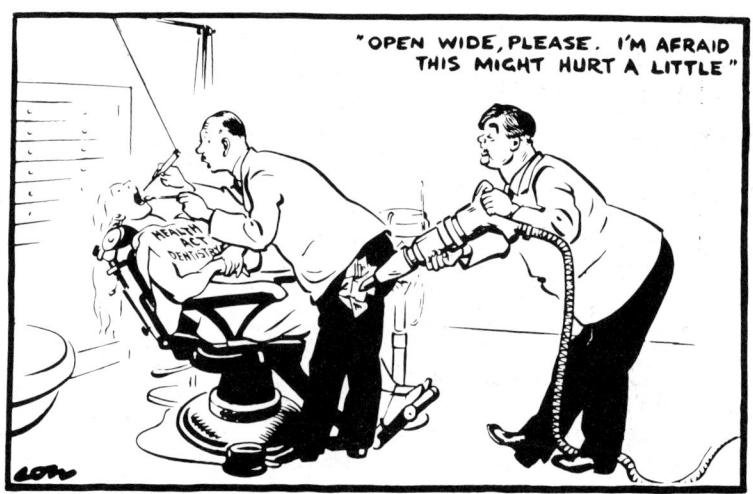

"OPEN WIDE, PLEASE. I'M AFRAID THIS MIGHT HURT A LITTLE"

The welfare state — *from the cradle to the grave*

Through social welfare the state tries to make sure that no one in Britain suffers from having insufficient money to cope with problems of health, handicap, everyday living or old age. It falls into three parts: 1. The National Health Service and 2. Social Security, both of which are run by the central government, and 3. Personal Social Services, which are run by local authorities. Some of the services are contributory, that is, they depend on the person having paid certain contributions to the National

Insurance Fund, and some non-contributory. People receive non-contributory benefits whether or not they have paid any contributions. Contributions depend on wages. Both employers and employees pay, but employers pay much more than employees. Even so, contributions make up only about one third of the cost of welfare, and the rest comes from general taxation such as income tax, VAT, customs and excise duties.

A few of the benefits, particularly supplementary benefit, which is

FREE (IF NECESSARY) MEDICAL, DENTAL, OPTICAL CARE, HOSPITALS, HANDICAP ETC.

SOCIAL SECURITY — CONTRIBUTORY

Unemployment benefit Payments are made for a certain time to people who are unemployed. There are additional payments for a wife and children. People who are still out of work when the time runs out may apply for supplementary benefit.

Retirement pensions are paid at 60 for women and 65 for men if they stop working. If they continue to work the ages are 65 and 70. If they still continue to work, the pension is reduced by a certain amount.

Widows' allowance and pension A widow may be given a weekly allowance for the first six months after her husband's death, and then a slightly lower regular weekly pension with extra money for children. Pensions cease on remarriage.

Sickness benefit is paid when people cannot work because they are ill or injured. The rates are similar to those for unemployment benefit. After a certain time you must apply for invalidity pension, which is slightly higher.

Maternity grant and allowance A small lump sum is paid for each baby. The mother is paid maternity allowances, similar to those for unemployment benefit, for 18 weeks, provided she does not continue working.

Death grant A small sum is paid to the next of kin to help with funeral expenses.

SOCIAL SECURITY — NON-CONTRIBUTORY

Child benefit (family allowance) is paid for every child under the age of 16, and from 16-18 if they are in full-time education

Supplementary benefit is paid on the basis of need. If people cannot manage on money they have coming in, they can apply for supplementary benefit but have to have a 'means test'. If you are not satisfied with the money granted you, you can appeal to a tribunal.

Invalidity pension is for people who are still sick, or unable to work, after receiving sickness benefit for a certain time. It is higher than sickness benefit.

Invalid care allowance is paid to people looking after severely disabled persons.

Mobility allowance is paid to severely handicapped people who are unable to get about easily.

Important note
Welfare benefits and contributions change from time to time and these pages may not be completely accurate. There are exceptions to almost all benefits and there is no room here to give all the details.

paid when people cannot manage on their normal income (some one-parent families, for example), are given only after a 'means test'. This means that anyone claiming supplementary benefit must give the authorities a full account of their income — wages, savings, etc., and of outgoings which they cannot avoid, to show that they are genuinely in need.

Many people think that the welfare state system is now so complicated that few of us can understand it properly. Some people who are entitled to benefits do not claim them because they do not know that they are available. You can find out more about the welfare state from local offices of the Department of Health and Social Security, which have free pamphlets about benefits. You might find it interesting to see how well you can follow the pamphlets.

Education 1850s - 1944

As industry and commerce became more complex in the nineteenth century, it was obvious that working people needed to be better educated. At that time no one had to go to school, and in the 1850s fewer than half the children did so. The churches tried hard to provide some education but often with only one master for several hundred pupils. There were some small dame schools, which were often little more than baby-minding establishments. Some towns had grammar schools founded in earlier times, but these were generally very poor.

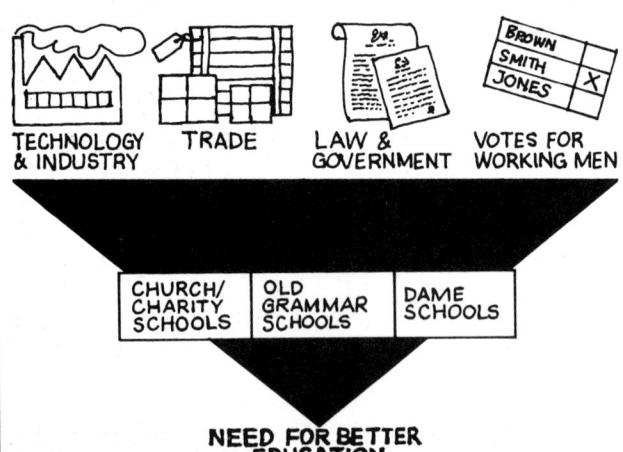

TECHNOLOGY & INDUSTRY   TRADE   LAW & GOVERNMENT   VOTES FOR WORKING MEN

CHURCH/ CHARITY SCHOOLS   OLD GRAMMAR SCHOOLS   DAME SCHOOLS

NEED FOR BETTER EDUCATION

The sons of the rich usually went to one of the public (boarding) schools. There were some very old ones and in the nineteenth century others were being founded all over the country. There the boys were often beaten; they learned Latin, Greek and the idea that they were superior to most people, but little else. Daughters of the rich were usually educated at home.

Public school boys (Westminster) learn French from a phonograph in 1909.

The universities too were for the wealthy, particularly in England. Until 1832 there were only 7 universities in Great Britain. Oxford and Cambridge did not allow anyone except Anglicans to take degrees until 1851. There were no women students. Other universities were opened in the nineteenth century, but very few students from ordinary working families were able to go to them.

Classroom drill in a board school, 1905.

In education England was far behind many other European countries and the position was becoming serious when the Education Act of 1870 was passed. This ordered every school district (usually a parish) to have a school. In parishes where there were no schools, a school board was elected with power to raise a rate for the building and staff. The act also made education from the age of 5 compulsory, but pupils could leave at 10 providing they had passed a simple test. Schooling was still not free, though it normally cost only a few pence a week. Free education had to wait until the 1890s.

1870   1902

Modern education began with the 1902 education act. This abolished the old school boards and made the county councils responsible for education. The new local education authorities were also allowed to build secondary schools, though this was not compulsory until after World War 1. The old grammar schools were reorganised to provide academic education for fees, but the act said that 20% of the places should be given to clever pupils whose parents could not afford the fees. This was the beginning of the 11 + examination which decided which pupils went to grammar schools (and possibly to university). The usual leaving age at secondary schools was 14. This act was the basis of the educational system until 1945.

An 'art' class in a state primary school in 1909.

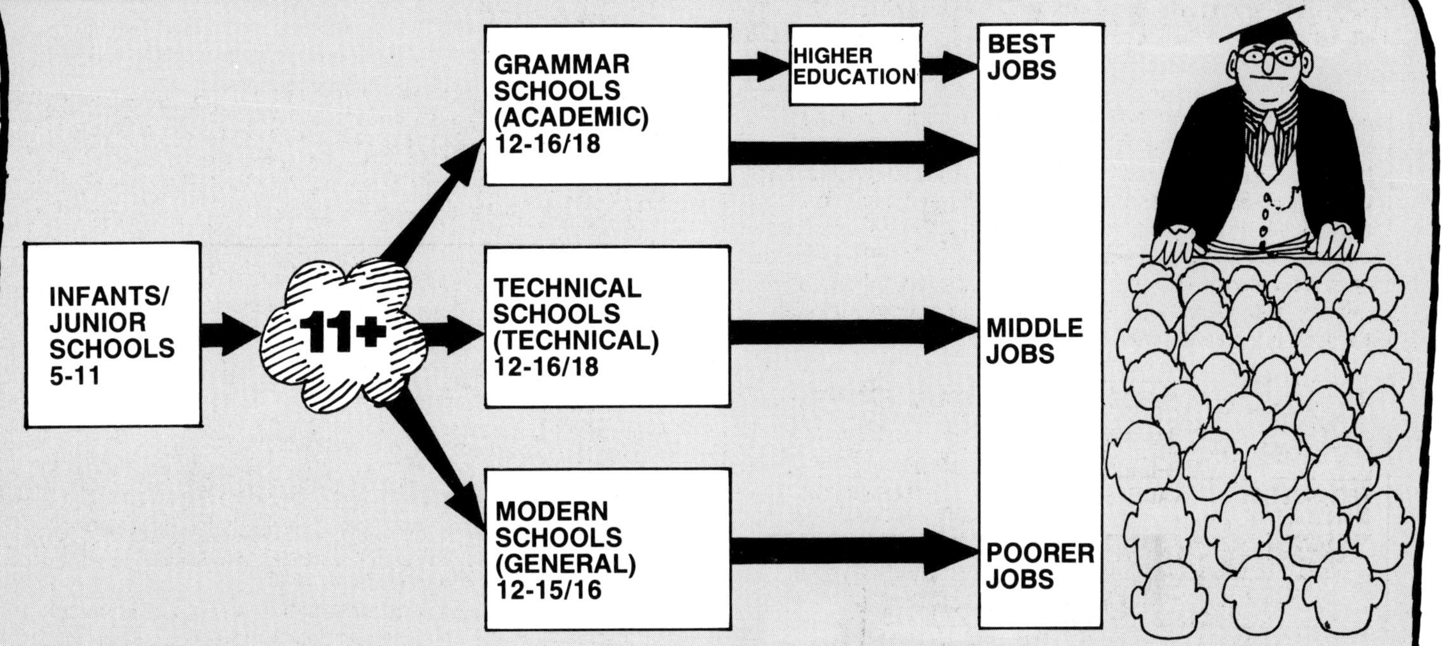

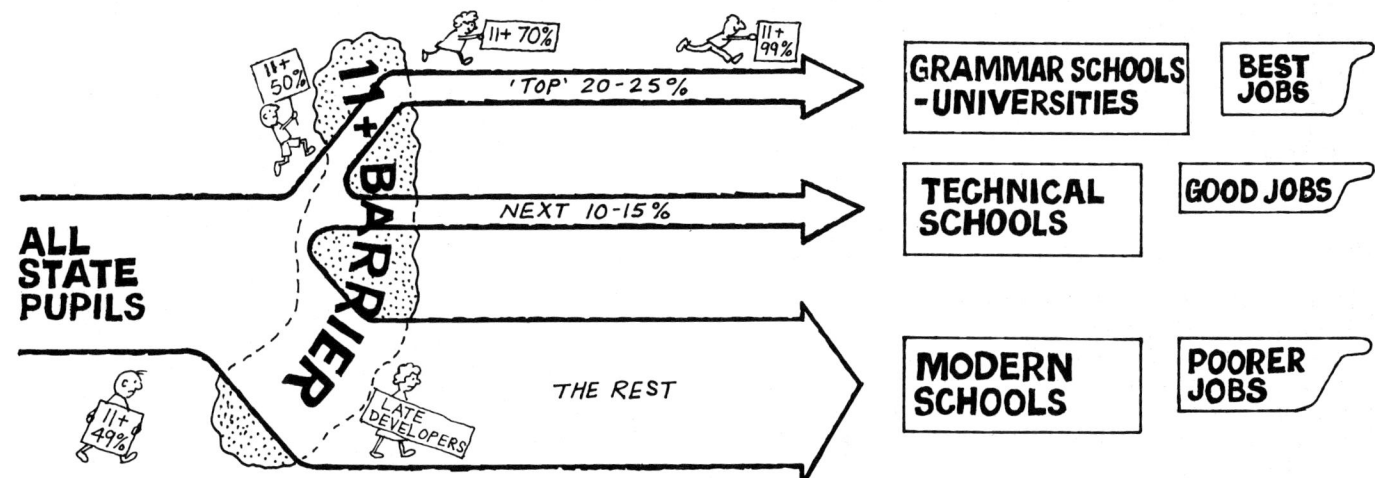

The 1944 Education Act

This act divided secondary schools into three kinds — grammar, technical and modern. At the age of 11 pupils sat an examination and on the results of this they were sent to one of the three types of school. The 'top' 20-25% went to the grammar schools, where they had an academic education until 16-18. Then they left for work or for higher education in colleges and universities. In some areas the next 10-20% went to technical schools until 16-18, when they usually went to work in industry. The remaining 60-80% went to modern schools, where they had a general, non-technical education until 15 (16 after 1973). Then they usually left for work.

Note

It is important to realise that this diagram gives the general effect of the 1944 act. There were of course children who did well and got very good jobs after going to modern or technical schools, and some who went to grammar schools and never did as well as expected.

The weakness of the 1944 act was that a child's whole education, and perhaps whole future, was decided by a single examination. There was little provision for 'late-developers', or even for pupils who had been feeling unwell on the day of the 11 + . Because the three different kinds of schools were usually in separate buildings in different parts of the town, and offered different kinds of education, it was difficult for a pupil to move from one type to another, even when it was obvious that he or she was much brighter — or duller — than the examination had seemed to show.

Because of this most authorities have set up comprehensive schools, where all pupils are housed in a single building or campus. The 11 + has been abolished in most places, and pupils can move from class to class, or set to set, according to their ability in a subject.

Many experiments in education are still taking place. Some of these are mixed ability classes, junior and senior high schools, sixth form colleges and the junior-middle-high school system.

Population

Governments have to keep careful records of population changes — the numbers of births and deaths, and the immigration and emigration figures — so that they can plan ahead. These are the figures for the United Kingdom from 1901-1981, with projections for 1991. Notice that the immigration/emigration numbers are small compared with the births, and for the period shown on this chart are only once greater than 100,000 a year.

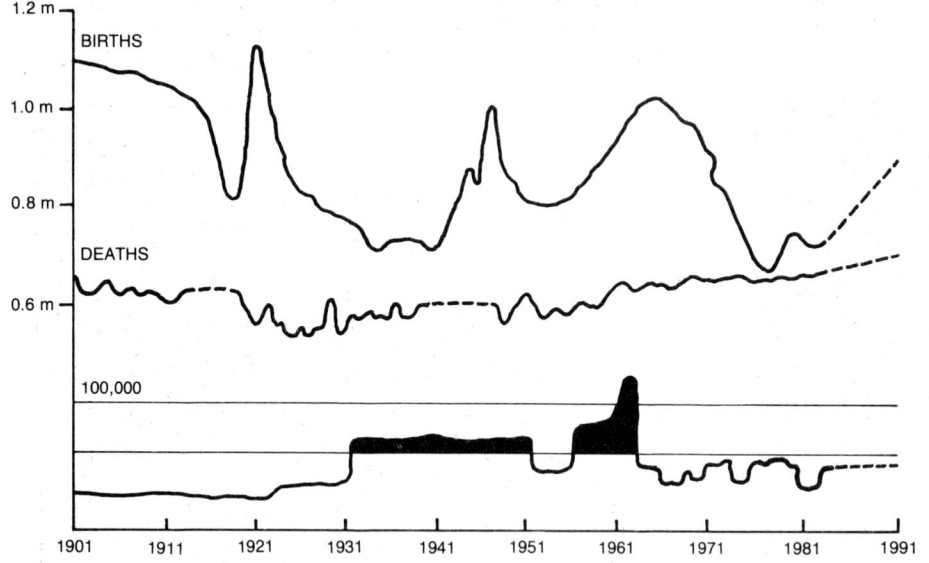

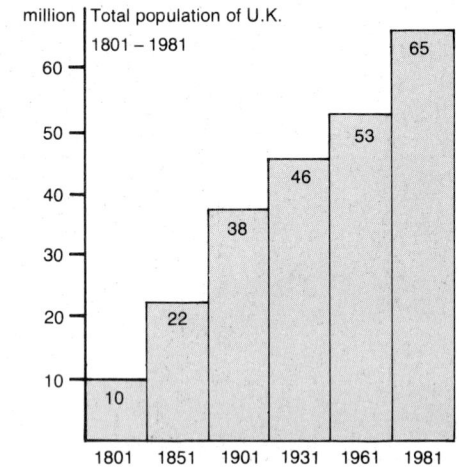

The young

While the number of older people increases steadily, the number of children is very variable. There were 'baby booms' in 1920-1921, 1946-1947 and 1963-1965, and 'troughs' in the 1930s, 1950s and 1970s. This makes it difficult to organise education. First there is pressure on the primary schools, then on the secondary schools. New schools have to be built and teachers trained (which takes four years). Later on the schools are half empty and teachers unemployed.

The adults

Governments and employers have to plan ahead for work — providing work for the numbers of students they know will be leaving schools and colleges. This is constantly being made more difficult by automation, which reduces the numbers of workers needed. It is very difficult to provide for unemployment, sharing out the work that is available and finding new ways of using leisure.

The elderly

Governments must know the number of older people in the population so that they can plan for pensions and the extra health care needed — hospitals, health visitors, etc. The chart shows how the proportion of people over 60 in the population has increased this century. The mounting costs of looking after these people have to be met by a decreasing number of people at work. The money has to be found from higher taxation or higher production.

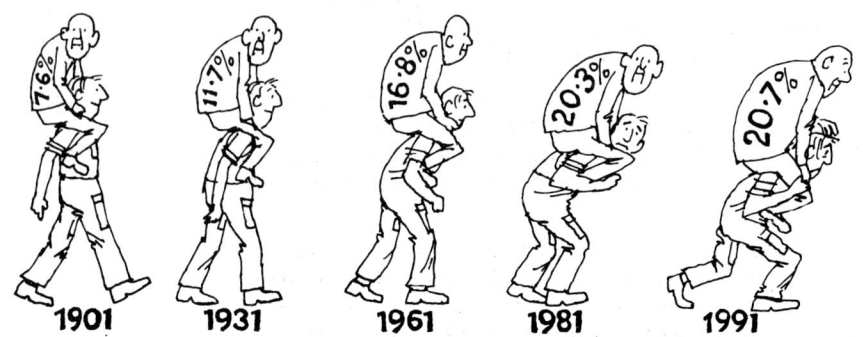

Housing: planning and new towns

Town planning is not new. The picture below shows the remains of Mohenjo Daro in India which was built about 2,000 BC with main streets 15 m wide, drains and indoor sanitation. The smaller streets often had right-angled bends in them to reduce wind nuisance.

In recent times the first town in Britain planned as a whole was Letchworth in Hertfordshire, which was begun in 1903. Soon after, the more famous Welwyn Garden City was planned as a complete town design — a pleasant place to live and work in, with town facilities and amusements, yet close to the countryside.

New towns

Since 1946 32 new towns have been set up in Britain, most of them based on small existing villages. Development corporations were set up to plan and design the towns, and to build houses, shops, factories and public buildings, which they sell or rent. The houses are designed for different kinds of families and income groups — from small inexpensive terraced or semi-detached homes for young couples with no children, to larger four- or five-bedroom detached houses for the better off. When the new towns are fully established, the development corporations will be wound up. The towns are planned to have populations of between 50,000 and 250,000, so that they do not become too large.

The new towns are light and spacious, with open spaces, gardens, shopping precincts, recreation and industrial areas all planned as a whole so that shops, schools and work are all within easy reach of residential areas, but do not spoil them.

The new towns of the 1960s onwards seem in many ways the perfect answer to housing. Indeed they do offer better housing and working conditions than many of the older cities, but there are a few problems.

1. Some new towns are too small to support large shopping or entertainment centres. As a result there is sometimes very little to do in leisure time, particularly for teenagers. This can lead to hooliganism and vandalism from sheer boredom.

2. The majority of the people in the new towns are young, so that the birthrate is very high, and the death rate low. This may in time cause problems for the services such as hospitals and schools which will have to change as the population that stays on grows older.

3. New towns are very efficient, but sometimes seem to lack interest. Some of the charm of older cities is that old and new stand side by side. New towns are almost entirely modern, built in a single period. Some are not wearing well and are beginning to look rather old-fashioned and shabby.

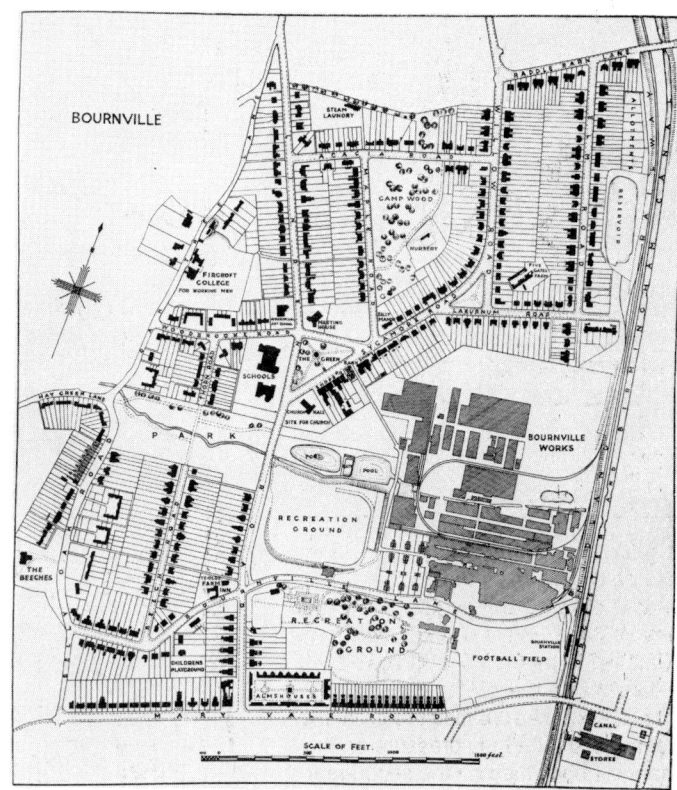

Early town planning in Britain. Bournville village, Birmingham, 1911. This was a 'model' town built for the Cadbury chocolate family.

World War 2 destroyed large areas of cities, leaving huge spaces for development.

Rising standards of living — people expect larger and better-equipped houses with fewer persons for every room.

Huge slum-clearance schemes to demolish small houses built in the nineteenth century which were thought to be unsuitable by modern standards.

Wider car-ownership in the last 30 years has meant that more people can commute to work in the cities and live well outside them.

1. Quick and relatively cheap to build by new building techniques. Walls or even whole rooms could be made in factories and assembled on the site. The huge numbers of people waiting for homes after World War 2 could be accommodated quickly.

2. Many more people could be accommodated on a given area of land than with any other form of housing.

3. Much better equipped than most of the older small houses they replaced — central heating and other amenities.

4. Fairly close to city centres so that people did not have to travel too far to work.

1. People felt isolated in the new tall buildings. The elderly and parents with small babies were often more or less prisoners in their flats.

2. Loss of community spirit. People did not know their neighbours and it was difficult to make contact with them. This had been easier in the old streets of small houses.

3. Practical difficulties of living many floors up — how to cope with bicycles, prams, refuse; what to do about play-space.

4. New building techniques had not always been properly tested, and some blocks were unsatisfactory, or even unsafe.

Tower-block (high-rise) buildings

To provide homes for many people as quickly as possible, many authorities built huge tower blocks on the sites of old buildings.

Completely new towns were created, sometimes based on existing villages, sometimes on empty farm land.

Huge low-rise housing estates, both private and local authority, were built further out from the city centres in what had been countryside.

The demand for housing began the age of planners and produced new methods of building which were quicker than traditional bricks and mortar.

1. Much better living conditions — much more space, gardens, provision for garages, easy access and storage for household items such as fuel, bicycles, prams.

2. No problems with lifts, stairs — especially important for older people and parents with small children.

3. Many fewer people per square kilometre.

4. Better living environment. Often good views and trees, grassed areas and gardens laid out by planners.

5. Well-planned estates can be very convenient with shopping areas, schools and other public places easily accessible to everyone.

1. More expensive and slower to build than high-rise developments.

2. Take up large areas of farming land, making towns and cities spread further and further into the countryside.

3. Can be very boring and lacking in character, with endless streets of identical houses.

4. Often lacking in amenities such as good shops and entertainments, so that people have to travel quite long distances to a town or city.

5. People on estates often have little in common and it can be difficult to build a community spirit.

Low-rise housing estates

Women in society

LEGAL CHANGES

1870/1882. Married Women's Property Acts

In the past women often had great power in private, but usually few rights in law. The first major step towards equality came with the Married Women's Property Acts. Before these everything a woman owned usually became her husband's personal property the moment she married. The two acts gave women the right to keep their money and property, and to use it as they liked.

1875. University Enabling Act

An act which allowed universities for the first time to award degrees to women. Although this affected only a very few women, it was an important step, because the chance of higher education did give some hope of a higher status. London University began to train women doctors in 1877.

1903-1914. The Suffragette Movement

This movement was a protest, often violent, to try to get votes for women. Many women went to prison for various offences, and in 1913 one killed herself by throwing herself under the king's horse in the Derby. Partly because of their efforts a Representation of the People Act was passed in 1917. This allowed women over 30 who were householders to vote in parliamentary elections.

1870 1880 1890 1900 1910

SOCIAL CHANGES

As well as the laws which have changed the position of women, there are slower social changes, many of which created the climate for the legislation to be passed. Towards the end of the nineteenth century many more women were employed in jobs other than the traditional ones of domestic service and textiles. New inventions made jobs for typists, telephonists, clerical workers, and offered a wider range of industrial employment. From the 1950s onwards there were further changes in industry, with many new jobs in light industry, electronics and computers, office work and entertainment. All these developments gave women wider opportunities.

Women's work in both world wars — in factories and on farms, as drivers, and — especially in World War 2 — in the forces themselves, made it perfectly clear that they were at least as capable as men. The suffragettes were mainly middle or upper class women, but the work of many ordinary women in World War 1 was probably the important factor which led to women being given the vote in 1917.

HOME ELECTRIC LAUNDRY COMPLETE

CASH DEPOSIT - £7 10s.

The Combined **UNIVERSAL** Electric Washer & Wringer

Tested and Approved 48 Good Housekeeping Institute

washes 6 sheets or the equivalent in 15 minutes without labour or the slightest damage to the most delicate fabric. The rinsing, blueing, and wringing are all done electrically without lifting heavy baskets or buckets. Wash-day the "Universal" way obviates those dreadful backaches and other anxieties.

GRAND Electric Ironer

dries and irons at the same time. It is truly the "wonder"

Labour-saving equipment, foods and materials in the home have freed housewives from much of the traditional housework and cooking. A home can be kept clean and meals prepared in a fraction of the time taken fifty years ago, so that women have spare time and energy for other things — jobs, entertainment, sports, travel and such outside interests as politics, which were once the privilege of men.

144

1928. Representation of the People Act
Gave all women over 21 the right to vote in elections. This gave them political equality with men. Many older people thought that the 'flapper vote' ('flapper' was a nickname for a wild young woman) would wreck the whole parliamentary system because most young women would know nothing about politics. In practice nothing changed.

1970. Equal Pay Act
This made it compulsory for employers to pay men and women the same wage for the same, or very similar jobs and to give both sexes the same conditions. There were job evaluation schemes to decide when different jobs were of the same value, and so deserved the same wages. Despite the act, the average woman's wage is still less than three-quarters of that of the average man's.

1975. Sex Discrimination Act
An act which makes it illegal to treat women differently from men in education and employment, and as buyers of goods and services. They must be allowed to take out mortgages if they can meet the conditions which apply to both sexes equally. It also makes it illegal to discriminate between men and women in job advertisements, so that phrases such as 'fireperson' or 'postperson' or 'housemaid, male or female' have to be used.

1930 1940 1950 1960 1970 1975

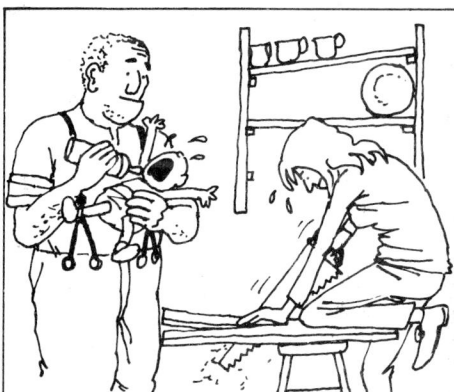

Rising standards of living. So many goods to make life more pleasant are now available that many families feel that they need two incomes. This means that both man and woman work, and share expenses. The division between male bread-winners and women earning 'pin-money' is gradually breaking down. This often leads to their sharing other things as well — household chores, child-rearing and leisure activities. The result is greater equality.

Reliable family planning has freed women from the round of regular pregnancy and child-bearing which occupied a major part of their active adult life in the past. They can have children only if they want them, and space them to suit their careers.

Changing social attitudes. Easy divorce, freer sexual relations, acceptance of men and women living together without marriage, abortion, males and females sharing all kinds of experiences on equal terms — holidays, pubs, clubs — have all helped in giving women more equality. It is difficult to say how much these changed attitudes are a cause or a result of the changing roles of men and women.

Although the role of women in society has changed considerably in the last hundred years, and especially in the last twenty, there are still big differences in the positions of men and women.

Education

Education might be thought to be one area in which there is relatively little sex discrimination. The chart shows the percentage of all school leavers obtaining A, B or C grades in important O-level subjects. What do you think accounts for the differences? Why do maths and science subjects seem to be favoured by boys more than girls? Is it a difference of attitude or ability? At 16 slightly more girls (3.7%) go on to A-level courses than boys (3.0%). The pass rate is about the same. But in 1981/2 22,800 males went on to higher education compared with 11,800 females. Why?

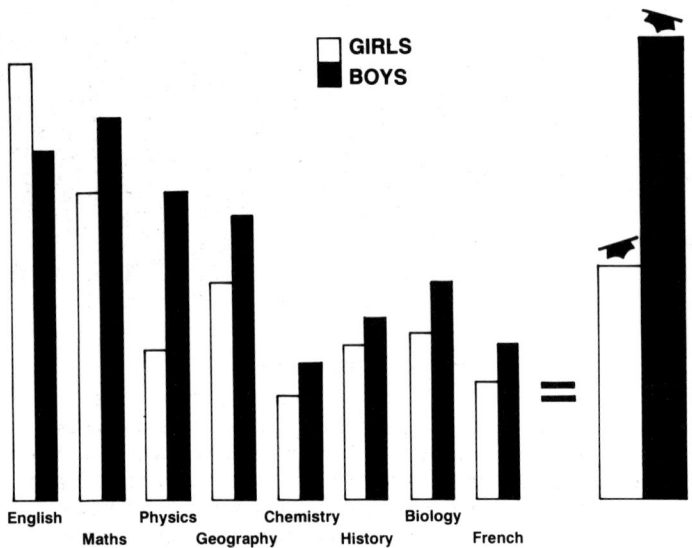

GIRLS
BOYS

English Maths Physics Geography Chemistry History Biology French

Conditioning

Are women conditioned to a specific role from their earliest days? From birth they are often dressed in dainty, frilly clothes, given dolls and domestic-type toys such as miniature kitchens and household equipment to play with, at school play different games (never rugby). Advertising creates a powerful image of what a woman should be — beautiful, shapely and desirable to men. What would happen if all children played in mixed soccer teams, and both sexes were given dolls and toy guns? Should more advertisements promote academic, financial and career success for women rather than the need to use beauty products or choose the right soap-powder?

HARESHEENE SHAMPOO
LEAVES HOURS FOR STUDY!

PASS THAT EXAM

EQUAL WAGES ACT 1970

288p hour
203p hour
451p hour
282p hour

Wages

In spite of the Equal Pay Act the average full-time manual worker in 1982 earned 288p an hour, the average female, 203p — about 70% of the male wage. The average non-manual male employee earned 451p an hour, the female 282p, about 63% of the male. This must mean that women have jobs with lower wages — domestic work, assembly lines, shop work, routine office/clerical work such as typing and filing. The chances of supervisory or administrative posts are often much lower for women than for men.

1	CHARTERED ACCOUNTANTS .... MALES
2	SOLICITORS
4	ARCHITECTS
7	SCIENTISTS
8	BARRISTERS
8	SENIOR CIVIL SERVANTS
9	DENTISTS
12	NATIONAL UNION OF JOURNALISTS
18	DOCTORS
34	ACTORS, MUSICIANS, SHOWBIZ, DANCE
60	TEACHERS
90% FEMALES	NURSES

Professions

Some people say that women should not be expected to do jobs which are dangerous (deep-sea diving), physically demanding (coal mining) or unpleasant (slaughterhouse work). Do you agree? If women want equality, should they expect to share in all its aspects? The professions have few of these problems, yet women do not seem to have penetrated them very far. The chart shows the proportion of women in certain professions. Why are so many in teaching and nursing? Is this because they are among the worst paid of the professional jobs?

Women now do more of the jobs once thought of as strictly "male". Here a corporal from the WRAF removes the main fuse from a bomb.

Promotion-career structure

The career prospects for the majority of women are not as good as those for men. The reasons often suggested are that a man's career is usually continuous, whereas a woman's is likely to be broken by marriage, by having children, by having time off when children or other members of the family are ill, and perhaps by moving to another district when a husband takes a different job. Do you think these are valid reasons? Should a husband move to suit his wife's work? Is there some reluctance on the part of men to work under a woman's authority? Does this apply in all types of job — manual, skilled and professional? Is it true that most women's loyalty seems to be first to their families and then to their work?

Socio-economic groups and women

Is there any difference in the male attitude to women in the different social classes? The percentage of women not at work is almost the same for all classes. Do working class males want the traditional type of woman — one who does all the housework and child-rearing, etc? Do non-manual and professional men have different ideas about it? If you are a female, what kind of male would you like to share your life with, or if a male what kind of female?

Best of both worlds?

Are women trying to have the best of both worlds — wanting to be treated just like men in everything but yet at the same time holding on to those privileges they had in earlier times? How do males feel about giving up their seats in crowded buses to females, apart from the elderly or ill? Do females like males to open doors for them, help them on with coats, pay for drinks or meals? Should females expect males to give them flowers or boxes of chocolates? Should it still be the male who proposes sex, or asks "Will you marry me?"

Innate differences?

Can we be sure that men and women are fundamentally alike? We know that there are physical differences — may there not be psychological ones too? Can you suggest characteristics, behaviour patterns and other attitudes which are typical of the majority of females, and other, different ones which are typical of the majority of males?

Leisure

Production of Morris cars at Cowley, Oxford 1930.

In the past the hours of work both at home and outside were longer than they are today. Until the 1940s — 1950s most people in industry worked a 5½ day week, with only Saturday afternoon and Sunday free. As late as 1961 the average working week including overtime was almost 48 hours. In 1961 97% of the total workforce had two weeks or less paid holiday a year.

By the 1930s housework was easier than it had been but it was still hard by today's standards. Ordinary homes did not have washing machines, driers, refrigerators, freezers, or electrical kitchen equipment such as mixers. Washing clothes and dishes was done by hand with soap powder or bars of soap which were much less efficient and mush harder to use than modern detergents. As synthetic fabrics like nylon and terylene had not been invented, most clothes had to be carefully ironed and many needed frequent repair. There were plenty of tinned and packeted foods, but none of the frozen or 'instant' meals that make catering easier today. The housewife's day was a long and wearisome one.

The last 30 or 40 years have seen a dramatic change in the amount and pattern of leisure — a change that will continue, and which can cause many problems.

A modern 1930s kitchen in London.

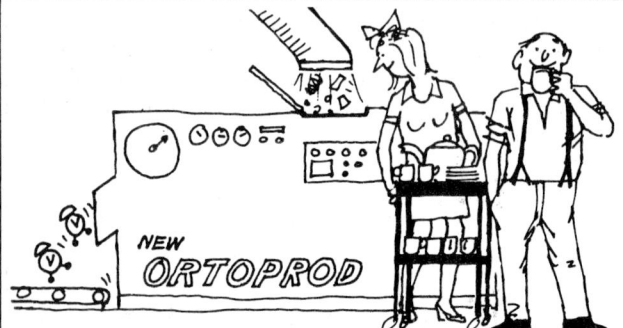

New production methods have meant increased output from the same number of workers. This has allowed shorter working hours and longer paid holidays.

A Co-op freezer centre in Lancashire.

Labour-saving devices and materials in the home (machines, easy-care fabrics, central heating, quickly-prepared foods) have meant that far less time is needed for housework.

There is more money to spend. Wages are higher than ever in history. The welfare state means that people need not save so much for old age, unemployment or illness.

There are higher expectations. In the past leisure was largely only for the rich, but today everyone rightly expects to share in the pleasure of free time activities.

Television and radio, as well as being enjoyable in themselves, help to show what other activities are available. They stimulate interest in travel, different sports, new crafts and recreational pursuits from archaeology and bird-watching to yodelling and zoology.

Basketry—continued	35*
Short courses	1*, 15, 18, 21
Willow	1, 2, 5*, 8†, 9, 14, 16, 17*, 18*, 21
Batik	18
Beadcraft	
Beauty Culture	2, 5*, 7*, 9, 12, 16*, 19, 20, (YC)
Beauty care and culture	20
Looking good and feeling fine—for people with learning difficulties (mental handicap)	12, 16†, 17†
Poise, dress and personality	1†, 18*
Bee-keeping	

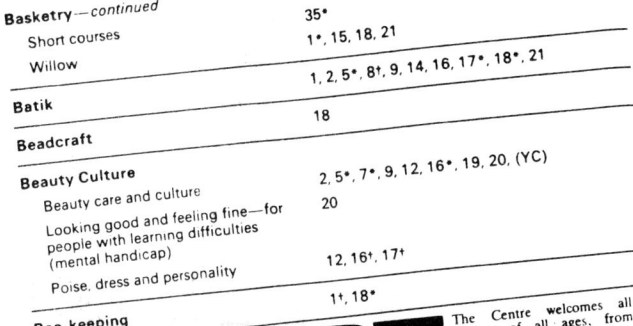

SPORT FOR ALL
Crystal Palace
National Sports Centre

The Centre welcomes all visitors of all ages, from absolute beginners to serious devotees. Come for fun, for training or for one of our many coaching courses. Come to watch major events, regular team matches and see our exhibitions. Relax in our bars or restaurant. For functions, ask to see our hospitality suite.

Some popular activities:
● WEIGHT TRAINING
● BADMINTON
● SWIMMING
● ATHLETICS
● AEROBICS
● KEEP FIT
● SQUASH

Advertising helps people to take part in new leisure activities. Travel agents and tour companies make holidays easier. Firms like sports companies list their recreational products and facilities, and local authorities publicise their sports amenities, leisure centres and a wide range of recreational classes in further education.

Passive leisure

This is always bound to be the major leisure area because it is convenient, cheap and comfortable. The number of radio and TV programmes are increasing in time and variety. The number of books, magazines, records, video tapes and electronic machines is growing. People are buying more alcoholic and other drinks and luxury foods. More and more things like armchairs and garden furniture are sold to make our passive leisure more comfortable.

Leisure can increase employment. People are needed to make equipment and clothing for sports and other recreational activities, to maintain sports fields, leisure centres, swimming pools, parks and gardens. Books and magazines catering for all interests are produced. People work as instructors, guides and assistants, as well as in hotels and restaurants. These service industries are labour-intensive, that is, they need a lot of people, and as traditional industries need fewer employees, more should be able to transfer to work associated with leisure. As the demand for leisure grows, new industries are created to cater for it. Firms make electronic games, videos, diving equipment, among many other things.

Active leisure

An increasing number of people want more recreations. A great deal of paid work is done sitting down, and people need physical activity. Often work is repetitive or boring, so that people need to use their minds and skills. This has lead to an increase in all kinds of sports, crafts, holidays, DIY, gardening and further education, for example.

149

Government statistics show that in 1982 the average family spent £19.23 or 14% of its total weekly household budget on leisure — and this did not include the cost of tobacco (13.5% of the household budget) and cars (16%). The chart shows how this was divided up for the nation as a whole, though of course not everyone spends their money in these ways.

£6.13	£3.99	£3.55	£2.44	£1.97	ALL OTHERS £1.15
ALCOHOL	HOLIDAYS	TV, RADIO ETC	BOOKS, PAPERS ETC	DIY MATERIALS	

Education for leisure

Just as no one expects a person to be efficient in a job without some training for it, so education is essential for people to make the most of their leisure. If left entirely to themselves they might spend most of their spare time in undemanding, passive activities. These may be worthwhile, but they may prevent people finding out about other recreations which they might find far more satisfying.

Should students be introduced to a wider range of sports and other activities at school so that they know more about the things which are available?

If people enjoy limited leisure activities — say spending every evening playing bingo, listening to records or drinking at a pub, is there any point in trying to get them to do something else?

Should certain activities be made compulsory? If they are optional, will not people stick with the ones they know and not try any new ones?

Should there be some control over recreations such as mountaineering and pot-holing where there is the risk of causing injury or death not only to oneself but also to others who might be involved in rescue?

Is there any justification for regarding some leisure activities as 'superior' to others — going to opera or classical concerts rather than rock concerts, or playing chess rather than bingo? How can these prejudices be broken down?

Should local authorities or national governments provide more facilities for people to try at low cost or entirely free specialised activities which require expensive equipment — gliding, polo or rowing, for example?

As working hours are likely to continue to grow shorter and work itself more automated, there will be an increasing demand for leisure facilities. Commercial firms and organisations will provide many of these, but national and local governments are providing more and more outlets for recreation.

National government

The state's contribution to leisure is largely to provide money for major museums, art galleries, opera and all kinds of concerts and exhibitions. The state also looks after large national parks and places of 'outstanding natural beauty'. These are usually left in private ownership but the state ensures that they are open to the public and that they are not spoiled in any way. The Forestry Commission also makes some of its woodlands available to the public. The Waterways Board maintains canals and other stretches of water for boating.

Local government

Local authorities spend large amounts of money on providing leisure amenities, most of which would not make a profit if run privately. These include parks and gardens, libraries, leisure centres, swimming pools, sports fields, picnic areas and some theatres and concert halls. Local authorities also have many schemes of further education, where people can study at very low cost arts, crafts, sports, DIY and practical subjects such as cooking, as well as academic subjects (foreign languages for travel, film and literature appreciation, creative writing, and many others).

Top: fell walkers in one of the national parks in Cumbria. Almost 20% of England and Wales is included in national parks or areas which have been designated by the government as of outstanding natural beauty.

Centre: most towns have public swimming baths which are run by the local authority as part of the amenity programme.

Bottom: despite the growth of television, more books are read than ever before in history. Small towns and larger villages have libraries — though not all as lavish as this one in Bebington, Cheshire. Smaller villages are visited weekly by mobile library vans from the nearest headquarters.

The media

Until the eighteenth century news travelled mainly by word of mouth, and could take days or even months to reach outlying districts. What eventually filtered through was entirely by chance, and the great majority of people did not hear anything but the most important items of national or international news — battles won or lost, deaths of kings. Even then the stories were told and retold so many times that in the end they were often very different from the truth. The outside world did not really concern most people — their world ended at the village or town boundary.

In the eighteenth century small newspapers of a single sheet with political, commercial and legal news began to appear in larger towns. They were expensive and had maximum circulations of a few thousands, which was all that could be reproduced on the slow hand presses. Often they were read aloud to customers in coffee houses and taverns. After the invention of the steam printing press in 1814, newspapers became more widespread, but they were dull, had very few illustrations and at prices ranging from a penny to threepence were too expensive for ordinary people to buy regularly.

The beginning of mass circulation came in Britain with the launching in 1896 of the Daily Mail, which had more illustrations, up-to-date news sent in by telegraph, and cost only a halfpenny. In four years it had a million daily readers, and was imitated in 1900 by the Daily Express. In 1904 the Daily Mirror was launched at a halfpenny, but was different from the other newspapers because it printed a large number of photographs. The age of the mass media had begun.

Moving pictures had been invented as a toy in the late nineteenth century, and jerky films lasting only a few minutes were a fairground amusement in the early part of the twentieth century. World War 1 gave a great boost to the cinema, and films became a major part of the media from the 1920s until their sharp decline in the face of television in the 1960s.

Scientists had been experimenting with radio since the end of the nineteenth century, and by 1912 a few ships were fitted with simple morse code transmitters. World War 1 developed radio considerably, and in 1922 the BBC made its first radio broadcast. With television in the 1950s the real age of the mass media had arrived. (The BBC started the world's first television service in a small way in 1936, but real development was delayed by World War 2.)

This TV was first developed in the early 1930's and was sold mainly as a scientific novelty at a price of about £20. The picture was very dim and flickered constantly. It was shown on the screen by means of a disc with holes along the edge and was only the size of a postage stamp. At the right of the set is a lens you looked through to see a proper image. The TV screen scans the image by lines and this TV only used 30 lines compared to the 405 lines used today.

The mass media give us a vast amount of news and comment from all over the world, often as things are actually happening. The impact of television is far more dramatic than that of newspapers. The written word lets us know what is happening, but the pictures in full colour almost let us be present. While a broader knowledge of the world and what is going on must be excellent, the mass media bring their own problems.

The media let us know what is happening, and can help to make it more easily understood by giving the background information.

The media can influence our opinion powerfully by giving us the news, and the aspects of the news which they want us to hear or see.

The mass media can break down our prejudices by showing us people of other colours, races, religions, political views.

By presenting the material in the way they decide, the media can strengthen our prejudices and create new ones (see page 155).

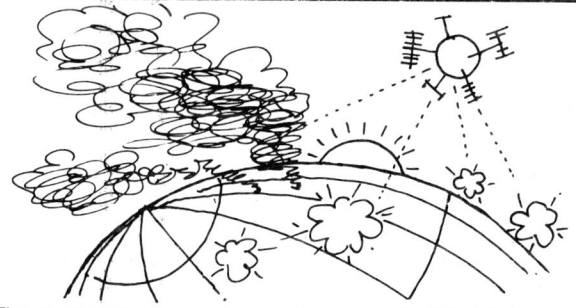

The media give a broad overall picture of all that is happening in the world, good and evil, and increase our understanding.

By mixing real news, documentaries, reconstructions and fiction, the media make it difficult to see what is real and what is entertainment.

The media, especially television, provide mass entertainment and are the largest single leisure activity. The tradition that in the past people produced their own entertainment is largely untrue; few people had particular leisure interests.

Television, especially commercial television, fights for bigger audiences (and thus higher advertising fees) and can produce an endless stream of undemanding popular programmes. Minority tastes are barely catered for, and there is a steady lowering of standards.

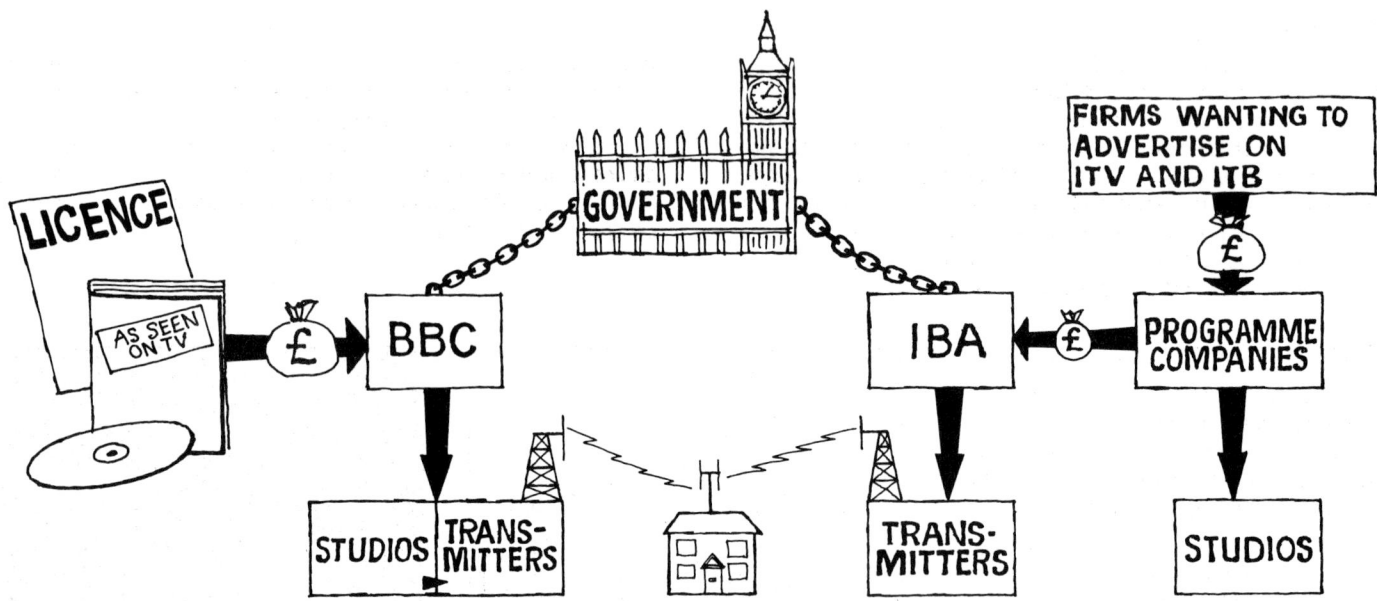

In Britain television is run by two public corporations, the BBC (British Broadcasting Corporation) and the IBA (Independent Broadcasting Authority). The BBC is different from all other broadcasting organisations because its income is mainly from the state, but at the same time it is independent — both Labour and Conservative governments have occasionally accused the BBC of being opposed to them. The BBC gets its income from the licence fees and from selling programmes abroad, as well as from books based on the programmes and from sales of *Radio Times.* With this money it builds studios and transmitters and employs staff to make and transmit programmes. The IBA owns transmitting stations, but rents them to programme companies such as Thames, Granada and Scottish Television. The companies make programmes (which have to follow broad principles laid down by the IBA) and make their money by selling time in the broadcasts to firms who wish to advertise. Different prices are charged according to the time of day. When more people are likely to be watching, advertising fees are higher. The companies buying advertising time have no control over the programmes in which their advertisements come. This is different from the situation in many other countries, especially the USA, where firms who wish to advertise often have their own programmes made. This can mean that they control what is in the programmes.

Newspaper circulation and audiences for radio, tv and cinema 1920 – 1982

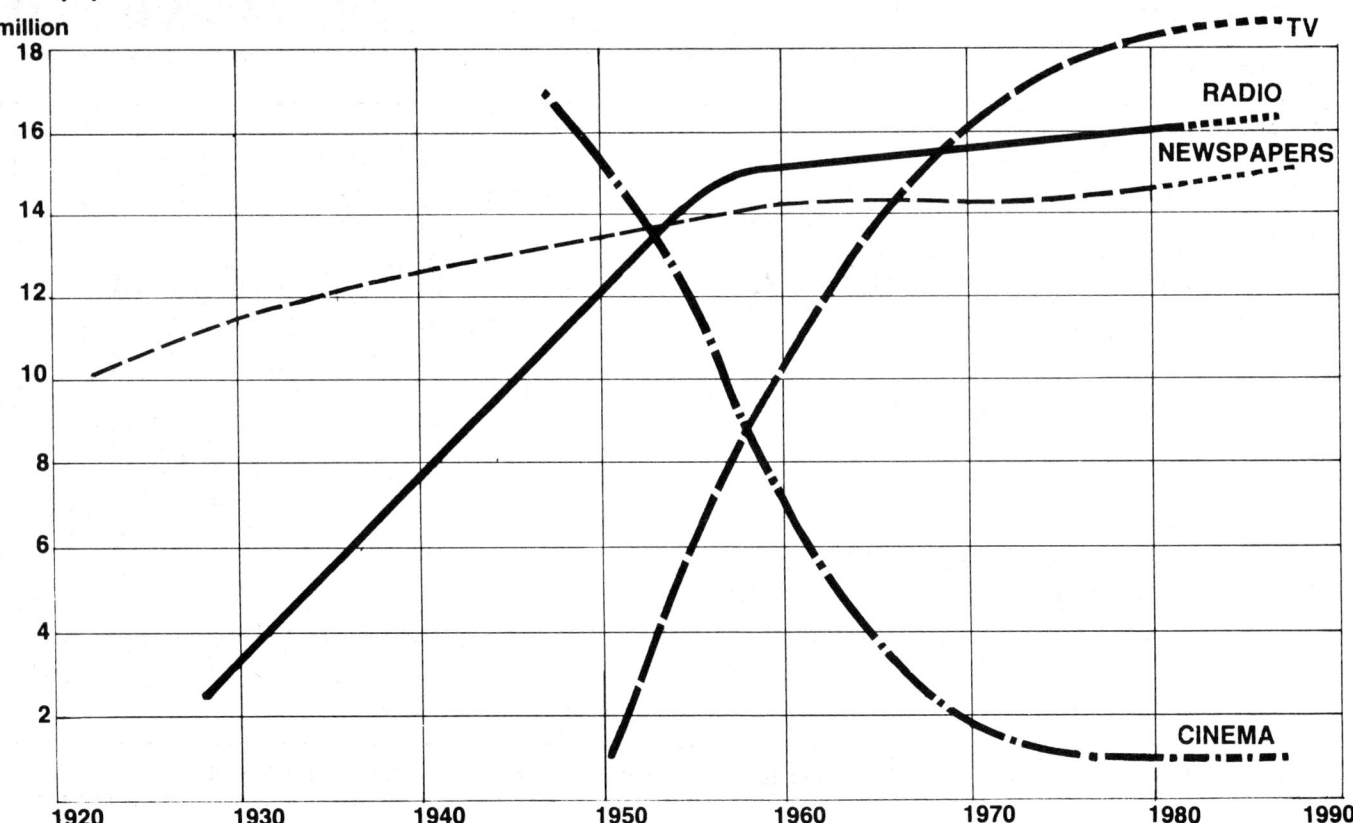

Propaganda

The media — press, radio, TV and (now less important) the cinema — are the most powerful propaganda tools of all. In states where the media are controlled completely by the ruling party, they can be organised to make sure that the people see and hear only what the leaders want them to. News, comment and even entertainment programmes can be presented so that the government or leaders always seem to be right — kindly, caring and peace-loving — while all opponent countries are wrong — warlike and aggressive.

In capitalist countries most of the media are controlled by private enterprise, that is, by firms whose aim is to make profits. These can hardly be expected to campaign for a totalitarian government, left or right wing, which would put them out of business by making the media state monopolies. This in itself is a form of censorship, though probably not as serious as those in completely totalitarian states.

Some propaganda methods

Selection of news to show the government or leaders in a good light. Serious setbacks, such as defeats in battle or in world politics, are not mentioned, or else treated so that they seem successes.

Only the ruling party view is given — there is no opposition anyway — and this is always seen to be right.

The leaders are portrayed as kindly, caring people, even though they may, like Hitler and Stalin, have caused millions of innocent people to be executed.

Constant repetition of untruths. The Nazi propaganda minister, Goebbels, said that if you tell people lies long enough and loudly enough, they will believe them.

Shifting blame for anything wrong to someone else — Jews, communists, capitalists, blacks, whites. The threat of an outside enemy unites people behind their leaders.

Convincing people that they are the best in the world: their history is the greatest; their nation is the source of every major invention and discovery.

Two faces of Amin, the ex-president of Uganda.

Nazi Goebbels shows a pleasant public face.

Left: Hitler reviewing his shock troops in 1932 and convincing them that he will become their leader in the general election and achieve great things for Germany.

Stalin tries to show his kindliness.

Do you think any of these methods are used in Great Britain? You will find it interesting to compare news items as presented in different newspapers, particularly if you do it over a period of time.

Some influences on Britain: 1945 -1985

Britain in the last quarter of the twentieth century is a very different place from the one people grew up in between the two world wars. These are just a few of the important influences and events which have shaped the Britain we live in today.

Welfare state

People today are no longer so haunted by the fear of what might happen if they are unemployed or ill, or when they get too old to work. There were of course provisions for these things before World War 2, but they were far more limited than they are today. Because people do not feel that 'saving for a rainy day' is so important, they spend more of their income and have a higher standard of living.

End of empire

Countries which were once colonies of Britain are now independent. This means that Britain is just one of the many equal sovereign states in the Commonwealth. This has turned her into a relatively minor power in the world politically. Economically it has made her turn more to Europe and the EEC for trade.

Collapse of old industries

The period since World War 2 has seen the collapse of industries such as ship-building, iron and steel, coal and cars. For some reason Britain cannot compete with countries such as Japan and West Germany. The blame might be laid on inefficient management, out-of-date equipment, powerful unions and attitudes of mind unsuited to the modern world. What is the 'British disease', as some people call it?

Unions and management

Both unions and management must take some of the blame for Britain's decline. Management often fails to see new opportunities and invest in modern equipment. It is secretive and does not take the workforce into its confidence. Unions do not wish to help control wages and are too concerned with keeping as many members as possible. Different unions often refuse to work together and share work in new ways.

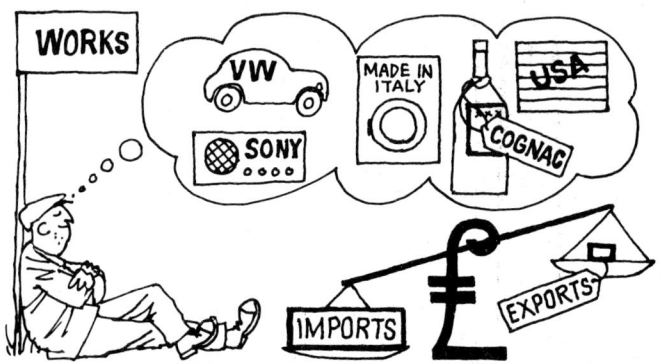

Balance of payments crises

The disappearance of older industries, the high price of British goods compared with those of competitors, and imports of many goods from abroad have meant that Britain has overspent. Often we buy things from abroad simply because British manufacturers no longer produce enough. Most of our kitchen and hi-fi equipment, for example, is imported.

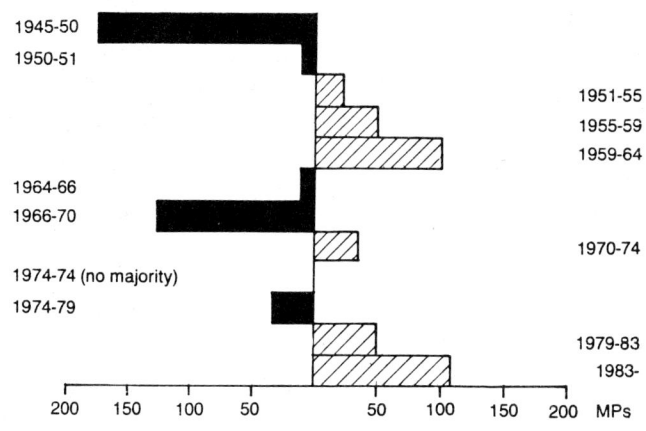

1945-50			
1950-51		1951-55	
		1955-59	
		1959-64	
1964-66			
1966-70			
		1970-74	
1974-74 (no majority)			
1974-79		1979-83	
		1983-	

200 150 100 50   50 100 150 200 MPs

Changing governments
In 40 years after World War 2 Britain had 12 governments, 6 Labour and 6 Conservative. Each had very definite ideas and spent much of their energy in reversing the laws of the previous government (for example on nationalisation). To make matters worse, 4 governments (3 Labour, 1 Conservative) had very small majorities, and so were very weak.

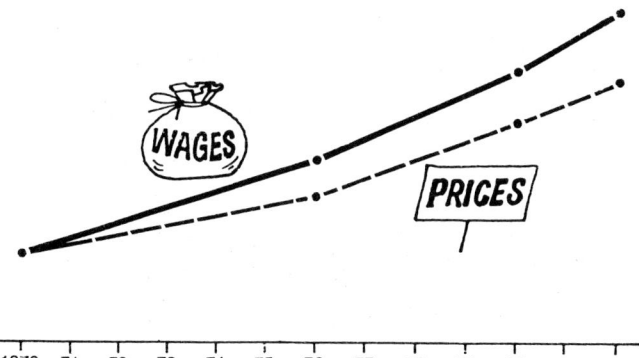

1970 71 72 73 74 75 76 77 78 79 80 81 82

Rising standards
The graph shows how wages have steadily kept ahead of prices over 12 years. This means that more money is available for spending. The average employee's home today has far more luxuries than a prosperous employer's would have had before World War 2.

North/South divide
There is a marked difference between the northern part of England and Wales and the southern part. The north has a higher death rate, a lower expectation of life, more violent crime, a higher rate of strikes, and more unemployment. Houses and land are much cheaper in the north. In the 1983 general election Yorkshire and the northern region returned 32 Conservatives, 54 Labour and 4 Liberal Alliance MPs. The south-east and south-west returned 74 Conservatives, 1 Labour and 3 Liberal Alliance MPs. This imbalance between north and south seems harmful and unfair to many people. How can we change it for the better?

Population
There has been a dramatic change in the age structure of the population. In 1941 9% of the inhabitants of Great Britain (4.5 million) were aged over 65. In 1982 it was 16% (8.5 million). This means a very big rise in the cost of pensions, medical care and other provisions, and the trend is still increasing.

North Sea oil
The discovery of huge quantities of oil in the North Sea came at a time when Britain seemed on the verge of bankruptcy through overspending. It is now the fifth-largest oil-producing country in the world, and the income from oil has done much to help the economy. Many people fear, however, that the oil may be used up before the revenues have been used to re-build British industry.

An oil rig off the coast of Aberdeen.

Index